D1429592

THE SOVIETS AND THE PACIFIC CHALLENGE

THE SOVIETS AND THE PACIFIC CHALLENGE

Edited by
Peter Drysdale

In association with
Martin O'Hare

M. E. SHARPE, INC.
Armonk, New York

Copyright © Australian National University 1991

First published in 1991 by Allen & Unwin
in association with the Australia–Japan Research Centre

This edition published by
M. E. Sharpe, Inc.
80 Business Park Drive, Armonk, New York, NY 10604 USA

ISBN 0-87332-866-3 C
　　　0-87332-867-1 P

Library of Congress Cataloging-in-Publication Data

The Soviets and the Pacific challenge / edited by Peter Drysdale
　　　p.　　cm.
　　Includes bibliographical references and index.
　　ISBN 0-87332-866-3 (cloth). ISBN 0-87332-867-1 (paper)
　　1. Soviet Union—Foreign economic relations—Pacific Area.
　2. Pacific Area—Foreign economic relations—Soviet Union.
　3. Soviet Union—Economic policy—1986– I. Drysdale, Peter.
　HF1558.5.P16S68 1991　　　　　　　　　　　　91-8373
　337.4709--dc20　　　　　　　　　　　　　　　　　CIP

Printed by Chong Moh Offset Printing, Singapore

Foreword

Under the worthy banners of 'Dialogue, Peace and Cooperation' an exchange of views is currently expanding and gathering pace on possible ways to transform the heterogeneous, but nonetheless unified, Asia–Pacific geographical area into an open region receptive to unifying political ideas.

Such ideas are not unknown in the history of continents. Even at the level of philosophical and political concepts they have served to draw countries together and defend their shared features against self-destruction. And today they form the basis for a common home of many peoples.

I am thinking here of the idea of Europe. And I venture to write, with full justification, of the existence of an Asian idea, the idea of Asia.

Experts on the Far East, orientalists, will challenge this assertion. But it is found in the great teachings of antiquity, whose common inheritance is a legacy to all humanity. All the religions of the world, springing from the East — from Christianity to Hinduism, from Buddhism to Zoroastrianism — hinge on the human being, and inspire mankind through the human being.

The idea of Asia can also be found in present-day thought, in political thinking directed towards the vast Asian community, even the world community — in the philosophy of non-violence, the Pancasila principles, the Bandung Declaration, and the Delhi Declaration on the principles of a world free of nuclear weapons and of coercion.

It is time for the Asian idea to come into its own, as the European idea has.

I have deliberately mentioned these two great continents in the same breath. In fact this does not come from me — it is history itself, and modernity, politics and geography, economics and culture that juxtapose them. Europe and Asia, East and West, have long been moving towards each other, surmounting the barriers, the self-imposed isolation of some countries, the nightmare of colonial rule and enslavement, regional conflicts, and unequal material wealth. The Great Silk Road transcended war and violence, the fine-spun silken fibre of history ran right through time and space. This is even more the case today, now that the slow-moving silk caravans have been replaced by optical fibres and electronics which draw together disparate worlds.

On the Pacific shore of the Soviet Union lies the beginning of the route which traverses the expanses of the Far East and Siberia, the European part of the Soviet Union, and Eastern and Western Europe, to reach the Atlantic coast.

From the summits of our Far Eastern hills we can see the great Eurasian expanse that is called the Soviet Union. If our political scientists and columnists are right in calling this 'the world of all worlds', then it must also be correct to suppose that it does not separate two distant worlds but links them. As the outstanding Russian philosopher Georgy Fedotov said, Russia must live politically in a complex world of European and Asian peoples alike.

I would venture to add that Russia and the other nations comprising that 'world of worlds' of Soviet Eurasia would like to promote in political terms the establishment of peace and good neighbourliness between them.

The unique situation of the Soviet Union may also perform an invaluable service in establishing the varied bonds of integration between Asia and Europe.

If in the past trans-Atlantic communications could be set in place, today, thanks to the new technologies, it is possible to create trans-Eurasian communications.

Our existing transport system may assist the process of integration. The Soviet Union's road, rail, and airline networks will provide access to vast markets and zones of unhindered joint entrepreneurship.

Nor should our space potential be overlooked. The Soviet Union could also make available its space technology for a wide variety of peaceful economic uses.

In brief, we propose that the potential of the Soviet Union be considered and appraised in the movement towards integration of Asia and Europe.

The division of Europe and Asia was to a great extent a result of the Cold War. Its frontiers cut across continents not only in Europe. Now that the Cold War is over, there are good grounds for speaking of the formation of a single Eurasian zone of security and stability. In this connection the idea of a decade of rapprochement between the two continents is timely.

We do not lay claim to any definitive truth. Here the markers cannot be set without constant and extensive exchanges of views, nor discussion and comparison of assessments and ideas, to ensure that we have correctly understood the state of the world, that we perceive accurately the trends shaping its development and have a sound basis for selecting a given course.

Above all, I believe, we need to ask ourselves what is happening in the world, and what lies at the heart of the present stage of human civilisation.

It is a commonplace of recent political analysis to say that we are living today in a rapidly changing world.

But was the world not changing ten years ago, or thirty years ago? Does the difference lie solely in the pace of change? I do not believe that it is merely a question of pace or scale.

First of all we should establish what is fundamentally new in the present situation.

It appears that we are now at that stage of the process of civilisation at which, in the terms of the great thinker Vladimir Solovyev, the growth of 'the body of mankind' reaches completion. For the first time perhaps, our world has reached its natural limits. For the first time we have become aware that vital resources are finite, and that it is essential to regulate many forms of human activity on a global level. Concurrently with this, another process has been gathering pace — the development of previously laid down infrastructures and the organisation of orderly life within them.

A period of speedy and radical change opens great opportunities, but also creates major, complex problems.

At a time of dynamic and sometimes dramatic developments, mankind must find a single axis of ethical coordinates, while learning to subordinate its individual components and bring their local and specific interests into line with those of the comity of nations as a whole.

Ethical self-determination in political life begins with the recognition of the equality of all and the rights of every individual, with the understanding that the individual's well-being must be the aim of the state.

This ethical self-determination of society, of the state, of the individual, manifests itself first and foremost with respect to violence and the use of force in relations between them.

The state punishes any assault on any individual's life, dignity, or property.

On the other hand, the state itself cannot exist without the protection of the law, without observance of international laws, for the alternative is every man for himself, which is to say anarchy and domination of the weak by the strong.

The world community cannot permit the rise of predatory states or piratical regimes, for this would lead inevitably to the erosion of international law and order and the destabilisation of international relations.

It is up to us to decide whether we are to live according to common perceptions of good and evil, or by cynically casting these aside, to shake the world to its foundations.

In view of the tensions produced by the crisis in the Persian Gulf, now is the time to ask this question.

The aggression against Kuwait is aggression against the trend towards positive change brought about in international life by the policy of new thinking.

We are all obliged to act in accordance with the resolutions of the UN Security Council.

It is inadmissible to permit even the thought of any option which would not restore the sovereignty, territorial integrity and legitimate government of Kuwait. Kuwait is, was, and will continue to be a member of the United Nations.

For the first time the world community has responded to aggression with such unanimity and singleness of purpose, and sought so energetically to eliminate its consequences. It is essential, however, to make every effort to do this by non-military means, and in such a way as to ensure that no external military presence is left in the region.

But a course aimed at a peaceful resolution certainly does not imply that the aggressor faces no risk. The aggressor risks being totally cut off from the rest of the world. We are convinced that sanctions will produce results, and will force the Iraqi leadership to heed the voice of reason.

The sense of unity felt by the states of the world on this matter is of great significance for all, including the Asia–Pacific region. A favourable basis is emerging for fostering and encouraging trends towards integration, and stimulating the process of shaping unified political, economic, scientific, humanitarian and cultural areas embracing whole continents.

The improvement in the political climate taking shape in the Asia–Pacific region is still far from stable, let alone irreversible. The level of mistrust, even hostility, remains high, fuelled by territorial disputes and ideological, ethnic, and religious factors.

A dangerously high level of military confrontation remains, especially on the Korean Peninsula. Deployment of nuclear missiles continues, and naval activity is increasing. The proliferation of nuclear technology and missile technology is cause for concern.

Observing and taking account of the diversity of the region, and its differences in structure and substance from other regions, we are prepared to seek specific 'Asian forms' to resolve problems of security and cooperation.

We cannot agree with those who underscore the unique nature of the situation in the Asia–Pacific region and in effect hold back the process of consolidation in the region of the positive trends in world politics.

In our view, reliable security at a substantially lower level of armaments — a level of sufficiency — making effective use of political means, may be applied to Asian realities as well.

Thus far, the statistics show that expenditure on armaments by some countries in the region is continuing to increase three or four times as fast as in European countries.

Is it really necessary to follow the path already trodden by others, to stockpile armaments, build military alliances and coalitions, and construct new military bases, only to discover later that they are not needed and re-channel the funds to the resolution of acute socio–economic problems.

Truly unique opportunities to do this have now arisen. The Cold War has ended, and with it a complex period of confrontation in the triangle formed by the Soviet Union, the United States, and the People's Republic of China.

A change without precedent has come about in Soviet–American relations. We no longer view each other as adversaries, and are beginning to build relations of partnership and interaction. These are no longer mere words, but large-scale actions working for peace.

No doubt progress will not always be smooth. Difficulties may arise. But it would be a serious mistake to fail to see the changes which have occurred in this crucial area, and the opportunities they open up.

In reflecting upon how to proceed to the establishment of bodies for negotiating regional issues, we have become increasingly convinced of the need for broad-based dialogue on regional problems.

Outside the Asia–Pacific region, comprehensive forums for discussion of major issues exist almost everywhere. In Europe, there is the Conference on Security and Cooperation, and a number of other structures; in America, the Organization of American States; in Africa, the Organization of African Unity. Of course, not all their work proceeds smoothly, but the existence of these bodies is not called into question. Interest in convening an Asia–Pacific forum in some format or other is increasing. The idea has been mooted of holding a meeting between foreign ministers directed towards this end. My Canadian and Australian opposite numbers recently declared themselves in favour of this.

Scholars and public groupings play an important part in developing the infrastructure promoting the convening of an Asia–Pacific forum. The Williamsberg conferences, the Kuala Lumpur round-table meetings, the New Zealand symposia, and the Vladivostok meetings all bear witness to the fact that a congress of representatives, official and unofficial, of Asia–Pacific countries, to discuss the political problems of the region, is not only possible, but increasingly urgent.

The need for broader and more regular parliamentary exchanges is no longer in doubt.

Taking account of the existing difficulties, we might proceed towards an Asia–Pacific conference incorporating political issues by stages, deploying a variety of political and diplomatic means and methods.

It seems to us unproductive to pose preconditions for the calling of such a conference. There is little point in waiting for all disputes and differences to disappear.

We propose an approach that seems to us more effective, namely this: to move towards the establishment of a multilateral negotiating mechanism, while increasing bilateral contacts and at the same time stepping up the drive to resolve conflicts, ease confrontation, and remove friction.

Where should we begin? How should we set this process in train?

We ought, for example, to consider holding a conference of a group of states with great military potential. This could be a working meeting of foreign ministers, open to observers from any other countries. The Soviet Union will be prepared to conduct the necessary consultations to prepare such a meeting and agree the agenda and the list of participants.

Given the broad interest in secure and unimpeded navigation on the high seas, it seems appropriate to consider and implement the idea of an international regional centre to guarantee the safety of maritime communications.

No single country, however powerful its navy, possesses the power to be a 'sole guarantor' of stability, or defender of the freedom of the seas. Furthermore, other countries would be wary if it attempted to do so.

We regard the development of a system of international guarantees as the best solution to the problem of ensuring the safety of maritime and aerial communications, including measures to combat terrorism and piracy.

I would like to restate one specific proposal: to invite to Vladivostok the foreign ministers of all interested Asian and Pacific states, in, say, the autumn of 1993.

This meeting could be planned as an open one, both with regard to the list of participants and to the range of issues for discussion.

The meeting might draft a joint statement setting forth the agreed political principles of the participants.

This statement could embody the changes which have occurred — a renunciation of confrontation and a move towards partnership.

Of course there will still be time, during ministerial and other contacts, for us to discuss the format and the concept of this conference, and to reach the required accord.

Further improvements in the situation in the Asia–Pacific region might be fostered by joint efforts to give the UN and other international bodies an increased role in resolving common problems.

Incidentally, why should an Asia–Pacific summit not be posed as our next objective?

As we seek optimal options, we should place more weight upon existing organisations and take account of trends and factors of a sub-regional nature, while endeavouring to combine effectively the UN's world role with the functions of these organisations.

We continue to support a conference on the Indian Ocean. In a draft agreement giving judicial form to the aims of the 1971 UN declaration which made the Indian Ocean a zone of peace, we consider it advisable to make provision for commitments by both the littoral states and the main users of the Indian Ocean, including the five permanent members of the Security Council.

The Soviet Union is prepared to initiate dialogue with all Asian and Pacific states on military problems and confidence-building measures. Confidence-building measures can be applied in Asia no less than in Europe.

I believe that this topic will also find an appropriate place in Soviet–Japanese negotiations and in our contacts with other countries.

We are not calling for an end to established military–political structures. Far from it; each country will itself decide, with its national interests in mind, how to build its relations with other states, including matters of security.

In addition to military–political concerns, there is anxiety in the region over the development of economic processes.

Of late there have been forecasts of a possible 'economic Cold War' both between Asia, Europe and America, and within the Asia–Pacific region. We must not permit a new North–South confrontation to arise. Now for the first time in history the prerequisites for the integrated development of the world economy and international economic relations based on principles of equality, mutual benefit and mutual aid are taking shape. We are seeing a noticeable development of East–West economic cooperation, the process of integration deepening all about us, and the growing interest of states in strengthening and heightening the efficiency of multilateral trading, economic, financial, and currency mechanisms.

These tendencies are fully in evidence in this region, which today is doing so much to shape the economic climate of the world. Here the processes of economic integration are gaining momentum. It is important that we impart to these processes, by our concerted efforts, an harmonious and democratic nature, lest they lead to trading and economic blocs, endlessly generating and regenerating economic friction, conflict, and even open trade wars.

We know that with regard to the Soviet Union's admission to a number of international economic organisations — the IMF, the World Bank, and GATT — certain prejudices remain. We hope that all these hangovers from the past will be left behind.

We realise how much remains to be done before the Soviet economic presence in the Asia–Pacific region reaches a level commensurate with Soviet economic potential and capability. Here some vigorous economic diplomacy is required of us, together with new forms of engagement in the economic life of the region.

To this end new internal measures are required to boost the development of the economy and the market in the Asian area of the Soviet Union and in the Far East, and to create a favourable political and legal environment for investment.

The realities are such that the transfer of our economy onto market lines, its greater openness, and the adoption of mutually-beneficial forms of external economic links are creating the basis for the inclusion of the Soviet economy in the economic architecture of the Asia–Pacific region, now taking shape. To overlook this is not only to limit substantially the potential for economic integration, but also to underrate the immense prospects of the Soviet Union's Far East, and the effectively unlimited opportunities for profitable investment aimed at the 21st century.

The Soviet Union cannot perceive its future development without the fullest possible participation in the world economy. Accordingly, it will seek partnership and linkages between the economy of the Soviet Far East and Siberia and that of the emergent Asia–Pacific economy.

We will do our utmost to promote the development of cooperative mechanisms for environmental protection. These could comprise, for example, an early-warning system for ecological dangers, an ecological first-aid service, an ecological fund, and cooperation in the exchange of advanced environmental protection technology. Here we see an opportunity for a major Asia-Pacific contribution to global efforts, including the work now under way to prepare for the UN Conference on Development and the Environment planned for 1992. It is important that we seek to coordinate the programs of all continents.

By way of a suggestion I would like to propose the idea of concluding a multilateral convention on conserving the marine and biological resources of the Pacific. Better still would be to draft a convention on the preservation of the environment throughout the region. Today the principal resource of any country is not its material wealth, but human intellect, human qualifications, and information. In short, science and technology are coming to the fore.

It is scientific and technological progress which will shape the destiny of humanity and the basic directions of social development on the eve of the 21st century. The future, therefore, depends to a great extent upon broadening and deepening international partnership in science and technology on both a global and a regional scale.

This cooperation is of particular significance for the countries of Asia and the Pacific and their links with Europe, America, and Africa. A glance at the map will show that these vast expanses of water and land can only be overcome by the use of advanced telecommunications, transport, and satellite links. It is here that we see the great potential benefits of the implementation of accords on the peaceful use of space recently achieved between the Soviet Union and Australia, and earlier with other states. This cooperation should have a marked Eurasian emphasis.

We propose discussion of the question of establishing an international centre for the speedy location and warning of the approach of tropical cyclones. Our country, with a fairly well-developed network of stations for identifying meteorological hazards, is prepared to share promptly the information received by these stations, including that from satellite facilities, with a future international centre.

There is a saying in the East that many roads lead to the summit. Of course, one is free to choose one's own road according to one's tastes and abilities, but if we pool our efforts and resources, determine the best route and help one another, we shall reach the summit that much faster, and at less cost.

We propose moving towards the summit together, guided by such interlinked precepts as respect, trust and cooperation.

Only by having respect for one's partner, the partner's choice of socio–political system and vital interests, is it possible to create an atmosphere of trust.

Trust will make it possible to implement measures in the political, military and economic areas, measures to remove suspicion and introduce into inter-state relations predictability, reliability and deep mutual understanding.

This volume makes a timely contribution to the development of mutual understanding through its constructive, but straightforward, discussion of the Soviet Union's present relationship with the dynamic economies of the Asia–Pacific region. The Australian National University and the organisers of the research and discussion on which the book is based are to be congratulated on their initiative and far-sightedness in bringing together scholars from all around Asia and the Pacific to work on this project.

From here the road leads directly to cooperation for mutually beneficial exchanges and links in all spheres, encompassing even the most diverse and complex areas for Asia–Pacific cooperation.

E. A. Shevardnadze
Former Minister of Foreign Affairs of the USSR

Contents

Tables

Figures

Preface

This book had its origins in an international conference organised by the Australia-Japan Research Centre, the Australian National University, in February 1990 on 'Soviet Reforms and Relations with the Pacific'. We were fortunate to gather in Canberra a very distinguished group of scholars from around the Pacific for a timely discussion of this issue. *The Soviets and the Pacific Challenge* is the product of that successful meeting. The papers in the volume reflect the frank and stimulating discussion from which they derive.

I am grateful for the enthusiasm and cooperation of the authors. They approached the difficult task of revising their papers in the face of ever-changing circumstances with great professionalism, in spite of the heavy demands on their time and expertise. Their wealth of experience and scholarly contributions have made this book possible.

We have been encouraged by the general interest in Soviet reform to have the book translated and published into Japanese and Russian. The Japanese edition is being published by TBS Britannica, through the agency of Tuttle–Mori of Japan. Our Soviet colleagues, from the Institute of World Economy and International Relations (IMEMO), facilitated the translation and publication of the Russian edition.

I am especially thankful to Eduard Shevardnadze, the Foreign Minister of the USSR, for the Foreword. I am also grateful to Dr Viacheslav Kuzmin from the Embassy of the USSR, Canberra, for assisting with the arrangement of the Foreword and for his support in liaising with IMEMO. Dr Vladimir Ivanov, of IMEMO, has been critical to this whole enterprise and I extend our special thanks to him for all his efforts.

I am grateful to my friends and colleagues Harry Rigby, Arthur Stockwin and Ken Heydon for their helpful comments on an earlier draft of Chapter 1. My wife, Liz, also made many helpful suggestions. Ben Underwood provided data and research assistance and Minni Reis did the typing.

The editorial work and liaison with the authors was undertaken by Martin O'Hare. His contribution to putting the volume together was essential. Debra Greer cheerfully undertook the difficult task of typing and typesetting the manuscript. Her work was completed by Kim-Lan Ngo and Minni Reis.

The bipolar hostility that governed international politics for most of our lifetimes has been replaced by a multipolar order that carries both hope and uncertainty. We live in an exciting and challenging era. The challenges for the Soviet Union in the Pacific cover a spectrum of political, economic, social and security issues. The successful political and economic integration of the Soviet

Union into the Asia–Pacific community will depend as much on the cooperation and goodwill of countries in the region as it will on the efforts of the Soviet people. *The Soviets and the Pacific Challenge* sets out the challenge for us all.

Peter Drysdale
December 1990

Abbreviations

APEC	Asia–Pacific Economic Cooperation
ASEAN	Association of Southeast Asian Nations
BAM	Baikal–Amur Mainline (railway)
CMEA	Council for Mutual Economic Assistance
COCOM	Coordinating Committee for Multilateral Export Controls
COMECON	Council for Mutual Economic Assistance
CPSU	Communist Party of the Soviet Union
DPRK	Democratic People's Republic of Korea
EC	European Community
FAO	Food and Agricultural Organisation
GATT	General Agreement on Tariffs and Trade
GDR	German Democratic Republic
GNP	Gross National Product
Gosbank	State (Reserve) Bank (USSR)
Gosplan	State Planning Committee (USSR)
IBRD	International Bank for Reconstruction and Development
IMEMO	Institute of World Economy and International Relations (USSR)
IMF	International Monetary Fund
INF	Intermediate-Range Nuclear Forces
Keidanren	Federation of Economic Organisations (Japan)
KGB	Committee for State Security (USSR)
LDCs	Less-Developed Countries
MTE	Market-Type Economy
NEP	New Economic Policy
NICs	Newly Industrialising Countries
NIEs	Newly Industrialising Economies
OECD	Organisation for Economic Cooperation and Development
PAFTAD	Pacific Trade and Development Conference Series
PBEC	Pacific Basin Economic Council
PECC	Pacific Economic Cooperation Conference
PRC	People's Republic of China
ROK	Republic of Korea
SDI	Strategic Defence Initiative
SOVNAPEC	Soviet National Committee for Asia–Pacific Economic Cooperation
SSBN	Nuclear-Powered Ballistic Missile Submarine
START	Strategic Arms Reduction Talks
STE	Soviet-Type Economy

Contributors

Peter Drysdale

Peter Drysdale is Professor in the Research School of Pacific Studies at the Australian National University, and Executive Director of the Australia–Japan Research Centre. He has written extensively on Pacific economic cooperation, Japan's foreign economic policy, Australia–Japan relations, Southeast Asia's foreign economic relations, minerals and energy trade and economic development issues. He was a co-founder of the Pacific Trade and Development Conference series and the first chairman of Australia's National Pacific Cooperation Committee from 1984 to 1987. He played a leading intellectual role in the development of PECC and APEC.

Alaster Edwards

Alaster Edwards is a Principal Geologist with the Exploration Department of BHP–Utah Minerals International. After graduating with a degree in geology from Melbourne University, he worked in the mineral exploration industry for four years before joining the staff of the University of New South Wales College in Broken Hill, specialising in petrology. Since joining BHP in 1979, he has undertaken applied research into the geochemical techniques used in both base metal and diamond exploration. He is currently responsible for the development of new exploration projects in the Asia–Pacific region.

Christopher Findlay

Christopher Findlay graduated from the University of Adelaide and the Australian National University (MEc and PhD) and has senior appointments with the Department of Economics at the University of Adelaide, and the Australia–Japan Research Centre at the ANU. He has written on Pacific trade in services, Australia and the Pacific economy, the Chinese wool textile industry, tourism, and steel industry development. He was a visiting fellow at the ASEAN–Australia Economic Relations Research Project and the Pacific Community Minerals and Energy Task Force at the Australian National University. Since January 1988 he has been the coordinator of the Minerals and Energy Forum of the Pacific Economic Cooperation Conference and is a member of the Australian Pacific Economic Cooperation Committee.

Vladimir Ivanov

Vladimir Ivanov, Doctor of Economics, graduated from the Faculty of Economics, Moscow State University in 1971. Until 1986, he was senior fellow and academic secretary of the Institute of Oriental Studies, Moscow. Since 1987, he has been head of the Department of Pacific Studies at the Institute of World Economy and International Relations (IMEMO). He is author and editor of many books, chapters and articles on political and economic matters in Pacific countries. He has served in the USSR Embassy in India.

Hiroshi Kimura

Hiroshi Kimura graduated in political science from Columbia University (PhD). He is currently Professor, Slavic Research Centre, Hokkaido University and Vice-President of the International Council for Soviet and East European Studies. His former appointments include Special Research Fellow, Japanese Embassy in Vienna, 1972–73; Moscow, 1973–75; Fulbright-Hays Visiting Professor, Institute for Sino–Soviet Studies, George Washington University, 1977–78; and Stanford University, 1982–83. His expertise lies in Japanese–Soviet relations. He is co-author of the book *Gorbachev's Reforms: US and Japanese Assessments*.

Ivan Korolev

Ivan Korolev graduated from the Moscow Institute of International Relations with a PhD in economics. He is a Professor of Economics and Deputy Director of the Institute of World Economy and International Relations, Moscow. He is the author of three books, and numerous articles.

Evgenii Kovrigin

Evgenii Kovrigin, Doctor of Economics, graduated from the Oriental Department of Leningrad State University in 1970. He has lectured on the history and economy of Japan, Japanese language, and the history of China at Leningrad State University. He is head of the Pacific Economy Group at the Institute of Economic Research in Khabarovsk. He has published around 50 scientific articles and three monographs.

Craig Littler

Craig R. Littler graduated from the London School of Economics (BSc and PhD). He has written extensively on industry and technology issues in China and Japan. He is author or editor of eight books, several monographs and numerous articles. He is Professor in the School of Management at the University of Southern Queensland, co-director of the Labour and Industry Research Unit, and the editor of the journal *Labour and Industry*.

Pavel Minakir

Pavel Minakir, Doctor of Economics, graduated from the Faculty of Economics, Moscow State University, in 1971. Until 1989, he was a Head of Department and Deputy Director of the Institute of Economic Research in Khabarovsk. He was then appointed the first Director of the Institute of Comprehensive Analysis of Regional Problems in Birobijan, the Jewish autonomous area in the Soviet Far East. He is the author and editor of many books, articles and chapters in collective monographs on the economy of the Soviet Far East and general problems of regional development.

Pu Shan

Pu Shan was awarded a PhD from Harvard University and an LL.D from Carleton College. In 1985, he became President of the Chinese Society of World Economy, Chinese Academy of Social Sciences, and since 1988 has been a member of the National Committee of the Chinese People's Political Consultative Conference.

Tsuneaki Sato

Tsuneaki Sato graduated in economics from the University of Tokyo. He has held academic positions at Aichi University, Tokyo Metropolitan Institute of Commerce, and Yokohama City University. He is presently Professor at Nihon University, Emeritus Professor, Yokohama City University and President of the Japan Association for the Study of Socialist Economies. He has written widely on economic issues and market forces in socialist countries.

Gerald Segal

Gerald Segal graduated from the Hebrew University of Jerusalem and received his PhD in economics from the London School of Economics. He is currently a Research Fellow at the Royal Institute of International Affairs in London, reader in international relations at Bristol University and editor of *The Pacific Review*. His recent books include *Rethinking the Pacific* and *The Soviet Union and the Pacific* .

Yu-Nam Kim

Yu-Nam Kim studied Russian and international relations at the Dankook University of Foreign Languages, the San Francisco State University and the University of California, Berkeley. He obtained his PhD in political science from the University of North Texas in 1973. He has held academic appointments at East Texas State University, University of Maryland, George Washington University and Georgetown University. From 1976 to 1984 he served at the Institute of Foreign Affairs and National Security, Ministry of Foreign

1 Soviet prospects and the Pacific economy

PETER DRYSDALE

This is a period of huge and important political, economic and social change in the Soviet Union, and for the entire world. In the last four and a half decades, the world has been ordered around the central balance of military and political power between the Soviet Union and the United States. All that has changed and, as one essay in this volume suggests, even the superpower status of the Soviet Union is itself in question.

The words *glasnost* and *perestroika* have become familiar, even to those of us who have been distant from the Soviet Union and Eastern Europe and there is generally a sense of relief that, in consequence of these changes, the risk of global conflict appears increasingly remote. There is an optimism that the prospect of mutual cooperation and closer economic interdependence between the former Eastern and Western blocs is achievable as the political barriers have come down in Europe.

At the same time euphoria is tempered by many uncertainties as Pu Shan hints in Chapter 9. On the one hand, there is uncertainty because of nationalist upheaval in the Soviet Union and because of the immense difficulties in the implementation of economic reform in both the Soviet Union and Eastern Europe, difficulties which threaten the pace and scope of the reform program. Littler considers the enormity and complexity of the task of economic reform in Soviet-type economies in Chapter 3. Through 1990, there has been little coherence in the implementation of economic reform in the Soviet Union and there is still a threat of economic disaster and political chaos unless greater coherence can be achieved through mobilising overstretched domestic energies and capacities as well as collective international understanding and support. On the other hand, uncertainty also arises because of threats to the relative stability in the central balance of power of the old era. The invasion of Kuwait by Iraq underlines this caution. The situation in the Middle East is symptomatic of the problems of, and the new requirements for, global system management in the post Cold War period, in which the relinquishing of direct superpower control and involvement increases the risk of regional adventurism and the threat to global stability from that source.

As I shall argue in this overview, it is precisely because of these developments that reconstructing the relationships with the Soviet Union in Asia and the
Pacific is such an important and urgent task. The Soviet economy is not yet, nor
for many years can it be, central to Asia–Pacific economic interests. But
building a new framework of political relations between the Soviet Union and
Asia–Pacific countries is a priority interest, both in the context of managing the
new international politics of the post Cold War period in the Asia–Pacific
theatre and in the context of exploiting the potential for growing economic interaction between the Soviet Union and the Asia–Pacific economies.

In this sphere, the most significant achievement thus far, as Segal observes in
Chapter 4, was the restoration of relations between the Soviet Union and the
People's Republic of China. The Gorbachev–Roh talks in June 1990 and
broader economic and other exchanges between South Korea and the Soviet
Union are another beginning. Yet, compared with the dramatic changes which
have taken place in East–West relations in Europe, progress in Asia and the
Pacific has been limited. A major stumbling block has been the inability to find
a way towards an understanding or treaty between the Soviet Union and Japan
consistent with the preservation of security interests and political stability in the
region and, thereby, to create stronger economic links between the Soviet Union
and the largest and strongest economy in East Asia.

ASIA–PACIFIC TRADE

A principal interest in the reconstruction of Soviet relationships with the
countries of Asia and the Pacific lies in integrating the process of Soviet
economic reform into the successful industrialisation and trade growth which
has taken place in East Asia.

East Asia's economies, which include Japan, China, South Korea, Taiwan
and Hong Kong, have grown more rapidly for longer than any others in world
economic history. East Asia's production has, in the last three decades, grown
from less than one-quarter of North America's to rough equality with that of
North America and almost one-quarter of the world's. In this time, East Asia has
been a main source of dynamism in international and especially long-distance
international trade. It has become the most important source of world savings
— larger than North America or Europe — and overwhelmingly the largest
source of surplus savings for international investment.

The shift in the world's economic centre of gravity towards East Asia has
brought with it large changes in the international economic and geopolitical
system, as well as in the analytic and ideological prisms through which people
all over the world now view reality. These developments are of particular and
strategic importance to many countries, including the Soviet Union, since there
is little doubt that East Asian industrialisation is bound to be a primary influence
on world trade and economic growth in the next quarter century and beyond; just
as it was around Japan's emergence as a great industrial power in the last.

The impact of successful economic growth in East Asia is reflected in the
immense shifts in regional trade flows. In the period between 1965 and 1989,

the share of the Asia–Pacific region (here including East Asia, North America, and Australasia) in world trade grew from around 30 per cent to almost 40 per cent. East Asian and Pacific countries transact almost 65 per cent of their trade with each other; in 1965 intra-regional trade was around 50 per cent of Asia–Pacific trade. Of total intra-regional trade in Asia and the Pacific, moreover, North American intra-regional trade represented a static or declining share. The proportion of intra-regional trade in Asia and the Pacific is now approaching that in Europe: in 1989, intra-regional trade amounted to 71 per cent of Europe's total trade. This regional trade growth, unlike that within the European Community, has taken place within the framework of discriminatory trading arrangements.

Table 1.1 sets out the geographic structure of Soviet, Asia–Pacific and world trade flows and the limited extent to which the Soviet Union has participated in the rapid expansion of trade within the Asia–Pacific region during the 1980s.

In the period 1980 to 1988, the Asia–Pacific share of world trade grew from 30 per cent to around 38 per cent, while that of the Soviet Union decreased from 2 per cent to around 1.4 per cent. Most Soviet trade is with the formerly centrally planned economies. In 1980, Soviet trade with other centrally planned economies was around 42 per cent of total Soviet trade, but in 1988 this share had risen to 49 per cent for exports and 58 per cent for imports. At the same time Soviet trade with Western Europe fell sharply, from 22 per cent to 15 per cent of all exports and 17 per cent to 12 per cent of all imports.

Trade with Asia–Pacific economies, other than centrally planned economies, is not large but nor is it insignificant. In 1988, it amounted to just over 4 per cent of Soviet exports (mostly destined for China and Japan) and 9 per cent of imports (mostly sourced from China, Japan and Australasia). The Soviet Union is not, however, a significant partner for Asia–Pacific economies, accounting for only 1.0 per cent of all their exports and 0.6 per cent of all their imports in 1988. While Soviet trade with China, and to a lesser extent with South Korea and Japan, has grown considerably since 1988, this growth in trade does not alter the fundamental picture described here — of a very limited trade and economic relationship between the Soviet Union and the Asia–Pacific region.

PROMISE OF THE SOVIET FAR EAST

The relative isolation of the Soviet economy from trade with Western economies and the extremely limited economic relationships between the Soviet Union and East Asian and Pacific market economies are, of course, a product of the politics of the Cold War and the closed nature of the Soviet economic system, more than of a lack of complementarity in economic structures. Indeed, the structure of Soviet trade and underlying resource endowments favours the expansion of trade with the labour, capital or technology rich, but resource deficient, economies of East Asia. The Soviet Union exports fuel and other raw materials and imports machinery, steel and chemicals. Fuel alone accounted for 42 per cent of exports in 1988. Heavy machinery, metals and chemicals accounted for 54 per cent of imports, while foodstuffs made up 16 per cent and

Table 1.1 Soviet, Pacific and world trade shares, 1980 and 1988 (per cent)

		Partner											
		China		Japan		Other NE Asia		ASEAN		Asia Total		Australia–NZ	
Reporter[a]		1980	1988	1980	1988	1980	1988	1980	1988	1980	1988	1980	1988
China	X	–	–	23.83	16.93	25.72	38.38	7.06	5.94	56.61	61.25	1.50	0.84
	M	–	–	27.12	20.62	2.99	22.37	3.43	5.67	33.54	48.66	6.40	2.83
Japan	X	3.96	3.79	–	–	11.88	10.84	10.22	8.54	26.06	23.17	3.17	3.08
	M	3.08	5.52	–	–	4.18	7.80	17.42	12.66	24.68	25.98	5.56	6.67
Other NE Asia	X	2.25	14.21	11.06	13.18	5.87	4.39	8.86	5.78	28.04	37.64	2.48	1.90
	M	6.92	18.82	25.73	26.20	5.10	3.71	8.31	7.67	46.06	56.40	2.76	2.70
ASEAN	X	0.98	2.62	29.82	19.84	6.62	8.04	17.00	18.09	54.42	48.59	2.89	2.51
	M	2.72	3.72	21.92	21.47	5.94	5.72	14.18	17.17	44.76	48.08	3.68	3.49
Asia Total	X	2.59	5.63	11.49	8.45	10.15	11.34	11.51	9.53	35.73	34.95	2.85	2.49
	M	3.64	7.69	12.34	13.66	4.69	8.15	13.76	11.56	34.44	41.06	4.58	4.53
Australia–NZ	X	3.53	3.22	24.16	26.36	5.15	8.90	7.78	7.71	40.62	46.19	6.47	7.99
	M	1.13	2.02	16.71	20.51	5.00	4.75	7.41	5.62	30.25	32.90	6.43	7.58
North America	X	1.59	1.71	8.66	10.71	4.34	4.48	3.48	3.29	18.07	20.19	1.89	2.09
	M	0.41	1.85	11.08	18.47	5.68	6.41	4.25	4.25	21.42	30.98	1.30	1.09
Asia–Pacific Total	X	2.14	3.85	10.77	10.20	7.07	8.30	7.41	6.78	27.39	29.13	2.61	2.57
	M	1.90	4.32	11.91	16.51	5.19	7.06	8.69	7.40	27.69	35.29	3.15	2.93
Soviet Union	**X**	**0.34**	**1.50**	**1.91**	**1.76**	**0.09**	**0.22**	**0.13**	**0.15**	**2.47**	**3.63**	**0.02**	**0.03**
	M	**0.33**	**1.30**	**3.99**	**3.00**	**0.03**	**0.07**	**1.33**	**0.31**	**5.68**	**4.68**	**2.11**	**0.70**
Other CPEs	X	1.67	2.59	0.46	0.82	0.03	0.18	0.25	0.69	2.41	4.28	0.11	0.19
	M	1.68	2.02	1.20	0.93	0.06	0.14	0.43	0.30	3.37	3.39	0.40	0.50
EC–12	X	0.38	0.63	1.03	1.98	0.83	1.17	1.12	1.20	3.36	4.98	0.77	0.84
	M	0.34	0.68	2.60	4.79	1.42	1.62	1.13	1.35	5.49	8.44	0.64	0.65
Rest of World	X	0.72	1.49	4.20	6.89	1.10	1.91	0.65	1.64	6.67	11.93	0.26	0.55
	M	0.98	1.88	7.14	8.57	1.74	2.99	1.47	2.63	11.33	16.07	0.59	1.00
World[b]	X	1.00	2.05	6.50	6.18	3.16	4.01	3.47	3.56	14.13	15.80	1.30	1.47
	M	1.01	2.30	6.76	9.79	2.70	3.85	3.64	3.82	14.11	19.76	1.55	1.62

Table 1.1 (Continued)

		Partner													
		North America		Asia–Pacific Total		Soviet Union		Other CPE		EC–12		Rest of World		World Total[c]	
Reporter[a]		1980	1988	1980	1988	1980	1988	1980	1988	1980	1988	1980	1988	1980	1988
China	X	6.62	7.97	64.73	70.11	1.35	3.11	6.24	3.41	16.33	11.11	11.56	12.43	100	100
	M	24.39	15.82	64.33	67.35	1.39	3.36	6.40	3.94	18.29	17.95	9.75	7.61	100	100
Japan	X	26.64	38.60	56.13	65.07	2.17	1.25	0.63	0.31	16.79	22.31	24.33	11.13	100	100
	M	20.76	28.29	51.44	61.41	1.33	1.55	0.18	0.39	7.39	17.09	39.67	19.61	100	100
Other NE Asia	X	32.10	33.66	62.74	73.31	0.03	0.04	0.11	0.11	20.74	17.69	16.39	8.86	100	100
	M	20.47	18.45	69.33	77.71	0.07	0.13	0.06	0.11	11.31	14.49	19.22	7.57	100	100
ASEAN	X	16.93	22.68	74.65	74.02	1.35	0.38	0.47	0.28	13.48	16.33	10.09	9.04	100	100
	M	16.34	18.19	64.85	69.85	0.17	0.28	0.39	0.60	15.00	18.26	19.63	11.04	100	100
Asia Total	X	23.98	31.55	62.83	69.17	1.47	0.97	0.83	0.54	16.71	19.05	18.22	10.32	100	100
	M	19.96	22.13	59.22	67.98	0.80	1.15	0.61	0.81	10.66	16.81	28.74	13.30	100	100
Australia–NZ	X	14.30	13.81	65.09	71.05	5.03	1.83	0.89	0.96	17.10	17.61	11.90	8.57	100	100
	M	23.17	24.09	60.98	65.23	0.11	0.11	0.39	0.36	26.08	28.73	12.45	5.58	100	100
North America	X	26.99	36.18	46.96	58.83	0.99	0.88	0.99	0.25	27.04	22.98	24.08	17.39	100	100
	M	27.19	29.05	49.94	61.14	0.17	0.14	0.40	0.38	17.27	22.00	32.23	16.35	100	100
Asia–Pacific Total	X	24.93	32.74	55.23	64.68	1.40	0.97	0.91	0.43	21.81	20.72	20.70	13.54	100	100
	M	23.67	25.85	54.69	64.23	0.45	0.57	0.49	0.56	14.70	20.11	29.69	14.56	100	100
Soviet Union	X	0.36	0.51	2.85	4.17	–	–	42.15	48.87	22.10	14.86	32.90	32.10	100	100
	M	5.23	3.55	13.02	8.93	–	–	42.95	57.95	16.86	12.29	27.17	20.83	100	100
Other CPEs	X	1.99	2.45	4.51	6.92	34.51	34.56	24.25	29.95	27.18	24.82	9.54	3.75	100	100
	M	4.68	1.39	8.44	5.28	35.27	38.25	22.07	29.48	26.07	23.72	8.15	3.27	100	100
EC–12	X	6.24	9.09	10.42	14.98	2.14	1.56	2.28	1.49	68.28	71.87	17.08	10.27	100	100
	M	9.38	8.12	15.60	17.28	2.64	1.68	1.97	1.55	59.81	70.24	20.10	9.33	100	100
Rest of World	X	32.02	34.53	38.97	47.01	2.16	0.73	2.22	1.23	38.15	40.13	18.62	11.05	100	100
	M	23.12	28.98	35.06	46.07	1.01	0.14	1.83	1.09	37.80	40.83	24.46	11.90	100	100
World[b]	X	15.32	20.08	36.88	37.49	2.13	1.45	2.86	1.48	46.38	48.24	17.92	11.48	100	100
	M	15.56	16.74	31.33	38.22	2.09	1.28	2.66	1.60	40.82	47.42	23.26	11.55	100	100

Notes: a The Reporter is the exporting/importing country. Each partner's share of its exports/imports is listed across the rows.
  b The World as a reporter gives the shares of the world's total trade by each partner.
  c The World as a partner gives the total volume of a reporter's trade and therefore has a share of 100 per cent.

Sources: IMF, *Direction of Trade Statistics*, International Economic Data Bank, Research School of Pacific Studies, Australian National University, Canberra. Data for the Centrally Planned Economies (CPEs) and the Soviet Union as reporters comes from *USSR in Facts and Figures*, Vol.12, 1988, and Vol.13, 1989; the USSR Academy of Sciences; and the Commercial Attache, Embassy of the USSR, Canberra.

consumer goods 15 per cent in 1988. This specialisation in international trade is highly complementary with Japan and the industrialising economies of East Asia.

Much of the promise of trade expansion between a Soviet economy, in the process of reform and internationalisation, and East Asia and the Pacific has been focused on the Soviet Far East. President Gorbachev, in his landmark speeches at Vladivostok in 1986 and Krasnoyarsk in 1988, highlighted the Soviet interest in promoting the development of the Soviet Far East through its integration with the Asia–Pacific economy.

Certainly the Soviet Far East, despite its difficult geography and harsh climate, is beckoning to the countries of East Asia. It is a huge region, larger than Australia and comprising 27 per cent of all Soviet territory. With a population of around 8 million, it holds 30 per cent of the Soviet Union's coal reserves and an estimated third of the nation's oil and gas reserves. The island of Sakhalin, in particular, has large offshore oil and gas fields and most of this energy capacity is unexploited. As well as abundant mineral resources (only partly explored, a mere 20 per cent of the territory having been geologically mapped and 1 per cent geophysically surveyed), the region is rich in forest and fisheries resources. At the same time, its vast distances and inhospitable geography make the economic exploitation of these resources, and development of the Soviet Far East region more generally, a very costly proposition. Internationally competitive resource projects require vast amounts of capital and large-scale investment. They will also require international cooperation, in assembling the necessary technology management capacities, markets and confidence in international participation. Despite its geographic size, the Far East economy is small. Only 2.6 per cent of the Soviet Union's people live in the region. Only 2.9 per cent of industrial production and 2.8 per cent of national income are generated in the Soviet Far East.

These data serve to emphasise that, despite its proximity and the complementarity of its resource endowment to that of the densely populated countries of East Asia, the Soviet Far East is only one element, and not necessarily the most important element, in the opening up of economic relations between the Soviet Union and the Asia–Pacific region. For the Soviet Union a primary interest is in access, across the back of Asia, to trade, capital, technology and economic assistance for its European heartland. For the Asia–Pacific economies access to the markets and investment opportunities in the Soviet West are of as much immediate interest as development of resource projects in the Far East.

WHITHER JAPAN AND THE SOVIET UNION?

In foreign diplomacy, the key question about the future development of Soviet economic relations with the Asia–Pacific region relates to Japan, as the second largest economy, the third largest trader, the largest exporter of capital, and a major source of technology in the world.

The visit of President Gorbachev to Japan in April 1991 catalysed efforts in Moscow and Tokyo to resolve the long-standing dispute between the two countries over the 'Northern Territories' issue and to develop a basis for the provision of substantial Japanese investment and other economic assistance to the Soviet economy. The origins and details of this issue are set out by Kimura in Chapter 6 and taken up positively by Ivanov in Chapter 12. Suffice it to observe here that the impasse on the territorial issue between the Soviet Union and Japan was deeply embedded both in the politics and security concerns of the Cold War period and in the long history of rivalry between the two countries.

Apart from military–security considerations, concessions to Japan on the return of the four islands raise, for the Soviet Union, larger questions of territorial integrity and the very authority of the Soviet state. Ultimately, these Soviet concerns must inform the Japanese approach to an understanding with the Soviet Union.

The Japanese government's uncompromising stance on the territories issue has also been complicated by the political advantage, in the management of foreign policy, of maintaining support for the security arrangements with the United States and increased sharing of defence burdens through appeal to the Soviet threat.[1] Significantly, analysts in Moscow have been sensitive to the effect of settlement of the territories issue on Japan–United States security arrangements and have sought not to disturb the Soviets' own fundamental interest in stable United States–Japan relations. Japanese concerns about the security arrangements with the United States must also inform the Soviet approach to an understanding with Japan.

The territories issue between the Soviet Union and Japan has been an extremely intractable problem, the solution to which requires a continuing and 'major input of effort, ingenuity, domestic political persuasion in both countries, flexibility and goodwill on both sides'.[2]

No party to any significant international negotiation yields the maximum concession in the early stages of negotiation so that neither the Soviet Union nor Japan, in their early approaches to defining a new relationship in the post Cold War period, were prepared to make any concessions on the return of the four islands. But the islands themselves are now a less and less significant element in the whole structure of intersecting military–security, political and economic interests between the Soviet Union and Japan, so that both countries need a path around their obstruction.

Of much more importance to the Soviet Union is active Japanese participation in the reconstruction of the Soviet economy, noted by Kovrigin in Chapter 7. The economic opportunities associated with more active involvement in this process are also of substantial importance to Japan. Despite suggestions that Japan now has little to gain from any additional resource and energy security which the efficient exploitation of the Soviet Far East might bring, the Middle East crisis underlines the ongoing interest in regional energy security.

Yet energy and resource security concerns are only one element in a much broader and collective Western interest in bringing to bear whatever influence can be brought to bear from outside the Soviet Union upon the successful transition from a command to an open market economy. This is, or ought to be, Japan's fundamental interest in structuring a new relationship with the Soviet

Union. This requires a total and strategic re-think of the major elements in a Japanese settlement with the Soviet Union and what it needs to encompass. Certainly a narrow bilateral settlement—the Northern Territories in exchange for project developments tied to Japanese financing and procurements in the Soviet Far East —may damage rather than assist the larger and more fundamental interest. A settlement limited in this way is likely to entrench, rather than assist with, the dismantling of the more irrational elements in Soviet economic organisation. It is likely also to add further grit to Japan's relationship with the United States since, while American corporations, with their superior technologies in the exploitation of energy resources, would have to be involved in any significant Soviet Far East project development, bilateral financing would tend to exclude more general international participation. This would damage relations with the United States and other countries as well as complicate the politics of Soviet–Japan relations. Commitment to a multilateral framework for the delivery of any Japanese financing of Far East development would insulate against these problems. An important interest is in active Japanese involvement in collective Western support for the process of economic reform in the Soviet Union. A belated but significant shift in the thinking of the United States administration on the role which can be played by the multilateral agencies, especially the World Bank and the IMF, in coordinating Western efforts and strengthening external disciplines on the processes of Soviet reform provides a new and important opportunity to direct a Japanese settlement with the Soviet Union to important collective purposes, thereby gaining for Japan international credit which it needs in the United States and Europe.

An integral interest for Japan, and its major partners in the Asia–Pacific region including the United States, is in building a new set of political relationships and a framework in East Asia and the Pacific, capable of sustaining confidence in the development of broader and deeper economic and political interaction among the countries of the region. Obviously Korea is a crucible within which these political and economic interests are mixed in a particularly volatile way. The Korean issue is explored by Yu-Nam Kim in Chapter 8. But strategic political interests are by no means confined to the management of events on the Korean Peninsula.

The geopolitical circumstance of the Soviet Union is of strategic concern to Japan and its Asia–Pacific partners. The Soviet Union is a huge bridge across the back of Asia to Europe. As Soviet Foreign Minister Shevardnadze observed in Vladivostok in September 1990, and elaborates in the Foreword to this volume, it is one of the few countries in the world with legitimate claims to a future both in Europe and in the Asia–Pacific region. Certainly Japanese reassessment of its relations with the Soviet Union needs to be cast in this light, with these larger strategic and long-term interests in managing its key relationships in East Asia and the Pacific a foremost consideration.

The return of two of the Kurile islands (the Habomai group and Shikotan) is an important first step in a more comprehensive understanding between Japan and the Soviet Union. This represents progress for Japan only if there are explicit understandings on subsequent steps, including the release of Soviet sovereignty over the Southern Kuriles (Etorofu and Kunashiri) within a defined time frame. Similarly, the Soviet Union requires recognition of its sovereignty over the Northern Kuriles and Sakhalin. Cooperative development of the Kurile islands and the energy and other resources on Sakhalin can be part of a comprehensive understanding, if there is parallel commitment by Japan to large-scale economic, technical and investment cooperation in the reconstruction of the Soviet economy. These are the elements in an historic settlement between Japan and the Soviet Union — a settlement which realistically cannot hope to achieve its primary purposes for either party without the close and cooperative involvement of Japan's main Asia–Pacific partners, especially the United States, and broadening Asia–Pacific political and economic dialogue to incorporate the Soviet Union.

Broadening political dialogue and the definition of a new framework for Asia–Pacific security in the post Cold War era are tasks for the future. Compared with the remarkable changes in political relationships which have taken place in Europe and the Atlantic, little progress has been made in the political sphere in Asia and the Pacific, which remains dominated by the divisions of the past. In Indo-China, on the Korean Peninsula and in the North Pacific, political change may be in the making, but has not yet been delivered. Various proposals have been put forward in the last four years — from Australia, the ASEAN countries, Canada and the Soviet Union — for restructuring the old political and security relationships to reduce the potential for friction and confrontation, but comprehensive political–security dialogue is only likely to evolve over a longish period of time in this region. One critical element of progress in this direction is, of course, an accord between the Soviet Union and Japan. A second is the political confidence built upon succesful management of the growth of economic interdepence in the region.

COOPERATION ASIA–PACIFIC STYLE

The development of dialogue on regional economic cooperation is much further advanced than political military or security dialogues. These dialogues have been driven by the pace of East Asian industrialisation and its impact through the intensification of Asia–Pacific economic interdependence (see Table 1.1) and by the need to define new commercial strategies and policy directions in consequence of these developments.[3]

These matters are at the heart of the change in the international economic regime now being cautiously but purposefully put into place by the Asia–Pacific Economic Cooperation (APEC) group of countries.

The ministerial level meeting on APEC in Canberra in November 1989 was the signal of a profound change in the whole regime whereby policies will be developed in the Pacific and international economy. The gathering of the most powerful and representative group of ministers responsible for foreign economic policy ever to assemble in Asia and the Pacific (from Japan, Korea, the ASEAN countries, Canada, the United States, New Zealand and Australia) testified, above all, to the growing imperative of regional economic cooperation. United States Secretary of State James Baker believes that the Asia–Pacific group could become as important in the international economic system as the Bretton Woods institutions. No one, least of all Baker, imagines this happening in the near term; but it is likely to evolve over the next decade or two.

It will be no easy task to build a coalition in the Pacific that will make the achievement of common policy goals manageable among the diverse economies and polities in the region, and ease the transition in international economic leadership responsibilities. One effect of economic change, and the domestic and international uncertainties it creates, is to make institutions, and the forums and settlements they make possible, much more important to the success of international economic collaboration.

The countries of the Asia–Pacific region have neither the example of a recent Armageddon such as that which impelled Europe towards the 1957 Treaty of Rome, nor the close economic, cultural and geopolitical interests which provide a ready basis for cooperation in North America. Yet despite the heterogeneity of Asia–Pacific countries, the process of establishing an infrastructure for closer economic cooperation was begun in 1980 through the Pacific Economic Cooperation Conference (PECC). The seventh PECC meeting was held in Auckland in 1989; the eighth meeting is scheduled for Singapore in 1991 and the ninth for the United States in 1992.

PECC's forums and task forces, which deal with regional cooperation in trade, agriculture, fisheries, minerals and energy, investment, monitoring macroeconomic trends, and transport, telecommunications and tourism, serve both policy and commercial strategic purposes. In this, their tripartite structure (with official, industry and academic participation) and quasi-official status are a considerable advantage. PECC's task force activities are fully open to expert participation from economies which have direct interests in Pacific economic cooperation but are not yet full PECC members. An important policy achievement, which grew out of consultations within PECC, was the development of Pacific support for the comprehensive round of multilateral trade negotiations currently under way (the Uruguay Round). Another achievement has been the facilitation and broadening of the economic dialogue between China and Taiwan. This will be an important advantage in drawing China, Taiwan and Hong Kong into the high-level APEC dialogues already begun.

PECC is the most comprehensive vehicle for consultations on economic cooperative interests in East Asia and the Pacific. Its essential features are: support for the enhancement of information about policy practices and economic data to assess policy interests; the opportunity for interchange on policy matters among officials of Pacific countries; and encouragement to seek policy convergence through the exploration of common interests and problems. PECC's unique structure and operating modalities, including the 'non-official' but informed character of its deliberations, are essential to its functioning (around the constraints of Asia–Pacific diplomacy such as those presented by China's relations with the region) and constitute a special strength in its role of policy development within the Pacific.

Compared with the elaborate mechanisms for consultation on economic policy matters that have evolved within Europe, or that are enshrined in the OECD, those in the Pacific are as yet quite rudimentary. Nonetheless, they incorporate features uniquely suited to the problems of encouraging policy coordination among Asia–Pacific economies. First, in no sense do the forums for consultation within the Pacific region constitute the formation of an economic bloc. Asia–Pacific countries have no interest in European-style union or the formation of a discriminatory trading bloc. Any such development would be inimical to the long-term interests of the region which is reliant on rapid trade transformation and global access. Rather, the aims of broadly-based Asia–Pacific economic cooperation are: to promote multilateral trade liberalisation and sharing of the responsibilities of world trade and economic leadership; to lower tensions between the United States and its East Asian economic partners over trade issues and payments imbalances; to reduce the risks to the region associated with a more inward-looking Europe; to accommodate new problems of competitive strength in East Asia; to manage whatever challenge the emergence of China, with its partially-reformed, centrally-planned system, brings when it returns as a major player in Pacific economic relations; and to define a new relationship with the Soviet Union.

Second, the mechanisms for economic consultation in the Asia–Pacific region do not require elaborate bureaucratic structures. In a commercial and policy environment that is subject to rapid change and immense political and cultural diversity, the need to anticipate new policy issues, to develop new policy approaches, and to increase the transparency of policy interests, recommend against the representation of policy positions, and their entrenchment, in a formal bureaucratic structure of extensive government-to-government arrangements. Government-level consultations do not, however, require elaborate bureaucratic structures.

The APEC meeting in Canberra was a logical step in a careful and, thus far, successful process of building the consensus on foreign economic policy approaches within the Pacific necessary to preserve and enhance the conditions for continued economic growth. It also signified an important change in gear.

The interests of Asia–Pacific countries as a group are converging on stronger support for an open economic system. There is a close consistency between regional policy objectives and international economic policy goals. The agenda of regional interests is huge and complex. These facts have defined the unique character and development of Asia–Pacific economic consultative mechanisms to date and for the future.

The central ideas are: **openness** in international economic policy and diplomatic approach; **evolution** in the practice of high-level consultation and cooperation; and **equality** in managing a growing economic partnership.

SOVIET PARTICIPATION

Uncertainty surrounding the immediate future of Soviet economic reform should not divert the Asia–Pacific market economies from inevitable involvement and substantial strategic interest in the progress and consequences of Soviet reform. From this standpoint, steps to engage the Soviet Union productively in the processes of consultation on Pacific economic cooperation are an important and necessary part of the agenda for establishing a new framework for ordering policy priorities and commercial strategies in the East Asian and Pacific region.

Already such steps have begun. Like the Latin American countries, the Soviet Union is now more actively involved, and interested in becoming still more actively involved, in Pacific economic consultation and cooperation. Successful reform in the Soviet economy will make more extensive economic cooperation with Asia–Pacific economies feasible. Meanwhile, within the framework of PECC and its task force activities, the Soviet Union has begun a modest dialogue in areas of particular interest — minerals and energy, fisheries, agriculture and trade policy — as too have the Latin American countries. The structured and non-exclusive character of dialogues within PECC gives Asia–Pacific economic cooperation at this level a policy and diplomatic stamp and openness appropriate to the pluralist constituency in East Asia and the Pacific.

As Korolev notes, in another but relevant context, in Chapter 2, the participation of Soviet policy-makers (and, in the PECC tripartite framework, industry leaders and economic analysts) is essential to successful management of the huge transformation of institutions, attitudes and capacities required for successful integration of the Soviet economy into the international marketplace. Sato argues in Chapter 5 that the convergence of interests between East and West leaves the West with no choice other than to support the reform efforts of socialist societies and encourage sensitively their integration into the international community.

The Soviet Union was among the non-member economies invited to send observers as guests to the sixth PECC plenary meeting held in Osaka in May 1988. Primakov, then Chairman of the newly formed Soviet National Committee for Asia–Pacific Economic Cooperation (SOVNAPEC), made a brief and effective presentation in which he explained the Soviet Union's interests in participating in the specialist working group meetings or task forces of PECC in the context of restructuring the Soviet economy, and the need to develop new approaches to international economic relations, especially with the economies of the Asia–Pacific region. Australia facilitated the participation of the first Soviet specialist in the Minerals and Energy Forum in Seoul in 1987. Effective Soviet participation in other PECC task forces is expanding steadily.

The non-exclusiveness and flexibility of the PECC process creates an ideal mechanism for countries with growing and different levels of interest in the practicalities of economic cooperation in the Asia–Pacific region to become involved in a constructive way. This provides a test of interest and commitment to PECC principles and the PECC process on which full membership of PECC can be ultimately based.

Membership of PECC requires: endorsement of the Vancouver Statement, which sets out the objectives and the principles of PECC; commitment to economic cooperation based on free and open exchanges; extensive economic activities in and with the Asia–Pacific region; an established and viable tripartite member committee; and substantial tripartite contributions in a number of PECC work programs (excluding PECC general meetings). In the admission of new members, PECC is also required to give full consideration to its capacity to absorb and productively engage the prospective member. While Soviet economic interaction with other Asia–Pacific economies is not yet so extensive as that required of present PECC members, the stage is now set for the progression of the Soviet Union to full PECC membership within a defined time frame.

Full and active participation in PECC, and the growth of Soviet economic ties with Asia–Pacific economies, would seem, in turn, a natural step towards an association, at a later stage, with APEC meetings.

For APEC the immediate priority in expanded membership is the inclusion of the three parts of China in its deliberations. This follows from the large and established economic relationship between the three Chinas and the rest of the region. As Soviet economic ties with the Asia–Pacific grow stronger and wider and special cooperative interests are taken up within a growing range of APEC meetings (such as that which considered trade policy issues in Vancouver in September 1990), the Soviet Union can expect to be drawn into these discussions. Meanwhile, there is immediate opportunity to make an input into the APEC process of policy discussion through participation in the work of PECC as it is being drawn upon in the development of the work programs and agenda of APEC.

PERSPECTIVES

The chapters which follow were the result of work and discussion organised in Australia to analyse the prospects for the Soviet Union in the Asia–Pacific economy. It is important to explain Australia's interest in this issue. Why should Australia take the initiative in work on the Soviet reforms and their impact on the Pacific?

Australia has a direct interest in the great changes that are taking place in the Soviet Union. If, indeed, some of the promise that was let loose at Vladivostok comes to fruition in the Soviet Far East, that region could emerge as a big competitor to Australia and other resource suppliers, like Canada and the United States, to the international market place. Although this prospect might not be so immediate, as Minakir's discussion in Chapter 10 indicates, consideration of the prospect is nevertheless important for Australia which is one of the largest and most efficient suppliers of resources to the world. It is also a prospect which Australia should welcome, whatever adjustment it may require, consistent with its position of support for, and dependence on, an open international economic system in which the right to compete on equal terms is a primary interest. But alongside that direct competitive interest, there is also a complementary interest, as Findlay and Edwards suggest in Chapter 11, since Australia's advantages and experience in the international market place for resource goods offer a strong basis for commercial and economic cooperation with the Soviet Union in the exploration, development and marketing of the resources of the Soviet Far East. Australia's direct interests in the effects of Soviet reform on the Soviet market extend well beyond the Soviet Far East, but they are also prominent there.

These direct interests are trivial, however, alongside Australia's much more substantial indirect interests in the impact of Soviet reforms on global, multilateral and regional systems and the stability and prosperity of the Asia–Pacific region. It is natural, although it was not inevitable, that Australia has taken some initiative in the whole process of establishing an infrastructure for Asia–Pacific cooperation through PECC and the important step of convening the first APEC ministerial-level meeting. Australia's economic and political interests are now deeply embedded in the Asia–Pacific region and forward-thinking about trends and developments in regional economic diplomacy is a sensible and generally valuable Australian preoccupation.

The chapters in this book (and the discussion that surrounded their preparation) provide the foundations upon which these specific and, earlier, general perspectives are based. No one foresees that the Soviet Union will soon become a major economic power in East Asia and the Pacific. Indeed, as a leading European power by history and political circumstance and an Asia–Pacific nation by geographic situation, the accommodation of the Soviet Union in the Asia–Pacific region presents problems quite different from those of its accommodation in a new European economic and political order.

Political and security issues drove a comprehensive accord within Europe, around a process of settlements set in motion through the Helsinki commitments. There is no such political focus for comprehensive accord in East Asia and the Pacific, although the long-term goal of establishing one is laudable. Rather, the motive force towards political accommodation in East Asia and the Pacific is overwhelmingly economic. Hence the critical and strategic role of the APEC group in the process of building political confidence and reducing uncertainty in a time of immense change, through successful management of the international diplomatic consequences of the region's dynamic economic transformation.

The Soviet Union is destined to play a critical political role, together with the United States, Japan and their allies, in containing important fragilities associated with the process of East Asia's own dynamic economic growth, and success with its own reforms would see its emergence as a small to middle-ranking economic player in the region within the next few decades.

The new international politics of the post Cold War period, and their articulation through the conduct of the Iraq-Kuwait crisis, highlight the political fragilities in East Asia and the Pacific. In this context there have been suggestions for the extension of political dialogues within the region. Yet, no nation with substantial regional interests, including the Soviet Union, is comfortable with a diminution in established regional security arrangements. A central element in these arrangements is the United States–Japan Security Agreement. These arrangements remain critical to regional political security but the development of broader dialogues on specific political and security issues in the North Pacific and Southeast Asia to supplement, but not replace, established arrangements and dialogues is now a more active interest. It is an active interest in dealing with tensions on the Korean Peninsular and also in resolution of the problems of Indo-China. It is also an active interest in the context of the fundamental reassessment of its own security environment being forced, by the new circumstance in international politics, upon Japan.

2 The agenda for economic reform in the Soviet Union: international dimensions and sequence

IVAN KOROLEV

The restructuring of the entire economic system of the Soviet Union is now underway. Somewhat ironically, economic reform is yet to produce radical change for the better in terms of the economic prosperity of the Soviet people.

There are numerous reasons for the current economic problems of the Soviet Union, some of which are similar to those in other centrally-planned economies attempting to become more market oriented such as Hungary, China and Poland. But there are also political and economic reasons specific only to the Soviet Union. There have also been mistakes made in Soviet economic policy over the last three years.

The economic mechanism formed in the Soviet Union seven decades ago is still in operation. The Soviet economy is still based on an excessively central-ised system of allocation of production resources, planning of output structure, budget financing of capital investment of enterprises and use of centralised norms and regulations. This substantially limits the Soviet Union's ability to self-regulate. The present economy has practically no incentive for scientific and technological progress or to increase the quality of products and services, and is still promoting monopolistic tendencies, unjustified growth of wholesale prices, and the dictatorship of producers. There is no wholesale trade in the means of production. Centralised rationing gives practically no incentive to enterprises in terms of economic initiative and a more effective utilisation of re-sources.

These economic problems are aggravated substantially by industrial minis-tries which, without any economic or legal responsibility, interfere into practi-cally all aspects of the activities of enterprises. Additionally, the Soviet Union is feeling the negative results of its previous investment policy. For many years the share of capital investment used for development in the social sphere of the economy, including housing construction, medical care, education and culture, has been falling. This policy is now changing but the process of rectification will be a difficult and protracted one.

In general, the economic situation in the Soviet Union since 1985–86 has not improved, and the financial and consumer market circumstances have deteriorated seriously.

BASIC DIMENSIONS AND SOURCES OF FINANCIAL INSTABILITY

An intensification of disproportions in the economy cannot but affect the financial sphere. A critical situation has developed in the sphere of money circulation. The non-secured monetary expansion has accelerated dramatically. In 1989 it reached 19 billion roubles, which is equal to the increase in money supply during the previous five years. The forced savings of the population (that is, pent-up demand because of shortages in the consumer goods market) are estimated to be at least 160 billion roubles, and are growing fast. Current funds of enterprises have also increased, creating excess demand for equipment, raw materials and intermediate products, leading to higher payments for supplies, design and development works. A considerable part of the funds of enterprises is leaking from the the non-cash into the cash payments sphere. All these facts disrupt the internal market and intensify inflation. At the same time, price increases have not led to increased production of scarce commodities and services. Therefore, incentives for productive labour are undermined sharply.

The nominal increment of money incomes of the population reached 64 billion roubles in 1989, against a yearly average of 15 billion roubles over the three previous Five Year Plans and 38.5 billion roubles in 1988. Nominal wages in industry and construction are now growing 1.2 to 1.4 times faster than labour productivity. This is not particularly significant given that the share of wages in the GNP of the Soviet Union is lower than in other countries.

What makes things much worse is that money incomes have grown faster than the supply of commodities and services in the consumer goods market. In 1989 the latter increased by only 30 billion roubles, with at least a quarter of the increase due to the rise of prices.

Usually cooperatives are the first to be blamed for such a growth of money incomes. According to the Gosbank data, their share in the total increment of money incomes is over 20 per cent. Net withdrawals from bank accounts for cash transactions of cooperatives reached 18 billion roubles in 1989. Cooperatives have concentrated their activities on intermediate trade which is largely speculative in the deficit economy. They are not yet interested in increased production of goods and services, trying instead to benefit from rising prices in times of shortage.

However, it is not correct to blame only the cooperatives for this situation. The state itself is guilty to a considerably greater extent. The destabilisation of the money circulation is largely connected with the budget deficit of 100 billion roubles. The basic reason for the deficit is the inefficiency of state expenditure over several decades and the low rate of return on investments in industry and agriculture. In 1986–88 the situation in the investment sector did not improve: the volume of non-completed investment projects grew by more than 80 billion roubles. During the last three years additional burdens on the budget were created by Chernobyl (direct expenditures alone amounted to 8 billion roubles) and the earthquake in Armenia (8 billion roubles). From 1987–89, the state budget was deprived of 40 billion roubles by the fall in world oil prices and about 36 billion roubles owing to decreased sales of alcohol. The conversion of the war industry is responsible for an additional expenditure of 4 billion roubles. The situation was also aggravated by a series of strikes in the summer of 1989.

ECONOMIC REFORM: LONGER-TERM AND IMMEDIATE EXTRAORDINARY MEASURES

There is a certain contradiction between the goals of radical economic reform and the extraordinary measures needed to rectify dangerous imbalances in the economy. Radical economic reform should be based on revolutionary (if it is an appropriate word) change in property relations to provide real pluralism, diversity and competition. This process will not be easy and a long period of time will be required to implement reform. One of the crucial issues — the ownership of the land — has remained unresolved for the last 130 years. Extraordinary measures are expected to give immediate results for the people and include first of all centralised measures. But in the long run these measures should provide better conditions for the implementation of market mechanisms.

The main elements of economic reform underway in the Soviet Union are:

— The rational combination of centralised economic management with the economic independence of state and republic-level enterprises, the cooperative sector and individual entrepreneurship.

— The reform of wholesale prices (especially for agricultural products) and retail prices. This reform was scheduled for 1989 but the situation in the consumer market made it impossible to implement. It was rescheduled for 1991. The reform of wholesale and retail prices will make conditions easier for the functioning of the real wholesale market of the means of production. For example, the price of fuel and raw materials is obviously too low in the Soviet Union (even compared with world prices at the official rate of the rouble) while the price of machinery, especially allowing for its quality, is too high.

— The improvement of the structure of output and capital investment into various sectors and branches of the economy and the increasing role of decentralised investment.

— The economic independence of regions and communities (not only Union republics). This process depends largely on the introduction of real pluralism in property relations.

— The increasing role of foreign competition in the Soviet market and the step by step integration of the Soviet Union into the world economy. At this stage, the priority should not be to increase the volume of foreign trade. It is simply not possible given the unnatural structure of the Soviet Union's exports and the potentially negative effect on the domestic economy. It is more important to effect change in economic mentality. The role of foreign enterprises in the development of contemporary market mechanisms in the Soviet Union is essential in this process.

All elements of Soviet economic reform are interconnected. In the long run, the ability to persuade foreign enterprises to open affiliates in the Soviet Union will depend upon the conditions regulating the day-to-day function of Soviet enterprises, regardless of their ownership — state, collective or private.

THE INTEGRATION OF THE SOVIET UNION INTO THE WORLD ECONOMY [1]

The furtherance of international stability, cooperation and understanding calls for the integration of the Soviet Union into the world economy. Foreign economic relations have become a crucial factor in the acceleration of economic, scientific and technological development. This fact is acknowledged by all socialist countries. There is also a growing understanding that participation in the world economy requires the establishment of an economic machinery capable of interacting positively with external markets.

The integration of the Soviet Union into the world economy is a complicated problem for numerous reasons. These include the very structure of the economy; the underdeveloped international specialisation; the lack of modern market elements in the economic machinery; and the inexperience of existing management to control external operations using generally accepted controls such as taxes, duties, interest rates and exchange rates. There are also certain subjective factors both in the Soviet Union and the West which restrict economic cooperation with the non-socialist world.

In addition, the integration of the Soviet Union into the world economy will be effected initially under unfavourable conditions. Indices of the efficiency of public production show the Soviet Union lags behind in productivity of labour, utilisation of fixed assets, energy and mineral resources. The infrastructure to conduct foreign economic relations is not well developed and the shortage of qualified specialists will be felt keenly, particularly in circumstances of entry into international economic organisations.

The main condition for an efficient integration into the international division of labour is the achievement of economic reform in the Soviet Union, that is, the transition to a self-controlled economy and the success of *perestroika*. In conjunction with this transition, the reconstruction of the foreign economic machinery is of great importance. The introduction of new foreign economic means such as efficient customs tariffs and real exchange rates for the rouble will only produce a positive effect in combination with the proper functioning of the general economic machinery. This will necessitate real non-financing by the state, direct relations and independence of enterprises, and elements of competition in the internal market.

Measures for the decentralisation and democratisation of foreign economic relations of the Soviet Union have been announced by the government. However, there are many unresolved problems in this area. These include the attraction and utilisation of foreign investments and the formation of joint companies in priority spheres to produce science-intensive products or mass consumer goods. A considered study is required to evaluate the benefits of establishing free economic zones or special export zones. Such zones should be considered in the general context of the utilisation of foreign capital. The effect on other sectors of the economy as well as the experience of other countries should also be considered in the evaluation.

The integration into the world economy presupposes an equal participation in international economic organisations and in the elaboration of norms and rules which regulate world economic relations. Organisations such as GATT, IMF, IBRD, FAO and various regional institutions are designed to regulate international economic cooperation for the mutual benefit of member countries. However, the United States and some of its allies hinder the entry of the Soviet Union into these organisations. Certainly, reform measures on the part of the Soviet Union are necessary for full-scale participation in such organisations and considerable efforts have already been made in this regard. However, at this stage, the main obstacle in many cases is a lack of good will on the part of some Western powers rather than the incompleteness of measures required for full and active participation.

Such is the far from complete list of problems facing the Soviet Union for a full-scale integration into the international division of labour. The problems associated with the reconstruction of the economy and the formation of corresponding economic machinery will need to be resolved by the Soviet Union itself. However, given the interdependence of the contemporary world, Soviet efforts to achieve reform will require a genuine desire on the part of all members of the world community to effect international cooperation. The Soviet Union is quite determined to progress along the road of reform and to meet its foreign economic partners half-way; a similar effort is required from the latter.

Unfortunately, economic factors still play a subordinate role in East–West relations. The relationship is determined primarily by the political climate. In spite of the recent positive changes in the international situation, a mutual suspicion towards countries of opposing blocks continues. Economic interdependence between the East and West is not yet a reality. Such interdependence will be necessary to provide radical solutions for military and political problems, global economic problems and ecological problems. Thus, East–West economic relations require additional political stimulation to further economic interdependence. The stimuli are, in the end, the same as those which motivated the East and West to reach agreement on disarmament.

INTERNAL MEASURES FOR A NORMALISATION OF THE ECONOMIC SITUATION

Radical economic reform cannot be exercised in an unbalanced economy. What is necessary in the shortest possible time are structural changes in the investment policy, a sharp reduction of non-efficient state expenditure and an abandonment of doubtful, expensive projects. Priority should be given to the distribution of state resources to achieve more balanced proportions in the economy. It is not important what general rates of growth are achieved in the meantime.

The weakest links in the Soviet economy are the manufacturing sector and the sphere of distribution. The Soviet Union produces sufficient industrial and agricultural raw materials yet is unable to satisfy the requirements of its enterprises or population owing to losses in processing. In comparison with other countries, the Soviet Union has an underdeveloped network in the wholesale and retail trades, especially in rural areas. Large investments are not necessary to remedy this problem. What is needed are organisational measures, especially at the local authority level. To this end, from 1990, half of the increased supply of foodstuffs and manufactured goods was left at the disposal of the republics and regions where previously everything was allocated within the framework of centralised supplies.

As for the financial sphere, the experience of many countries introducing radical economic change shows that the main problem is to keep consumer prices and wages under control to ensure maximum stability. A concerted anti-inflationary policy that includes monetary and credit measures is required. In implementing this policy, interest rates, taxes and exchange rates serve as market instruments of macro-economic management under conditions of greater decentralisation of the economy. Purely administrative measures will be also necessary during the transitional period at the central, regional and local levels to provide the population with the basic necessities. Some of the measures adopted by the Supreme Soviet of the Soviet Union include:

— legislative restrictions on monetary and credit expansion;
— a radical reduction of centralised investment and an austerity regime for all state expenditure;
— a sharp increase in interest rates on credits, bank deposits and state bonds;
— the leasing of small enterprises and shops to workers' collectives or cooperatives;
— an issue of 'target bonds' which give subscribers the right to purchase scarce goods such as motor vehicles;
— tax deductions and other benefits for state-owned industry, cooperatives and individuals that produce consumer goods as well as an expansion of the supply of decentralised construction services;
— the transfer of state housing to personal property; and
— an expansion of non-cash transactions.

The government also proposed an instantaneous, one-step price reform involving price increases for foodstuffs. This proposal is now opposed strongly. There is a danger that such a reform would give an additional impetus to inflation and aggravate social tension. Moreover, new prices alone will not create a competitive market mechanism nor become objective criteria for economic activity. The alternative to instantaneous price reform is the stage-by-stage reform of pricing in conjunction with other measures. These include a transition from distribution to trade in raw materials, intermediate goods and means of production; the encouragement of competition in the banking sphere; and the formation of a new tax system. The reconsideration of the attitude towards price reform indicates a strengthening of the position of proponents of a sober and pragmatic approach to the transition to a market economy.

There is, however, one question which should be decided without delay. This is the sale of plots of land as personal property to encourage the development of individual farming and housing construction. I believe such a measure could prove to be a particularly efficient one. The decentralisation of property should begin with land and, in hindsight, Soviet economic reform should probably have started with this measure. There will be at least three favourable effects of such a measure: (1) the state will receive billions of roubles; (2) competition between individual farmers and collective farms will be encouraged; and (3) opportunities for foreign investment in the Soviet Union will expand.

EXTERNAL ECONOMIC AND MONETARY MEASURES

Foreign trade has the potential to improve the situation in the consumer goods market quickly. For this purpose, it is unnecessary to resort to additional credits as some Soviet economists have suggested. A temporary reduction of centralised investments will allow the Soviet Union to reduce imports of some types of equipment, rolled ferrous metals and a number of other semi-manufactured articles. It will then be possible to increase imports of consumer goods, medicines and other commodities important from the point of view of social stability. Some of these measures have been partially introduced. In adopting these measures, the Soviet Union will simultaneously change the structure of agricultural imports, reduce the importation of raw materials, and increase purchases of finished goods and tropical commodities such as coffee and fruits.

I consider the importation of commodities for production purposes for cooperatives and individual labour activity to be a sensible proposition. These purchases will ensure high budget efficiency, and increase the supply of consumer goods from these sectors of the economy.

An urgent rationalisation of the structure of our exports is necessary. The Soviet Union often exports products without taking into account the costs and the effect on the internal market. In 1989 the Soviet Union exported 37.5 per cent of washing machines produced, 27 per cent of cars, 21.5 per cent of household refrigerators, 13.9 per cent of receivers and 12.8 per cent of television sets. The receipts from these exports are not considerable. However, given the acute shortage of these commodities in the internal consumer market, their sale in the country would have a beneficial economic and social effect.

To achieve a more optimal export and import structure there are plans to use currency instruments more widely. The question of rouble convertibility is a more remote goal which will be addressed after the stabilisation of its purchasing power in the internal market. Under the present conditions, I see three directions in the sphere of the exchange rate policy: (1) the introduction of a more realistic commercial exchange rate for the rouble; (2) the expansion of the internal wholesale trade with payments in foreign currencies; and (3) the development of currency auctions. These measures will not only stimulate exports from the Soviet Union but, what is no less important, promote the development of the internal market.

A matter of special significance for the Soviet Union in both the long and short-term is the attraction of foreign capital. As of today, the results in this field are far from impressive. There are serious obstacles. The main obstacle is not the non-convertibility of the rouble but the underdeveloped internal wholesale trade in raw materials, intermediate goods and equipment as well as the absence of an internal monetary and financial market.

Foreign investors are naturally interested in increased sales to the Soviet market. So is the Soviet Union but, at present, there is no currency for a transfer of dividends. If foreign investment becomes larger in scale, however, such opportunities will appear.

What is the way ahead? It seems that the East and the West should be interested (at least from a political point of view) in stimulating foreign investment into the sphere of distribution of the Soviet Union (including trade and banking), thereby forming an infrastructure which would allow foreign companies to use rouble returns from sales in the Soviet market for reinvestments including export-oriented ones.

Concessions could be the quickest way to attract foreign capital into the Soviet Union to solve problems of raw materials processing and to produce products which are now imported. Provided foreign firms strictly observe ecological requirements, mines and mineral deposits, industrial facilities, individual enterprises, hotels and tourist complexes may be transferred for their long-term exploitation over 20, 30 or even 99 years. Concessions could be made to exploit forestry reserves, mine deposits of metallurgical raw materials, extract fuels and process oil and gas, establish natural and ecological reservations and develop foreign tourist resorts.

Certainly, clear guidelines for the mutual benefit of all parties will be required. These might include legislation regulating foreign economic relations; state guarantees of the inviolability of concessions for an agreed period; a system for the evaluation of the objects leased; and an introduction of an economically justifiable exchange rate for the rouble.

Finally, let me return to the matter of the Soviet Union's membership of international financial organisations. From the long list of problems in the Soviet economy, it is clear that participation in the IMF and the World Bank is not the highest priority for the Soviet Union. Nevertheless, participation in these organisations would be useful for the Soviet Union. And here I do not agree with the statements of a number of officials in the West that the Soviet Union could not participate in these organisations due to its economic system or the inconvertibility of the rouble. The Soviet Union (one of the founder-countries of the IMF) has an indisputable legal right to participate in these organisations. It is another matter that the Soviet Union may not gain direct commercial benefit from participation in the IMF, the World Bank or GATT under existing conditions in the Soviet economy. But participation in these organisations will provide an additional channel to mould a modern economic outlook in the Soviet Union. Moreover, the West will gain a better understanding of the problems of the Soviet Union through its membership of international financial organisations. The integration of the Soviet Union into the world economy is hardly possible without mutual understanding and cooperation.

3 The dynamics of reform in Soviet-type economies: comparative perspectives

CRAIG LITTLER

The huge changes taking place in socialist societies all over the world need to be placed in comparative and systemic context. The primary touchstone is the development of economic reforms in China and the parallels and contrasts with the Soviet reforms. The aim here is to connect the experience of all the Soviet-type economies (STEs). This broad focus raises a number of basic questions:

— How should state socialist societies be characterised? What are the essential features? This study treats state socialist societies as distinctive economic systems with dynamics which are peculiar to themselves. If this is so, then the basic characteristics which have marked off state socialist economies from capitalist economies need to be understood.

— Why did such societies reach a watershed during the 1980s, a crisis-point which seems to have been general across all the COMECON members and which became more apparent in China at the end of the 1980s?

— What are the basic driving forces of change and the basic contradictions of such societies? Is it a question that there is a fundamental contradiction between socialist principles and the conditions of economic efficiency?

— What are the dynamics of economic reform?

This chapter considers each issue in turn. At this historical juncture, these issues are critical ones for the 1990s. However, events are moving so fast in Eastern Europe and the Soviet Union that this study can only be tentative.

One major conclusion is that Soviet-type economies have suffered from an historic failure, not just in relation to the traditional model (see below), but from a failure of the reform process. Up to 1990 no stable reformed model has been developed in any society. The Tiananmen massacre of June 1989 was a symbolic statement of the failures of the Chinese strategy.

24

SYSTEM-SPECIFIC FEATURES OF SOVIET-TYPE ECONOMIES

In his book published in 1972, Brus set out a list of the main features of the traditional Soviet-type economy.[1] Similarly, American authors such as Grossman have delineated the key features of the Stalinist model.[2] Ellman, in a recent revision of his widely-known text, draws some of the institutional features together and suggests the following model:[3]

Table 3.1   Ellman's list of key features of the state socialist economies (traditional model)

• State ownership of the means of production.
• Political dictatorship.
• A mono-hierarchical system.
• Imperative planning.
• Physical planning.

However, this characterisation of the Stalinist model remains a listing rather than an ideal type. An ideal type is based on a specific rationality, or principles, which mark out some features as fundamental and some as contingent. As discussed later, this issue is a critical one.

The basic rationality of the traditional, or Stalinist, model was that of socialism — however distorted it may have become over time. There were three basic dichotomies underpinning the notion of socialism:
— social ownership of the means of production versus private ownership;
— central planning versus the anarchy of the market; and
— egalitarian income distribution versus a class-based distribution of income.

The left-hand side of these dichotomies (social ownership, planning and the ideology of an egalitarian income distribution) constitutes the 'Socialist Trinity'. They have been the core features of Soviet-type societies *at the level of the relations of production*. Other characteristics are contingent or derived. Political and ideological structures underpin Soviet-type economies and they must be analysed as political phenomena.

The criterion of the ownership of the means of production constitutes a fundamental set of institutions of any socio-economic system. The dichotomy is between private ownership and social ownership. What does 'social' mean in the context of ownership? The answer given in practice is that 'social ownership' and 'state ownership' have been treated as synonymous. Until recently in China, state ownership has been regarded as the highest, or most progressive, form of ownership. The process of economic reform has brought this assumption into question and Yugoslavia was the first state socialist country to embark upon a process of radical reform whereby the leadership accepted significant changes in property rights as acceptable within the framework of socialist ideology.

Secondly, state socialist societies are characterised by bureaucratic coordination as opposed to market coordination. The economies are not market-linked networks of competing firms, but a system of enterprises controlled by ministers and local authorities and subordinate to the polity. Kornai refers to this system as 'bureaucratic coordination' in which the 'plan' plays a significant role.[4] The emphasis in bureaucratic coordination is on vertical relations which are not necessarily monetised. Under market coordination the transactions are generally monetised.

The notion of an egalitarian income distribution (the third factor in the Trinity) has been embedded in a particular way. Sabel and Stark argue that there is an implicit social contract between urban populations and state socialist regimes, a legitimating ideology which has buttressed the regime:

> Thus the context for social conflicts in Eastern Europe is formed by: the ideology of continuous economic advance; the centralisation of economic control in the hands of self-proclaimed custodians of a higher rationality; and a system of price and employment guarantees that vindicate, though in a stunted way, the elite's claim to protect the interests of the otherwise defenseless.[5]

In a recent book, Granick takes the embedded consequences of this ideology as the means to develop an alternative theory to explain the functioning and malfunctioning of Soviet-type economies. He argues that STEs are characterised by (1) each worker being protected from dismissal or from being forced to take an inferior job within his enterprise; (2) the maintenance of overfull employment; (3) the equitable allocation of the available work, or required degree of idleness, so that each worker can 'earn' his/her income as opposed to receiving unemployment benefits with the associated loss of dignity.[6]

As is well known, the Socialist Trinity has been linked to a specific set of political principles. In China, for example, the Trinity has been linked into the 'Four Principles', which have been stubbornly supported by Deng Xiaoping since 1978. These Four Principles are the socialist path, the leadership of the Communist Party, the dictatorship of the proletariat and the relevance of Marxism-Leninism and Mao Zedong thought. I will not focus on these specific political aspects of the STEs for the rest of this chapter.

However, there is another dimension to the general argument. The features of the Socialist Trinity were inserted into a particular set of contexts relating to the level of development of the society. As has often been noted, socialism did not emerge from the growing contradictions of the advanced capitalist economies. Instead, socialism emerged in societies which were peripheral, with the exception of the GDR and, perhaps, Czechoslovakia. Socialism, in the sense of the Soviet-type model, became associated with varying degrees of peripheralisation.

If this linkage to peripheral societies is noted, then it raises the issue of interpreting socialism as it historically existed in a developmental perspective. The difficulties of doing this have been exacerbated by a narrow focus arising in part from the persistence of the Cold War on the economic systems of the East and West. Comparative analysis has focused almost exclusively on the advanced, Western, market-type economies (MTEs) and the Soviet-type economies. In surveying the existing literature, Winiecki argues:

> Few scholars venture beyond the ideal type MTE and its real life exemplifications, usually the USA and a country symbolising extensive planning and control among

MTEs (France or, more recently, Japan) on the one hand, and the ideal type STE (usually the War Communism period in the USSR) and its real life exemplifications, normally the USSR and a string of STE mutations on the other. Not only ideal types, which necessarily represent the two ends of the continuum, but also exemplifications cluster very near each end of the continuum, leaving its broad middle range empty. This empty terrain has for a quarter of a century been filled with (no less empty) considerations about economic systems convergence, made plausible by assuming away the politics/economics interface and disregarding other institutional features of both systems. Theoretical and empirical comparative economic studies have followed the pattern almost without exception.[7]

Thus, if this limited focus is put to one side, then socialism can be seen for what it became: a development strategy without perceived alternatives under conditions in which capitalism had failed. Socialism has taken on the historical functions of overcoming traditional structural obstacles to development, obstacles which are constitutive of peripheral-capitalist societies. Consequently, the Soviet-type model as a set of relations of production, historically has been inserted into a specific developmental context leading to economic outcomes which are, arguably, contingent.

The fact that these outcomes may be contingent is pursued by Winiecki. He argues that if our range of comparisons shifts to comparing the STEs with less-developed countries (LDCs), then this comparison suggests 'strikingly similar outcomes of inward-oriented, state-controlled development strategies in LDCs and centrally-planned strategies bordering on autarchy in STEs. Costly neglect of agriculture, overgrown and underperforming heavy industry, low product quality and weak innovative performance of insulated economies, foreign trade bottlenecks and the like — all plague both groups of countries'.[8]

Thus, the Soviet-type model has three fundamental characteristics at the level of the relations of production combined with a developmental context which is contingent but which sets up tensions in terms of the basic model.

There is a second level of contingency in relation to the Soviet-type model. The model is often portrayed as a specific model of industrialisation and modernisation. Historically this has been the case, but the strategic choices made and enforced have depended on historical conjunctures. The Soviet model emerged from political debate, discussion and conflict during the 1920s to be consolidated in 1930–34 as a tool of rapid industrialisation. However, some of the characteristics involved in the Soviet model had little to do with socialism and much to do with intellectual ideologies and fashions of the 1920s. This can be indicated in terms of three illustrations:

— the emphasis on mechanised, large-scale, prairie-type agriculture;
— the emphasis of large-scale, mass production industries linked to Fordism and Taylorism; and
— the emphasis on heavy industry as primary in the process of development.

During the 1920s the American model of production seemed to be the most advanced and progressive. This perspective influenced Soviet decision-makers. The agriculture of the American prairies, which was large-scale, mechanised and capital-intensive, was seen as the agriculture of the future. However, it reflected particular factor relations peculiar to North America — virtually limitless land, ample capital, high labour costs and labour shortages. These factor costs did not apply in the Soviet Union and were totally irrelevant to China. Nevertheless, the model was followed in the Soviet Union in conjunction with violent collectivisation. Gray puts the issue bluntly:

> ...is it really necessary to have a thousand people milling about in one huge field doing rather badly what they could be doing better in their individual field? Is this a necessary part of socialism?[9]

This, of course, is a rhetorical question and any answer would depend on the task structure involved. Several commentators point out that the Hungarian economic reforms in agriculture have resulted in a differentiation of tasks whereby the cooperatives concentrate more on the production of grain and fodder, which lend themselves to larger-scale operations, leaving the private household farms to concentrate on labour-intensive products, such as fruit, vegetables and dairy products.

Additionally, the Soviet-type model of industrialisation absorbed the ideas of Fordism and Taylorism from the United States of the 1920s. Industrial production, it was assumed, should be mass production utilising economies of scale, standardised equipment and standardised products. Small-scale industries were out of date. This has resulted in the size distribution of manufacturing firms being skewed in favour of large units in state socialist economies compared to capitalist countries *with the important exception of China*. Ford's mass production methods were widely copied in the Soviet Union and Russian engineers visited Ford's plants in Detroit in the 1920s in order to learn Fordist methods, whilst over a hundred skilled mechanics from the Ford plants came to the Soviet Union in the early 1920s in order to assist the setting up of production at the Moscow Automobile Factory. Associated with this one-sided absorption of mass production technology was an endorsement of Taylorism. This led to a fierce controversy during 1918–24 in the Soviet Union. As is well known, the major figure was Alexi Gastev who promulgated through his Central Labour Institute a narrow, elitist, technocratic interpretation of Taylorism. He advocated nothing less than 'Soviet Americanism':

> The metallurgy of this new world, the motor car and aeroplane factories of America, and finally the arms industry of the whole world — here are the new, gigantic laboratories where the psychology of the proletariat is being created, where the culture of the proletariat is being manufactured. And whether we live in the age of super-imperialism or of world socialism the structure of the new industry will, in essence, be one and the same.[10]

In part, this focus on mass production was linked to an emphasis on heavy industry. Partly, this was driven by a munitions mentality (the war machine took precedence), but partly it was a logical confusion of the production chain with the policy scheme of priorities: heavy industry comes first and consumption comes last. It is true that this law of the priority growth of the producer goods department (Department 1) was put forward by Marx, but it was suggested in a rudimentary fashion and it was Stalin who converted it into an economic law binding on Soviet planners. However, this was a misreading of history. During the early processes of industrialisation in Western Europe it was the expansion of consumption powers and the development of *services* which provided the dynamic for the growth of manufacturing capacity. This currently accepted historical view is a reversal of the Stalinist view. Despite the arbitrariness of Stalin's interpretation, the priority of heavy industry development has been enormously influential and has shaped the development path of all STEs. The influence in China can be seen in Table 3.2.

This set of processes was recognised by Chinese analysts themselves during the 1980s. For example Bensi Xing says

...we copied the Soviet experience with its priority development of industry, especially heavy industry, and failed to give proper attention to the advancement of agriculture and light industry. Although in theory we recognised the planned development of [a] socialist economy on a proportional basis, in practice the balance of industry and agriculture, light and heavy industry was seriously upset. We subsequently realised the faultiness of our views and shifted the priorities... However, we were unable to change completely the old economic strategy, which did not correspond to the concrete conditions of China, because even the bad aspects of the old practice pass away with great difficulty.[11]

Here Bensi is alluding to the fact that the heavy industry lobby (organised by the Ministry of Machine Building in China) became entrenched and resistant to new policy directions.

Thus, it is possible to conclude from these three illustrations that the nature of state socialist economies has been significantly determined by the range of economic and industrial strategies which were available to the Soviet leadership at the point of regime formation. During the 1920s it was the Utopian view of 'Soviet Americanism' which became dominant. This selection process of economic and industrial strategies was reinforced by the mechanisms of centralised planning. It was easier to plan large-scale, capital intensive production systems in contrast to small-scale, flexible production systems or an array of service provisions. The planning system did not dictate the nature of these production systems, but it did reinforce them over time.

So far, I have argued that the system specific features of Soviet-type economies derive from three sources:

— the fundamental ideology of socialism leading to a basic model embodied in the Socialist Trinity and the Four Principles;
— a set of contextual characteristics deriving from the level of development of the state socialist economies; and
— a set of economic and industrial strategies, derived from historical conjunctures at the point of regime formation, which were transmitted from the Soviet Union to all the other STEs, including China.

If this three-fold analysis is correct, then it has dynamic implications. The social and economic formation of state socialist societies has been such as to set up specific patterns of contradictions. Moreover, these contradictions have been intensified as these societies have attempted to move from an extensive to an intensive path of growth. Contrary to traditional Marxian arguments, Senghaas argues that the more developed and complex a society is *the less relevant are socialist development policies.*[12]

The next section looks at some of the major economic dynamics of state socialist economies based on the work of Brus, Kornai and Winiecki. Following this, the processes of economic reform and the stages of transformation are

Table 3.2 Accumulation and investment in the three branches of industry, China, 1953–82 (per cent)

	Rate of accumulation	Agriculture[b]	Light industry[b]	Heavy industry[b]	Heavy industry/ Light industry + Agriculture[a]
First Plan 1953–7	24.2	7.1	6.4	36.1	268
Second Plan 1958–62	30.8	11.3	6.4	54.0	307
1963–5	22.7	17.7	3.9	45.9	213
Third Plan 1966–70	26.3	10.7	4.4	51.1	339
Fourth Plan 1971–5	33.0	9.8	5.8	49.6	317
Fifth Plan 1976–80	33.4	10.5	6.7	45.9	267
Sixth Plan 1981–85					
– 1981	28.5	6.6	9.8	39.0	238
– 1982	29.0	6.1	8.4	38.5	266

Notes: a   This column gives the ratio between the amount of investment in heavy industry and the amount of the sum of investment in light industry plus agriculture in per cent.

b   For a given period the total of the column is not equal to 100 as the Chinese distinguish other sectors.

Sources: Pairault, *Politique Industrielle et Industrialisation en Chine*, 1983, pp.33–37; *Statistical Yearbook of China*, 1982; *Zhongguo Jingji Nianjian*, 1983.

examined. It is argued that economic reform faces a series of barriers in all state socialist societies.

THE DYNAMICS OF STEs PRE-REFORM

Kornai's conceptual framework for analysing STEs has been most widely used for understanding the economies of Eastern Europe and the Soviet Union. More recently, it has been applied to China and Chinese developments.

The economic context of management

In his book *Economics of Shortage*, Kornai argues that the key factor in relation to state socialist economies is the phenomenon of shortage. Shortage is defined as systemic, pervasive and self-reproducing. Shortage breeds shortage. The pattern self-reproduces because the shortage phenomenon plagues enterprise directors who react by the hoarding of inputs. This leads to very high ratios of input inventories to output inventories compared to the Western, capitalist societies.[13]

In Soviet-type economies, enterprise managers are frequently monopolists of some particular good and are subject to what Kornai calls a 'soft budget constraint'. In other words,

> incentives at the enterprise level, for managers and workers alike, have always been positively correlated with the volume or value of output in a Soviet-type economy, but not at the same time, negatively correlated with the costs of material inputs and factors of production. In consequence, enterprises have been encouraged to expand production at any cost, or continuously increase their demand for material inputs, using them wastefully, expanding their inventories, and disregarding the possibilities of material-saving innovations.[14]

Thus, the link between input usage and the production of outputs is severed and the economy continually faces excess demand. In addition, these soft budget constraints and orientation to volume outputs and not inputs results in the well-known high resource intensity of production in the Soviet-type economies and the low priority given to product quality. The resource intensity of state socialist economies compared to West European market economies is indicated in Table 3.3.

Table 3.3 only compares the state socialist economies with the West European economies; a comparison with the Japanese economy would demonstrate even more startling comparisons. The Chinese use of energy is clearly the most wasteful: relative to GNP, China's use of energy is about three times the average for either low income or middle income (industrialised market) economies. The reasons for this pattern of energy use is not that China is at a particular stage of development, which some Chinese economists argue, but from system-specific causes. As the World Bank Report puts it,

> More important, however, has been the lack of incentives in China to economise on energy: as with other materials, enterprise managers have, until very recently, had little reason to limit the energy use of installed capacity, or to demand new and more fuel efficient equipment from their suppliers — whom in turn have been under little pressure to undertake appropriate research and innovations.[15]

Table 3.3 Resource intensity of state socialist economies and market economies, 1979–80

Countries	Energy intensity in 1979 in kg of coal equivalent consumption per 1000 US dollars of GDP[a]		Steel intensity in 1980 in kg of steel consumption per 1000 US dollars of GDP[a]
State socialist economies			
Bulgaria	1464		87
Czechoslovakia	1290		132
Hungary	1058		88
GDR	1356		88
Poland	1515		135
Soviet Union	1490		135
China	2500		—
Average unweighted (7)	1525	Average unweighted (6)	111
West European market economies			
Austria	603		39
Belgium	618		36
Denmark	502		30
Finland	767		40
France	502		42
Germany	565		52
Italy	655		79
Norway	1114		38
Sweden	713		44
Switzerland	371		26
United Kingdom	820		38
Average unweighted (11)	657	Average unweighted	42

Note: a 1979 US dollars
Sources: *World Development Report 1981*, Appendix, Tables 1 and 7; Winiecki, 1987, Table 1/1; *World Bank Report on China*, 1981, Table 4.13

Prior to 1979, there were few price or administrative incentives for enterprises to conserve energy and despite price hikes in 1979 the price structure has not been conducive to energy conservation.

One consequence of the high resource intensity of state socialist economies is the continuing tendency to suck in raw materials and intermediate goods, leaving less hard currency for technology transfer, or creating reoccurring shortages. In the East European economies, raw and intermediate materials have accounted for more than half and in some cases up to three-quarters of the total imports. The material dependency of the East European economies is not a consequence of their resource base; the same system-specific tendencies are apparent in China as well. For example, though China produces more than 50 million tonnes of steel per year, its very high steel intensity in manufacturing industry results in imports of 20 million tonnes per year at current rates. Partly, these figures reflect quality problems of Chinese steel production and increased demands for specialist steel products (such as steel pipes), but these are not adequate factors to explain the pressure of Chinese demand.

Complexity and changing industrial structures

In general, the complexity of inter-industry and inter-enterprise linkages increases with the level of economic development. In recent years there has been a shift away from industries based on economies of scale in which vertical relations predominate (for example, steel, cement, bulk chemicals) to ones based on innovation and flexibility and involving a mesh of horizontal linkages. This has formed the basis of the 'Post-Fordist' debate in the Western literature. Even in simple economies the central authorities are partially ignorant of the detailed situation throughout the economy because of distortions of information, aggregation errors, the screening out of information and inadequate techniques for data processing. These problems have been compounded by the shift in industrial structures which have taken place in the Western economies in the past twenty years. Emulation by state socialist societies is increasingly difficult under a centrally-planned model. China, with very limited managerial, accounting and statistical personnel, is in an even more difficult situation as it watches the development of the Taiwanese economy, Japan and the other Southeast Asian economies.

Lack of specialisation

Winiecki argues that one critical, system-specific feature of state socialist economies is the twofold lack of specialisation of their industrial structure. On the one hand, policies of import substitution have led to a situation where the potential advantages of the international division of labour are not realised: the Soviet-type economies 'turn out too large an assortment of products, especially intermediate products, in too small production runs, with outdated technology and using too many material inputs and factors of production. In consequence, many of these products are costly, technologically obsolete, of low quality and largely uncompetitive on world markets'.[16]

But there is another level of lack of specialisation which increases economic waste. Given the chronic and endemic shortage of supplies and components, enterprises display an extreme do-it-yourself tendency. To reduce the levels of uncertainty on the supply side, enterprise managers prefer to produce as much as possible within their own organisation. They try to do all the phases of processing, producing components and parts as well as the finished products. Consequently, the scale of the enterprise does not equal the scale of production. It is interesting to note that this lack of specialisation is seen by East European economists as a system-specific characteristic rather than the outcome of Maoist ideology with its emphasis on self-sufficiency or the result of the scale of the Chinese economy. However, decentralisation to local government levels, which has occurred spasmodically in China and has occurred under economic reforms, increases the lack of specialisation and wasteful investment.

Innovation and risk aversion

The bureaucratic system of state socialist economies generates, as is well-known, risk-averting behaviour at all levels. For example, enterprise managers are primarily interested in fulfilling plan targets for the current planning period or, to be more precise, managers are concerned to maximise the gap between the perceived capacities of the production system and performance results. What is important from the management perspective is the difference between the two magnitudes and not plan fulfilment in and of itself. Even if a proposed innovation might result in increased production, the risks of delays whilst the new technology or techniques are installed and mastered and the possible disturbances to production schedules push managers towards conservatism. Given the lack of competitive pressure or the threat of financial failure, risk aversion pays off. This process of risk aversion extends to organisational innovations and human resource management. Indeed, these areas are highly politicised in state socialist economies such that most innovations and experimentation in this area originate outside of the enterprise.

Distortion of information flow

Economic systems involve power, information, motivation and constraint. Information flows are a critical element. In market-type economies, information about scarcity is generated by markets and conveyed by prices. However, STEs are report-based systems not profit-based systems. This implies that enterprise managers and economic agents are rewarded by the production of 'good reports' to bureaucratic superiors. This has always involved distortion and misrepresentation. For example, Mandel argues that:

> Within the Soviet economy, given the bureaucracy's material interests in getting the maximum possible resources for the minimum possible goals for the plan, not only is open information between the enterprises and the higher bodies not assured, it is practically excluded. It is even limited within one enterprise. The bureaucratic management system works largely on the basis of wrong information, as is recognised by all those concerned. That is what the former Hungarian Communist Prime Minister, Andras Hegedus, called 'generalised irresponsibility'.[17]

However, the enormous extent of distortion is only just coming to light with the break-up of existing regimes in East Europe. For example, at the 'August 23 Factory' in Bucharest which produces trains, rolling stock and underground carriages, one of the worker's leaders is reported as follows:

> This is how it worked. We can make maybe 300–500 engines a year, but the management claimed that we made 1,000. Ceausescu before a visit... would tell the minister: 'Only 1,000? It should be 2,000'. Then he came and told the workers: 'I see you have the capacity for 4,000'. And by the time he left he was talking about 10,000 engines.[18]

As can be seen from this illustration, economic data were based on a fantastic pyramid of deception, each official changing production figures upwards until the upper levels of bureaucracy were satisfied. Underlying this problem is the fact of unified control of the means of economic information. Within the political sphere the Party and the security organisations can and do act as alternative channels of information. Within the economic sphere, expertise is lacking and this results in a single pattern of information flow.

The shifts in the economic and technological trends in the world economy through the 1960s and 1970s have slowly exacerbated the endogenous, system-specific causes of the difficulties of the state socialist economies. Moreover, these accumulating problems have led to a set of social-cum-political difficulties which intensify the issue further. All state socialist economies, except China, have witnessed a 1980s cycle of falling or static living standards creating communal pessimism and low expectations leading to cynical alienation and, in turn, leading to reduced worker effort.

One solution to these accelerating problems of STEs has been economic reforms in the direction of marketisation. This is discussed in the next section.

ECONOMIC REFORMS: THE STAGES OF TRANSFORMATION

Economic reform is not a recent concept for STEs. It began in Yugoslavia in 1950–51, was discussed in Poland and Hungary in the mid-1950s (giving rise to several key works), introduced in Czechoslovakia during 1967–69, Hungary in 1966–68 and in China in 1978 and has spread to the Soviet Union and the rest of East Europe during the closing years of the 1980s. It is useful to set these events out in a table (Table 3.4).

As can be seen from Table 3.4, China's experience follows that of Yugoslavia and Hungary. Hungary, in particular, was a model for the Chinese reformers. Equally, China's strategy has influenced the reform planners in the Soviet Union.

The path of economic reform in STEs is never straightforward. The processes of marketisation can never be isolated from political and social issues. Nevertheless, there have been some similarities of events and these can be understood in a stylised way. In an ideal-typical way, it is possible to suggest the following stages to the process of economic reform:

— Reform typically starts in agriculture and/or small-scale urban services. This is the first phase, as it was in Hungary in 1966 when mandatory plans were abolished for agricultural cooperatives. This phase is seen as experimental, as it was in Sichuan province in the late 1970s. In both Hungary and China, reforms in agriculture and the small-scale private sector have proved successful. However, in relation to the latter in particular there has been an oscillation of encouragement and discouragement over time. At one point 'entrepreneurship' is welcomed, at other politico-economic moments 'profiteering' is denigrated. (It was notable that during the July 1989 miners strikes in the Donbass and Kuzbass coalfields that there were demands that cooperatives should be closed down on the basis that they obtained rapacious profits from reselling state goods.) This oscillation leads to insecurity of the economic agents and short-term profit-making. In many ways the problems during this phase are ideological in nature — how to encourage the economic development of agriculture and services without undermining state socialism at an ideological level.

Table 3.4   The diffusion of economic reforms

	Country	Continuing or not
1950–51	Yugoslavia	Continuing
1966–69	Soviet Union	1969 - Marketisation reversed
1966–68	Hungary	Continuing
1967–69	Czechoslovakia	Soviet invasion
1978	China	Continuing
1988	Soviet Union	Continuing
1989	Poland	Rapid switch to a market economy from 1990
	Czechoslovakia	Shift to a market economy
	East Germany	Incorporation in West Germany's market economy
	Bulgaria	'Socialist market economy'
1990	Romania	Outcome uncertain

The Soviet Union, though it has followed the path of encouraging the growth of small-scale private services, has *not* moved to reform agriculture. Up to 1990 economic *perestroika* has affected agriculture to a lesser degree than other sectors of the economy. Agriculture in the Soviet Union has been large-scale, collectivised and industrialised for a longer period than elsewhere and the problems of reform are correspondingly greater.

During the reform process agricultural units move into non-agricultural activities (for example, light industry sub-contracting for state-owned industry; construction and services). This happened in both Hungary and China. The development of collective enterprises in rural areas generates pressures on urban enterprises to reform and tends to undermine rigid controls on distribution and materials allocation.

—The second barrier to economic reform is the problem of transferring the successes of market liberalisation in agriculture and small-scale services to industry. How is the urban, industrial sector to be sorted out? There are greater problems of management, information, technology and infrastructure. In 1984, after a few years of cautious experimentation, the Chinese leaders decided to extend reforms to urban industry.

—The solution to the second barrier (how to solve the industry problem) is moves towards monetisation of economic exchanges and, typically, an increased market orientation for consumer-goods firms (perhaps involving joint ventures with the West or importation of Western plants) with a continued form of planning for producer goods industries and enterprises. Markets for capital goods (steel, machine tools and so on) are slow to develop and continually subject to bureaucratic constraints. Thus the third barrier is that of the producer-goods industries. Up to 1989, most state socialist economies had not really crossed over this boundary. China has experimented with a so-called two-track system for producer goods since 1985. This involves a state-set price for planned supplies and a higher, market price for a proportion of supplies. In early 1986 the planned allocation of, for example, steel was 57 per cent, with the remainder traded between enterprises. However, there has been a periodic reimposition of central controls over the distribution of producer goods, a process which appears to have been happening from late 1989 to mid-1990.[19]

— Underlying the problems of transferring marketisation to the industrial sector is the pressing problem of capital markets or profit retention. The central bureaucracy creates continual resistance to an independent banking or credit system. Even in Hungary, which has undergone processes of reform for over 20 years, the emergence of a capital market has been shadowy. Kornai concludes that 'the first vague contours of a credit and capital market are emerging but the Hungarian economy is still far from overall 'monetisation' and from the solidified institutions of a full-grown, well-operating, flexible credit and capital market'.[20] In China, the first stock market opened in Shanghai in 1986, but the overall development of capital markets has proceeded very slowly and is now stalled. This, then, is the fourth barrier.

One general point should be noted in connection with this ideal typical sequence — the sequence of reform measures tends to follow the *complexity of transactions*, plus, to some degree, the extent of need for cultural and institutional change. For example, commodity market transactions involve exchange of goods or services for money at one point in time — a 'spot' transaction. In contrast, transactions in money markets involve the exchange of monetary purchasing power at different points in time. The increasing complexity of market transactions requires a greater degree of institutional and cultural underpinning.

— The last phase is the issue of ownership. Do the patterns of state ownership provide intrinsic barriers to economic reform? Do they inevitably mingle the economic and political? Does the Party always have to be in the factory? Until 1989, this barrier had not been crossed in any significant way by any STE. Small private firms have been allowed (usually in the service sector) with strict limits on employment levels. Xiaokai Yang makes clear that the last stage of the reform debate in China before the Tiananmen massacre focused on ownership rights and the possibility of extensive privatisation.[21]

One significance in conceptualising the reform process as a series of barriers or phases is that it cuts across the all too frequent, implicit notion that economic reforms are a linear process. On the contrary, all the evidence and experience indicates that they are oscillatory and cyclical. Secondly, it cuts across the notion that specific problems are 'transitional'. In one sense this is correct, but *in the context of repeated transitions*. Moreover, resources at each point of the cycle tend to become more exhausted whilst technology falls further behind the West. The idea of transition implies something: it implies that there is an identifiable end-state towards which the policy-makers are moving. However, there is no theoretical conception of this end-state nor any explicit consensus amongst the policy-makers. This 'feeling the stones with one's feet in crossing the river' syndrome adds to the uncertainties and the cyclical nature of the process.[22]

It is not clear how long an economic reform process will take. The historical transition is unprecedented. Fei and Reynolds chart a prescriptive sequence of initial monetisation, establishment of commodity markets, followed by the creation of capital and labour markets (see Table 3.5). However, they see the sequence as taking 25 years or more in the Chinese context. Will the politics of the events wait?

At various points the economic reform process creates social and political tensions. These tensions can, and do, accumulate. The expectations associated with the reform process continually outrun the realities (inflation, continued shortages, job insecurities) and people do not comprehend the cyclical reversals. Kornai goes so far as to suggest that Hungary and the Hungarian experience (up to 1986) represent the limits of economic reform in state socialist societies. The recent events indicate that this is not so. The failures and cyclical setbacks associated with the reforms create a momentum for *political* changes and this momentum can break through the envelope of bureaucratic inertia and political constraint — to create what?

Tragic Utopias?

The preceding sections have attempted to outline some answers to the questions posed at the start of this chapter — How should state socialist societies be characterised? Why did such societies reach a watershed during the 1980s? What are the basic driving forces of change?

The first point to underline is that STEs have proved through the 1980s to have shared systemic features. At the start of the decade, there was a literature analysing Poland and the 'Polish disease' — a term which implied unique dynamics to the Polish situation. For example, even insightful scholars like Nuti wrote, 'Polish political developments are unlikely to spread to other East European countries and the Soviet Union. They are deeply rooted in Polish conditions and there are no effective mechanisms of transmission'.[23] Events of the 1980s have demonstrated that the Polish situation, whilst having specific characteristics, was a *good indicator* of the system-based problems of STEs. Few observers in 1980 predicted this.

I have argued that STEs cannot be typified in a simple manner. Instead, the system-specific features derive from three sources: the basic ideology of socialism (the Socialist Trinity and the Four Principles in the case of China) combined with, firstly, a set of contextual characteristics deriving from the level of development of the specific society. This varied between the different cases, but nearly all of them tended to be underdeveloped, peripheral economies. In addition, the nature of STEs needs to be understood in terms of a set of economic and industrial strategies which derive as much from historical conjunctures as from socialist ideology.

This threefold social and economic formation leads to specific patterns of contradiction. In some ways Mao Zedong thought embodies these contradictions in the sharpest form. Faced with the Marxian notion that 'tractors preceded collectivisation', Maoism simply attempted to reverse this order by an act of political will — 'collectivisation, rapid accumulation, then tractors'. These

Table 3.5 Program for total reform of the economic system (1986–2006)

	1949	1958	1978	1986	1990	1994	1998	2002	2006
A Socialist transformation	Totally politicised system		Transition period to a depoliticised economic system						Chinese Socialism (exclusively indirect control)
			Initial period	Middle period			Late period		
B Sequential order for establishing various markets			Advent of money economy (government monetary guarantees persist)	Establishment of a commodity market			Capital goods market	Labour market	
				(I)		(II)	(III)	(IV)	(V)
C A five-stage reform program (post-1986)			Dispersion of economic and political decision-making process	Price system reform (government acts as guarantor for: i Smooth urban-rural exchange; ii Successful outcomes for state enterprises)		Reform of interest system	Reform of profit system	Reform of financial property	Reform of human relations
D Content of each reform			i Agriculture: collapse of communes; marketisation; privatisation ii Collectives pursue profit iii Tax replaces profit in state enterprises	i Prices float ii Government deficit controlled iii Free purchase and sale iv Inflation controlled		Establishment of a loanable funds market	Production efficiency profit (Marshallian profit)	Capitalised future profit, risk and embodied technical change are basis for value of capital goods	Labour mobility

Table 3.5 (Continued)

E Sequential establishment of a management culture in state enterprises	Individual initiative begins to replace command system	Business/politics separation (concerning current operations)	Business/politics separation (concerning long-term growth)	Business/politics separation (halfway to profit/loss responsibility)	i True profit/loss responsibility ii Enterprise a legal entity iii Property rights depoliticised	i Firm now pure production unit ii Labour contract system iii Labour/management relations depoliticised
Attitudinal basis for legal system	State enterprises develop sense of independence	Commercial cost culture established	Commercial interest/debt culture	Profit culture (profit apolitical)	Entrepreneurs: group identity, social status	Workers: sense of integrity and independence
F Reform of the legal system	Gradual separation of party and government			Independent judicial system		
	Rule still primarily by party or political force; sprouts of legalism	Antitrust spirit, private legal system	Banking laws	Corporate income tax law	Bankruptcy and contract law	Labour relations law
G Rebirth of traditional Chinese cultural values	Family values	Spirit of independence; self-reliance	Trust and honesty	Apolitical entrepreneurs	Respect for intellectuals	Independence of labour class; Cultural revival (basis for reunification)

Source: Based on J. Fei and B. Reynolds *Journal of Comparative Economics* 11, 1987.

contradictions have led some observers to interpret the recent history-breaking events in terms of the idea that the STEs are reverting to capitalism and that the entire 73 years experience can be written off as the choice of a 'painful route from pre-capitalism to capitalism'.[24]

However, this is only one perspective on events. Turning to the second question, there have been various explanations of the traumatic events of the late 1980s (and early 1990s?). In general, there have been six key factor explanations put forward by observers:

— an upsurge of nationalism — the new politics of STEs are simply the old politics;

— an upsurge of demands for democracy and greater representation;

— a specific legitimation crisis of communist parties associated with changing generations, the Afghanistan factor or continual economic failures;

— economic collapse — food shortages, inflation, unemployment, budget deficits, and loan burdens.

— working class revolts in opposition to a corrupt, elite bureaucratic class; and

— pervasive and systemic changes in the forces of production rendering Fordist-type production systems (which are the basis of all STEs) inflexible and redundant.

None of these key factor explanations is adequate in terms of itself and it will take some time to sort out the pattern of events. Nevertheless, some threads can, perhaps, be disentangled. Nationalism and ethnic unrest cannot be treated as an adequate key factor explanation. Demands for national self-determination have been constants in the situation through the 1950s, 1960s and 1970s and yet the events of 1989 did not occur earlier. Similarly, the demands for participation in decision-making may ebb and flow, but are a repeated theme of each new student generation. Consequently, nationalism and democratisation demands should be seen as the surface events, the group phenomena to be explained in terms of broader processes. It seems to me that we may be living through a period of social and economic revolution equivalent to the end of the 18th century in Europe. As Jin Guangtao points out, 'The experiment of the Socialist-system and its failure is the most important legacy of the whole human society this century'.[25] If the processes of change are of that magnitude, then we have enough sociological knowledge about revolutions to say something useful. During a revolutionary period, there is an explosion of possibilities, an explosion of social and political groups advocating different paths and realities in various localities and parts of society. Simultaneously, the integument of legitimacy of the regime is cracked open and the social mechanisms which limit possibilities (police, security forces, judiciary) have diminishing efficacy. This means that to stop someone or some group from constructing an alternative social order, it is actually necessary to go out and physically stop them (the Lithuanian scenario). In other words, there is an increasing tendency for all political conflicts to turn into military conflicts. In this light, the nationalist, ethnic, regional and working class revolts can be seen as the cumulative outcomes of the destabilisation, not the initiating circumstance. The latter has been the *rate of change* of economic events during the 1980s.[26] These considerations underlie the analysis in Figures 3.1 and 3.2.

Figure 3.1   A suggested model of events in STEs during the 1990s

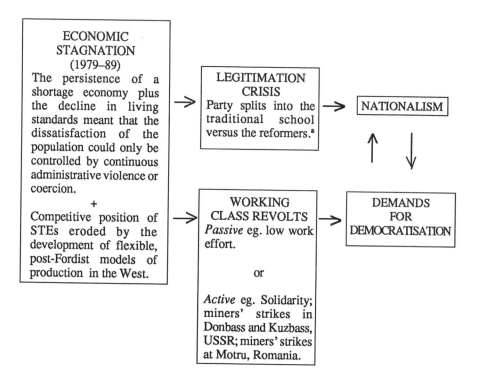

Note: a The 'traditional school' tends to attribute the economic and political problems to the weakening of discipline and the low political consciousness of the masses. The 'reformers' tend to attribute the source of the problem to the system and its inherent malfunctioning, such that a comprehensive process of reform is required.

If the economic events are taken as critical, then a general model can be suggested before looking at the differences for the Chinese situation (see Figure 3.1).

However, as already shown, this model of events does not simply apply to China. During much of the 1980s China went through a rapid period of growth and food supplies and consumer goods supplies improved significantly, even if total factor productivity in industry did not. In addition, the events in China, unlike all the other STEs, were not marked by, nor did they generate, surges of nationalism. China has its minority groups and its linguistic variety, but, with important exceptions (for example, Tibet and the Muslim population in the northwest and the southwest), the Han Chinese form the dominant part of the population. Consequently, one ingredient in the East European situation is largely missing from the Chinese context.

If the above points are accepted, then it is necessary to typify the events in China rather differently (see Figure 3.2).

Figure 3.2   A suggested model of events in China during the 1980s

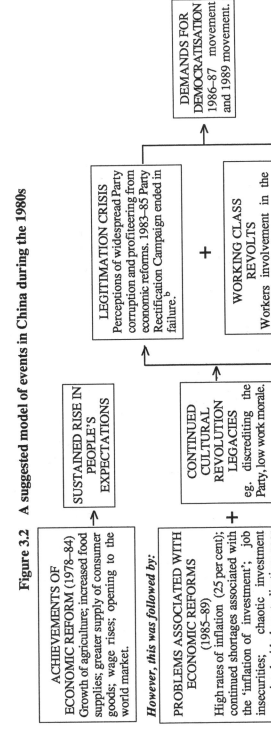

ACHIEVEMENTS OF ECONOMIC REFORM (1978–84)
Growth of agriculture; increased food supplies; greater supply of consumer goods; wage rises; opening to the world market.

SUSTAINED RISE IN PEOPLE'S EXPECTATIONS

However, this was followed by:

PROBLEMS ASSOCIATED WITH ECONOMIC REFORMS (1985–89)
High rates of inflation (25 per cent); continued shortages associated with the 'inflation of investment'; job insecurities; chaotic investment associated with decentralisation; poor performance of agriculture (1988, 1989).[a]

+

CONTINUED CULTURAL REVOLUTION LEGACIES eg. discrediting the Party, low work morale.

LEGITIMATION CRISIS
Perceptions of widespread Party corruption and profiteering from economic reforms. 1983–85 Party Rectification Campaign ended in failure.[b]

+

WORKING CLASS REVOLTS
Workers involvement in the 1986–87 democracy protests and the 1989 democracy movement. Widespread strikes in 1987.

DEMANDS FOR DEMOCRATISATION 1986–87 movement and 1989 movement.

Notes: a   After increasing living standards between 1978 and 1984, the situation deteriorated. An unpublished All China Federation of Trade Unions study showed that during 1987, the real income of the urban population fell by 21 per cent. By the beginning of 1990, Chinese wage earners had not received a formal wage increase for two years despite the high rates of inflation, and the demand for consumer items had collapsed.

b   Party splits have been a factor in China too. With Zhao Ziyang's dismissal in 1989, two General Party Secretaries had been dismissed within two and a half years. The dismissals represented splits along East European lines — Maoist traditionalists plus bureaucrats believing that 'the political consciousness of the masses needs to be raised' versus reformers. However, after the Cultural Revolution (1966–76), avoidance of major political conflicts was a policy priority for all concerned. Party corruption has been the major corrosive issue.

Arising from Figures 3.1 and 3.2, one key issue remains to be addressed: namely, in trying to trace the pattern of causation of events are the economic failures and economic collapses being attributed to pre-reform economics or to the impact of attempted reform?

Clearly in the cases of Bulgaria, Romania, Czechslovakia, Poland (to a significant degree, though it is a mixed case[27]) and the GDR, the history-breaking events owe little or nothing to the impact of market reforms. However, this is not the case in connection with Hungary, the Soviet Union nor, indeed, China. In all of the latter three countries, it can be argued that the dynamics of reform (inflation, unemployment or threats to job security, perceptions of profiteering, cycles of reform, and so on) exacerbated the legitimation crisis of the ruling communist party; they have aggravated the systemic crisis they were intended to alleviate.

The implications of the above are in some ways positive and in some ways horrendous. Romania and the execution of Ceausescu teaches that hard-line, traditional, Soviet-type economies will not survive. However, Hungary, the Soviet crisis and the Chinese crisis (it cannot be called anything less) imply that the transition to 'market socialism' is no easy solution. As I have pointed out, up to 1990 no stable reformed model has been developed in any society. The reason for this in the ultimate is that a pervasive use of the market system (affecting commodities, credit, capital and labour) would destroy the complex set of exchanges which have been established under state socialism. For example, there has been a fragile social contract between the party and labour based on a double compromise — low wages but full employment, shortage of consumer goods but a relative egalitarianism in income distribution. Unstitching these types of socio-political compromises requires more than the mechanical prescriptions of Fei and Reynolds in relation to a sequence of reforms.

It is too early to write the epitaph for state socialist economies, but to carry out reform or restructuring under the banner of communism is increasingly impossible. Silviu Brucan (one of the new leaders in Rumania) put it like this:

...the Rumanian Communist Party, all communist parties, have been politically discredited for having put psychopaths at the head of their organisations, the Ceausescus, Pol Pots, Maos and Stalins. They have no future any more...they can exist only in socially backward countries.[28]

Pope John Paul II (not a neutral observer) has attempted to write the epitaph nevertheless. Communist regimes, he is reported to have said, were 'tragic utopias which brought an unprecendented regression in the tormented history of humanity'.[29] I do not think that the scorecard is so negative — but too many people (including most Chinese) *believe* that it is. That belief has had, and will have, potent consequences. Not the 'end of history', but the beginning of a new politics.

4 The Soviet Union and the Pacific

GERALD SEGAL

INTRODUCTION

Time-worn standards and stereotypes are particularly tenacious in politics, to say nothing of political thinking. It seems to us that with regard to many problems of the Asian Pacific region mass perceptions and consciousness are dominated by views and approaches whose roots lie in the experience gained by us in European and Soviet-U.S. affairs...It would evidently be premature to claim that the Asian Pacific region has already taken up a proper place in Soviet foreign policy. We have unquestionably begun to concern ourselves with the region, but unfortunately this is not enough.[1]

The Soviet Union may not be a natural East Asian power, but it is very much a natural Pacific power. Yet with all the fashionable speculation about an impending Pacific century, it is striking just how little attention is paid to the Soviet factor. To be sure, it is only in recent years that the Soviet Union itself has begun to take the Pacific as anything more than an arena of naval competition. But Mikhail Gorbachev has clearly placed parts of the Pacific very high on his agenda for foreign policy reform and he has already engineered major foreign policy triumphs in the region. Thus the central questions to be answered are: what does the Soviet Union now want from the Pacific region, and how has Soviet policy towards the Pacific been reformed?

While there have been earlier studies of Soviet policy in Asia or even East Asia,[2] it is in keeping with the Soviet Union's own blinkered past that there have been few attempts to understand Soviet policy towards the somewhat different region called the Pacific.[3] A Pacific-wide perspective is essential not only because of the trend of Pacific-chic in other Western studies, but also because the Soviet Union itself has begun to take the Pacific region seriously.[4]

In order to tackle the diverse and difficult subject of the international relations of the Pacific in the Soviet perspective, it is essential to train the binoculars in the opposite direction too, and assess the way in which the states of the region see the Soviet Union. One of the most striking features of the new Soviet policies in the Pacific is the extent to which the Soviet Union is learning from what its neighbours are telling it about the problems with Soviet policy.

The main theme of the analysis is that the Soviet Union is likely to become a different, and perhaps in the long term a more important, power in the Pacific.

45

Moscow has recognised that if it is to stand any chance of succeeding in its objective, it will have to reorder drastically its priorities in the region. It has discovered, much as the United States did, that military power gives only an illusion of influence. There is always a danger of imperial overstretch in the vast and increasingly vibrant Pacific region. Economic and political influence must also be developed. The process of reforming priorities is already underway. As a result, the international politics of the Pacific is being transformed and the balance of power shifted.

These changes in Soviet foreign policy and in the Pacific region are both affected by, and in turn are helping reshape, Soviet domestic politics. The key to the success of the new Soviet policy in the Pacific lies in domestic reform, and especially the reform of the politics and economics of the Soviet Pacific territory. With so much uncertainty surrounding the great experiment in *perestroika*, there must also remain some uncertainty about the prospects for continuing reform of Soviet policy in the Pacific. Yet, in the short term, reform there must be; the Soviet Union has no option.

Looking forward

Imagine if you will the dream as the leadership of the Soviet Union wakes up on 1 January 2000 and gazes eastward from the Soviet Pacific coast:

—The domestic reforms have gone very well and the massive investment plan in the Soviet Pacific has attracted a flood of new immigrants from European Russia.

—The storehouse of raw materials is being efficiently exploited and the processing of some of them is driving an export boom that has at least tripled Soviet trade with the Pacific.

—The Soviet Union has become a major market for other members of the Pacific as well as a major supplier of commodities, much like Australia and Canada.

—Light industrial products from China and the NICs have vastly improved the quality of life in the Soviet Pacific as the natural trade is unhindered by political divisions or military conflicts.

—Japan has joined in multilateral economic joint ventures with the communist states of Northeast Asia, and Japan has also begun investing large sums in joint ventures in the export processing zones in the Soviet Pacific.

—The NICs and ASEAN states are also buying Soviet commodities and investing in dynamic new Soviet projects.

—Socialist East Asia has been revitalised and Vietnam is beginning to undercut the price of Chinese light industrial products.

—The Soviet Union has new friends among Pacific islanders because of the Soviet Union's booming international mining and fishing industries.

—Soviet military power is still the second strongest in the Pacific but it concentrates on naval operations close to home and in maintaining a skeleton force along the Sino–Soviet border.

—Confidence-building measures have been negotiated with China and Japan and multilateral talks are underway with others in the region.

—The inhabitants of the Pacific now visit resorts on the Soviet Pacific coast and Soviet airlines and trains serve as a 'landbridge' connecting East Asia and Europe.

An impossible dream? Perhaps, but the possibility that the Soviet Union will finally begin to fulfil its promise as a Pacific power is in many ways now more likely than ever. It is doubtful that the 21st century in the Soviet Pacific will look anything as fine as the dream recounted here, but neither is it likely that we are in for more of the same in the mould of the Brezhnevian 1970s. Even if the Soviet Union's full dream of the 21st century seems unachievable, at least it seems almost as unlikely that the nightmare of past Soviet policies will return.

Important changes in Soviet policy are already underway. One could play safe and focus on the vast bulk of what has not changed in Soviet policy towards the Pacific. But it is more revealing to look at the margins where reform takes place and concentrate on what is likely to change. It is true that there are formidable obstacles to reform and the reality of the Pacific often changes faster than the Soviet Union can cope with. But we have already seen some sweeping and impressive changes (for example, Sino–Soviet detente) and we need to focus on what may follow. After all, so much discussion of things Pacific is in the realm of what might be, and thus it is only fair to apply the same principles of positive thinking to Soviet policy in the region.

THE ENDURING REALITIES

There may be much that the Soviet Union might like to change about its position in the Pacific, but there are some things which are relatively immovable. In the 300 years of a Russian seat by the Pacific, or the 75 years of Soviet power in the region, certain relatively consistent features have set the scope for the policy-makers in Moscow. Some of these features are positive, some negative, and some have elements of both. No matter what else changes in Soviet policy towards the Pacific in the 21st century, these features are likely to remain of vital importance.

Territory and population

The Soviet Union will continue as a Pacific power that looms from the north across vast stretches of inhospitable territory. Despite being the largest country in Asia, its population will remain one of the smallest in the region.[5] Even with rapid reforms, any likely influx of people will at best take the Soviet Union to the present-day level of the population of Taiwan (20 million). In the longer term, a cynical Soviet optimist might hope for a serious deterioration in the greenhouse effect because global warming would vastly increase the prospects of the Soviet Far East.

But in the near future, the people of the Soviet Pacific will, as in the case of Canada, be mostly spread out along the southern border: in the Soviet Union's case, meaning the frontier with China and especially in the corner where Japan, China, Korea and the Soviet Union come together. Thus the frontier spirit is likely to remain. With successful reforms it will be a positive spirit that encourages enterprise and experiment. With failure to reform and open up to the outside world, it will be a spirit in awe and fear of its surroundings.

China on the mind

For similar reasons of geography, the Soviet view of the Pacific will be dominated by China.[6] If there is an enduring lesson from the Russian experience in the Pacific it is that failure to get on with China presents serious difficulties for Russian policy. China has a legacy for Russia in that it is both necessary for Russia to get on with China but also to be aware that China is the Soviet Union's main rival in the region. Like the superpower relationship, the lesson is that mutual security is an imperative for both sides and at best they can only have a stable relationship of competition and coexistence. Such uneasy detente will always be subject to the machinations of outsiders, but Moscow abandons detente with China at the peril of its entire Pacific prospects.

The elusive Japan

Japan has always been the second most important object in the Russian perspective of the Pacific.[7] Given the continuing successes of Japan, this offshore presence can only continue to complicate Soviet calculations. In the broad sweep of Russian experience in the Pacific, relations with Japan have rarely been warm.[8] Despite the distinctive sort of complementarity of the two countries' economies, it is hard to see why the two should get on especially well. The enduring Soviet priority given to China and the clear orientation of Japan to the global capitalist economy means there are few avenues for close collaboration. To a large extent, as in the case, say, of Anglo–Soviet relations, the reasons for the distance of Japan from the Soviet Union do not all come from the Soviet side. The upshot is that Japan is likely to remain the most difficult major power for the Soviet Union to deal with in the Pacific.

An outsider in the global economy

Although there have been times when Russia was more closely involved in the Pacific economy, its reach has rarely been a long one. The problems stem not merely from the continental Russian tendency to underestimate naval power. They are now aggravated by the fact that the Soviet Union's adopted political and economic system has kept it out of the mainstream of success that has so transformed the Pacific. To the extent that the Soviet Union ever had a role in the regional 'division of labour', this was largely focused on bilateral relations with China. Trade patterns are difficult to shape and sustain in a region divided between several competing centres of influence, especially when there are others, such as Canada or Australia, which have similar products to sell and much closer political affiliations with the intended markets.

The not-so-hidden powerhouse in this global economy remains the United States. For all the talk of the decline of the superpowers, the United States remains the most powerful economy in the region and much of the reason why people 'think Pacific' at all rather than just in East Asian terms.[9] It is true that there have been extensive periods of Pacific history when Russia and the United States have made common cause.[10] Although conditions have changed since 1945, the enduring lesson for the Soviet Union is that good relations with the United States may be an easier way to ensure an active part in the Pacific system than the struggle to forge a warm relationship with Japan.

Regional diversity

One of the enduring differences between the Atlantic and Pacific worlds is the much more diverse political world in the Pacific. From the Soviet point of view, this diversity is both a problem and an opportunity. If Moscow is intent on building region-wide cooperation or formulating a similarly general strategy for the Pacific, this will likely be wrecked on the rocks of diversity. The opportunity in the diversity is that for a country seeking entry into an otherwise successful international system, diversity allows the Soviet Union to pick and choose its opportunities with less fear of making a fatal blunder. It is true that most states in the Pacific system of international relations have not seen Russia as a major actor in the past, since they have focused on the capitalist world. But because of the very diversity and rivalry within the region, there will be many, such as China or Indonesia, who will welcome a new Soviet player as an excuse for reshuffling the deck.

REFORMS IN SOVIET FOREIGN POLICY

Of course, change in the post-1945 international system must always be on the margins because that great facilitator of past change, major war, is not a useful instrument of policy. As a result, real change is harder to spot because it happens in the margins of the old system. There are some smaller wars, and some striking personalities, which do manage to help mark the transformations. But in an age of increasing interdependence and loss of sovereignty by states, the more far-reaching changes often take place because of reforms in the domestic politics of a number of states. Recent events in Eastern Europe are a striking example of such change in communist systems. The changes in Soviet policy in the Pacific are not (yet) nearly as successful an example of domestic reform driving foreign policy reform, and then domestic politics in turn affected by the international system.

Confusion about socialism

Whether Mikhail Gorbachev's reforms in the Soviet Pacific were inspired by the example of successful competitors like Japan, or whether they are driven by the stalled state of the Soviet economy and society, reform was urgent. For a one-party state with a supposedly guiding ideology, the first reform had to be the acknowledgement that past strategies were wrong. Socialist hubris has been consigned to the background as the leadership experiments with reform. Yet

Soviet leaders still claim that no matter what the reform, the essential character of the Soviet Union will remain socialist. Whether reforms can have such limits seems increasingly doubtful, and yet it is also likely that change in the Soviet Union will not be quite as 'anti-socialist' as it has been elsewhere in Eastern Europe.

But because reforms are also being pursued in many other Pacific socialist states, neither the uncertainty nor the limits necessarily means that socialism will be meaningless for the Soviet view of the Pacific. It may well remain easier for the Soviet Union to get on with socialist states, if only because, as events in China in 1989 suggest, 'bourgeois ideas' can be especially dangerous to reforming communist leaders. It is not yet clear whether the Soviet Union will react like the Chinese and see events in Eastern Europe as evidence for the need to draw a line somewhere to defend socialist power. Of course, 'shared' ideology has not prevented a number of inter-socialist conflicts in the Pacific, but it is often insufficiently understood in the West that ruling communist parties who see threats from capitalist ideology will seek some solace in cooperation with socialist comrades. It certainly would be short-sighted on the part of any Soviet (or Russian) leader to abandon close relations with the socialist states of East Asia, especially as much has already been invested in developing a presence for the Soviet Union.

But the new, reformed socialism, has already begun to change the domestic base of the Soviet Pacific. The decision to play a greater part in the international division of labour has already been taken. The decisions to open a special economic zone and encourage joint ventures, particularly in the Pacific, are already being implemented. These are major reforms that have come about faster than most thought possible. As the Chinese experience suggests, these reforms do not have to be immediately profitable before they begin having an important effect on the role of a socialist state in the Pacific economy. To be sure, a great deal remains to be worked out about how these reforms will develop in practice (see below), but there can be little doubt that there is a Soviet determination to reform its home base and join the Pacific economy. This may well draw it further away from 'socialist-internationalism' and closer to the global market economy.

Detente with China

Sino–Soviet detente began before Gorbachev came to power and at least in the early stages was as much a Chinese reform as a Soviet one. But after a mere five years of power, Mikhail Gorbachev achieved the normalisation of Sino–Soviet relations that had eluded his predecessors. It is not an exaggeration to suggest that there has been no single improvement to the post-war strategic position of the Soviet Union that is as important as Sino–Soviet detente. If Gorbachev achieves nothing else, he will have taken the most important step in transforming the Soviet position in the Pacific.[11]

Of course, this detente will remain a mix of competition and coexistence. For example, as the Soviet Union revises if not abandons much of its ideology, China has grown more disturbed at the impact that close relations with Moscow might have on any state seeking to remain socialist and run by a communist party. After a hard struggle to improve Sino–Soviet relations, it seems likely that relations will now deteriorate for the same reasons they improved: shifts in domestic politics in both states.[12] But it makes possible the revitalisation of the domestic Soviet economy in the Pacific and the target of tripling trade with the Pacific by the year 2000 suddenly becomes reasonable. Sino–Soviet detente sets a new agenda for Soviet policy in the Pacific, and to some extent also sets a new agenda for the region as a whole. Until the recent revolution in Eastern Europe, Sino–Soviet detente was the most important shift in the strategic balance since the American detente with China in 1972.

Declining use of military force

The withdrawal of the Soviet Union from more direct involvement in regional conflict has been taking place both inside and outside the Pacific. The specific changes in the Pacific, including troop cuts, less out-of-area naval operations and pressure on allies to lower regional tension, have been made quickly. They will eventually save money and therefore play their part in the broader process of domestic reform. But their main purpose is to help improve political relations in the Pacific. Although the political impact has been uneven, these changes in Soviet policy have already had a positive effect. Soviet relations with ASEAN are improved by pressure on Vietnam to end the Kampuchean conflict, much as relations with Japan are improved by pressure on North Korea and troop cuts in Northeast Asia. While none of these changes is irreversible, any decision to undertake such a reversal would need to explain why the benefits should be lost.

Of course, if the Soviet Union puts less emphasis on military power, admits to having made ideological mistakes, and has not yet developed a strong economic presence in the Pacific, there will be less reason to consider the Soviet Union as a superpower in the Pacific. Are we witnessing the slimming down of the Soviet Union into the mere shape of a great power? That implication alone might lead to a re-evaluation of the lower military profile.

Dealing with the NICs

Nothing illustrates the new Soviet pragmatism in the Pacific as much as Moscow's improved relations with the NICs. Singapore has always had the best economic relations with the Soviet Union and will be the key to Soviet plans to establish a presence in Southeast Asia. Taiwan is likely to increase in importance as a trade partner, but political relations will be limited by the far more important detente with China.

It is the detente with South Korea which is of greatest importance.[13] Not only does South Korea sit in the more vital Northeast Asian region, but its larger population and rapid repeat of the Japanese miracle makes it a more important trade partner. While successful detente with China will account for the largest part of the improvement in the Soviet position in the Pacific economy, the improved relations with South Korea may well be the next most important reform for the Soviet Union. Moscow expects that once South Korea becomes involved with the Soviet Union, Japan will not be far behind.

Accepting the United States

It was a major reform of Soviet policy towards Western Europe when Moscow accepted that the United States could not be excluded from discussions of European security. The ensuing arms control and confidence-building measures were built on the implicit recognition of the variety of American links with allies a long way away. Similarly, the acceptance of the United States as a Pacific power in Gorbachev's Vladivostok speech of 1986 marked the maturity of the Soviet view of the Pacific. While it can be expected that there will be periodic Soviet attempts to make mischief in the United States' relations with its allies, it is now more possible that a more stable security in the Pacific, including arms control agreements, can be negotiated.

And yet one needs to keep the American role in perspective. It was not American action that caused any of the other, already mentioned, shifts in Soviet policy, although American policies did have an impact on how Sino–Soviet detente developed. It is true that the fact the United States was more willing to challenge Soviet power in the Pacific in the early 1980s made it easier for China to improve relations with the Soviet Union. But the overall importance of superpower relations is far smaller than it has been in the European theatre.

CONTINUING DEBATES[14]

Reform, especially at the pace and scope now underway in the Soviet Union, inevitably results from, and encourages further debate. All of the changes already discussed can be reversed as a result of changes in domestic and external politics. In many cases, it is still hard to distinguish between the reality and rhetoric of reform. Because the reforms are so fast and far-reaching, some reversal, however temporary, seems likely. Therefore it is well to be prepared for what those debates might lead to, and the implications of the likely outcomes.

The speed of the general domestic reform

The myriad debates in the Soviet Union about reforms in all sectors are too complex to be recounted here.[15] Almost all have some importance for the Soviet Pacific. Without macro-economic reform, and more micro-level problems as a convertible rouble, real interchange with the Pacific will be restrained. Without new ideas about management, no joint venture will succeed. Without rethinking of the role of military power as part of a reassessment of military doctrine, the temptation to intervene in regional conflict will remain. The list is seemingly endless. But the main point is that an understanding of the success of Soviet policy in the Pacific requires an appreciation of the struggles in Moscow, and indeed in the towns and villages of European Russia.

Maritime or continental

Perhaps the most vociferous debate at present in the Soviet Union is that between the inward-lookers and those urging a genuinely more independent development strategy. In the Soviet Pacific, as indeed elsewhere in the Soviet

Union, there is a serious need to look towards the outside world for finance, ideas and even people to make the Soviet Pacific flourish. In China this more outgoing strategy was described as the 'open door' strategy, and it has clearly run into its biggest crisis in its ten years of operation. In the Soviet Pacific such a strategy is best described as a 'maritime orientation'. Its supporters call for greater freedom in the region to experiment with new ideas, rates of pay, systems of management, types of investment and types of partners. With downtown Moscow seeing itself as the arbiter of reforms in the Soviet Pacific, it is not surprising that bureaucrats often stifle local initiative. The absence of a powerful regional decision-making apparatus means such problems are likely to persist for some time. Therefore it becomes clear why, as one Soviet observer notes, there is a freshly-painted 'welcome' sign put up in the Soviet Pacific, but the old sign of 'keep out' is still visible beneath it.

The more conservative, continental school urges less regional differentiation, more balanced growth and less reliance on the outside world. There is even a 'green' strand to the argument that sees the perils of rapid development. So far, the maritime school is in charge, but its ability to remain there depends on successful reforms at home and interest from the outside. It also depends on how the various sub-categories of the maritime school, with some supporting concentration on opening to Europe rather than Asia, manage to resolve their differences. So far, there is strong evidence that those wishing to pay proper attention to the Pacific have at least been able to hold their own. Hence the Vladivostok initiative, detente with China, opening to the NICs and a form of military retreat.

A Pacific aquarium or processing zone

The factions are complex, and even within the maritime school there are differences of opinion. The strategy for the Soviet Pacific in the 1970s was to draw foreign finance and technology to aid an essentially Soviet program of exploiting the raw materials in the region for export. Since then, the reformers have argued that the plan to wait for a trickle down of investment from European Russia — the continental approach — will not work. But the maritime school has not yet agreed on just how much of the opening to the outside world can be achieved without relying on the old strategy of raw material extraction and selling fish. One reformer notes the similarity of contemporary caution and that of the pre-Peter the Great Russia which thought only of 'timber, hemp and blubber-oil'.

The more radical reformers are convinced that the service sector, for example, in providing tourist facilities, can, as in the case of China, provide vital experience and finance for other industries. The intention would be to take advantage of the better-trained Soviet labour force in order to produce light industrial and even electrical goods in export processing zones with foreign investment. Soviet raw materials would be extracted, but they would be processed first in the Soviet Pacific territory and then exported to Pacific markets. This argument is probably still too far out in front of the main group of reformers, but it may well provide the most successful long-term basis for growth of the

Soviet Pacific. Yet the specific options for the Soviet Union depend very much in a detailed assessment of specific industries and international markets.

Northeast Asia or the wider Pacific

When the Soviet Union thinks Pacific, what does it see? As already suggested, China and Japan dominate the view. Because of the diversity of the Pacific, it is harder to invest time and thought in other parts of the Pacific, especially at the early stages of reform. Thus the emphasis has so far been on Northeast Asia, including the Koreas, and tacitly even the United States. The Soviet Union has tended to see the Pacific as the North Pacific.

But there is a school of thought, and curiously enough, mostly associated with a less ambitious idea of the Pacific, that wants to concentrate on a socialist base. This school looks to Vietnam, the third most populous communist state, as a vital part of the Soviet strategy in the Pacific. They see Laos and Cambodia as additional elements to be developed. Some also see China as something larger than just the Amur basin and see possibilities in wider contacts with those parts of China in the heartland that have not had the benefit of coastal contacts with the West.

These divisions are often thin and even overlapping. There are some who look beyond Northeast Asia and are attracted by the ASEAN states, and there are even those who still think more in Asian than in Pacific terms. Many of these differences stem from regional specialisation, for what country one has studied often determines what one thinks is important. The main point is that the diversity of the Pacific may distract the Soviet Union from the northern part, where the easiest and most important gains are to be made.

Territorial concession

A much more specific debate concerns the vexed question of territorial concessions. The agreements with China on settling border disputes have yet to be completed or published. But they seem to include the Soviet Union's return to an earlier position that recognised some Chinese claims, especially along the river border. But little if any territory is expected actually to change hands. By all accounts, there were those who argued that even such a limited shift in the Soviet position should not have been made for fear of leading others to believe that they could reclaim territory from the Soviet Union. It was the 1975 Helsinki agreement in Europe, in the Soviet perspective at least, that codified the principle of no change in post-war borders.

In the early part of the 1990s, the major territorial debate in the Soviet Union will concern Japan's claim to what it calls the Northern Territories. At a time of major territorial concessions and changes in Europe, the old certainty that the Soviet Union will be unwilling to give up territory in East Asia must be revised. As is already evident, there are those who are willing to return some islands to Japan and are prepared to return to the compromise of 1956. The less ambitious are not prepared to budge at all. The outcome may well depend on the extent to which Japan is prepared to compromise, for it was the Japanese who scuppered the deal in 1956. But one thing is clear, without some arrangement on the territorial issues, Soviet–Chinese and Soviet–Japanese relations will be worse than they need to be. The apparent Sino–Soviet deal and change in Eastern Europe suggests that those willing to trade territory for peace and prosperity are taking charge of Soviet policy.

WHAT IS TO BE DONE?

As one Soviet specialist described the challenge facing the Soviet Union in the Pacific: 'The dilemma before us is that either we will adopt radical structural decisions for our ship to gather headway, or the pace of growth will remain slow...time is no ally of (our) country'.

Under such pressure of time, we will probably not have long to wait in order to see how successful the Soviet Union will be in transforming its position in the Pacific.

In the decade before the millennium, there is increasing evidence that the Soviet Union has already begun to improve its standing in the Pacific. But it is not yet clear whether, like an energetic acrobat having performed a somersault, the Soviet Union will end up facing the same direction and problems as when it started. It seems likely that the Soviet Union will reach its modest targets of tripling foreign trade, improving the standard of living in the Soviet Pacific, attracting more immigrants to the region, and becoming more integrated into the prosperous pattern of international relations in the Pacific. But unless it does a great deal of all of these things, it will not have moved forward very far.

Thus the result of the game of picking a scenario for the future of the Soviet Union in the Pacific depends on the type and depth of reforms that the Soviet Union chooses to adopt. The reaction of other states is important — for example China may change its policies and worsen relations with the Soviet Union — but the primary variable for Soviet success is its own responsibility.

Perhaps the worst of the most likely outcomes for the Soviet Union would be the gradual decline of the Soviet superpower. This might result from half-hearted reforms which produce little real change in the Soviet domestic scene and therefore less change in its international economic position. Having retreated militarily and still tinkering with an obsolete ideology, there will be less reason than ever before to take the Soviet Union seriously. Like the Turkish empire, it might gradually crack apart, with all the destabilising consequences for international security that surrounded the death of the Turkish empire. Of course, even if it loses all its republics, Russia remains a vast country with the same presence by the Pacific. Under such circumstances it might even be a leaner and fitter player in the Pacific region, and certainly less encumbered by the effects of imperial overstretch.

A more likely but still less than satisfactory scenario would result from more significant success in Soviet reforms, but which result in more efficiency in the present system rather than any systemic change. The Soviet Union might then be a poorer version of Canada or even possibly Australia. It might end up as a 'hewer of wood' for the resource-poor economies of the Pacific, but still with a decent standard of living. Assuming, as one must in the short term of any of the positive scenarios, that the Soviet Union pays less attention to its military power in the Pacific, then it will be better armed than Canada or Australia, but not much more influential.

The 'best' scenario would depend on massive reform along the lines of the 'maritime strategy' outlined above. At best, the Soviet Union would be wealthier (more like Canada and Australia) and more integrated into the Pacific region. But it is hard to imagine this taking place with a growing Soviet military presence in the Pacific. Integration into a booming Pacific economy seems to require a less threatening posture. If the United States is satisfied with this state of affairs, and other powers such as China and Japan do not try to take advantage of the new balance of power, then the Soviet military weakness might not be a problem.

If the Soviet Union does end up travelling the road that takes it to the status of an Australia with atomic weapons (and this is not meant to be an epithet), it will not have reached it, even by the year 2000. The task facing the Soviet Union is enormous. But it must be in the interest of other states in the Pacific that the Soviet Union and its friends do become more integrated into the region. As the Soviet Union is likely to remain the second largest military power in the Pacific for some time to come, it is in the interest of all those who want to have a prosperous international economy that, at a minimum, the 'normalisation' of Soviet power in the Pacific be managed peacefully.

Irrespective of which scenario eventually comes to pass, it is no exaggeration to note that with less than ten years to go to the year 2000, the Soviet Union's position in the Pacific is probably better than at any time in its past. What is more, the improvement has been attained in a remarkably rapid five-year period. Of course, as they say, 'that was the easy bit'. In order for the Soviet Union to keep pace with change in the Pacific, and especially if it wishes to enhance its position even further, then the past reforms will only have been a warm-up for the bigger game to come.

5 The new detente and the reforms in socialist countries

TSUNEAKI SATO

The dramatic changes in the countries of Eastern Europe represent the most important political development since the Second World War. Their radical transformation, democratisation and initial integration into the world economy affect far more than the internal political and economic situations of the individual countries. The new alignment of forces in Europe, emerging on the basis of the reforms now being carried out, raises the issue of new economic, military–political and strategic relations, and this course of development cannot but have an effect on external actors.

The events which took place in Eastern European countries in the course of 1989, particularly in its second half, could be termed 'revolutionary' given the breath-taking speed with which they occurred, the depth of the transformation they brought about and the unprecedented scale of their people's involvement. The West, preoccupied with the Soviet Union and the constraints under which reform attempts in Eastern Europe have operated, was surprised by the swiftness of the changes in Poland, Hungary, East Germany and Czechoslovakia. The reforms even extended to Bulgaria and Romania, which had been considered bulwarks of conservatism in Eastern Europe. Few could have believed that a ruling mono-party would voluntarily surrender power and become a by-player in the coalition government headed by a non-communist intellectual, such as occurred in Poland.

Moreover, we are now witnessing an historic opportunity for the successful implementation of long overdue reforms in Eastern European countries. At this time, the interests of the Soviet Union coincide with those of Western nations. In the case of Eastern European countries, it is therefore a unique occasion in their post-war history when the interests of the superpowers and great power nations have combined to support their aspirations to establish stable democratic governments and, hopefully, prosperous market economies.

Even if the external conditions at the moment seem favourable for democratic transformation in Eastern Europe, one should not forget that there is a long way to go before these countries attain the goals they have set. There are many obstacles on their path to a dual transition from an authoritarian political system to a parliamentary democracy and from a bureaucratically-controlled economic system to a market economy.

We should also be warned against the efficacy of multi-party coalition governments, although this is undoubtedly a welcome symbol of democratic transformation and dramatic progress in an historical perspective. In the case of Eastern European countries, where reform is taking place in a climate of deep economic crisis, there is a real danger that the strong political leadership urgently needed to implement emergency, sometimes unpopular, measures for economic recovery might be paralysed by pluralist coalition governments. This could be called the economic dilemma of political democratisation.

Nonetheless, we face an historic opportunity to discard the legacies of the Cold War whose origins date to around 1948 when Eastern European countries were absorbed into the socialist camp after a few years of modest attempts to evade that pattern of development. Moreover, just as the Berlin Wall collapsed, there exists a real possibility that the 'Great Wall', which has hitherto divided East and West, may fall down or be dismantled so significantly as to make it unnoticeable.

The democratic transformation in Eastern European countries, with their strongly expressed orientation towards both a market-type economy and social-democratic pattern of political administration, should be seen against this background. Should the transformation succeed to a significant degree, the barriers between East and West will be reduced further in both a political and economic context. The two hitherto rival systems will become closer to one another. At any rate, it can be said that we are witnessing, for the first time in post-war history, a positive interaction between democratic transformation in socialist countries and the New Detente which is beginning to unfold.

In this context, we will examine the qualitative changes (discontinuity) brought about by the radical transformation in Eastern Europe, with the major focus on economic and political aspects.

CRISIS OF THE SYSTEM

Let me first address the causes of these changes. The changes became inevitable due to a combination of deep and compounding crisis in Central and Eastern Europe and the influence of the global socio–economic system. It is commonly accepted that the Soviet model of economic and social development that imposed industrialisation and collectivisation in the early 1930s has long since exhausted its potential. Its negative aspects have become increasingly clear. Forcibly transplanted to the countries of Central and Eastern Europe, this model and its corresponding socio–political system became a source of unsound development fraught with frequent crises and a distorted socio–political order.

In countries of *Mitteleuropa* with their deep-rooted European political cultures, pluralist political order and a mixed economy were preserved in the initial post-war period. The hegemonic imposition of the Soviet model and its forcible maintenance by a combination of internal coercion and outside interference (actual or potential) were an insult to the national dignity of Eastern European countries. Whenever the situation permitted any latitude in the expression of their needs and aspirations (1953, 1956, 1968 and 1980), the peoples of these countries tried to shake off the model of 'quasi-socialism' as economically inefficient, politically undemocratic and at variance with their national and civic requirements.

Sporadically-attempted reforms failed to produce any major or lasting results. The reforms were usually partial, as they involved but one part of the society — the economy — and did not touch the entirety of socio–economic and political relations. Even the reforms in the economy were half measures striving to remove some of the defects of the existing system, rather than substantially changing its structural elements. Consequently, after the initial vaguely-praised results, the reforms were checked, suffocated and finally abandoned. All this time the problems and contradictions inherent in this system continued to accumulate.

The failure of reforms in the 1950s and especially in the 1960s constituted a missed opportunity for East European countries to reform and modernise their structure at a time when the West was forging ahead rapidly. The gap between the East and West began to widen further after the two oil shocks of the 1970s. Western economies responded to the shocks with energy-economising high technology, while the East stagnated on the same technological level of the 1960s. The unfavourable developmental trend of the East was aggravated further by the emergence of the newly industrialising economies (NIEs) which demonstrated their vitality and capability to absorb and assimilate high technology transferred from developed economies. This contrasting development became obvious in the early 1980s when even the GDR and Czechoslovakia, the so-called 'honour students' in the COMECON region, began to lose ground in exporting machinery to OECD markets.

Over twenty years have been lost to countries of Central and Eastern Europe since the mid-1960s when the opportunity to reform and modernise the economic structure was missed. The pressure of lost time gave a special impetus for radical political as well as economic transformation. So it was not surprising that a structural crisis developed during the 1980s and the situation came close to one where the cup of popular discontent overflowed. Importantly, Gorbachev's *perestroika* removed the constraints within which popular discontent and aspirations could be contained by replacing the notorious Brezhnev Doctrine with the principle of non-interference in internal affairs of other countries. This not only created conditions conducive to change but marked the beginning of the long-deferred transformation.

But what kind of revolution is now underway in the countries of Central and Eastern Europe? In my opinion, the transformation underway is revolutionary insofar as it is trying to win back the civil populace which has until now been absorbed into the structure of 'party equals state socialism'. The possibility exists that transformation in these societies may exceed the framework not only of the traditional notion of socialism, but also any kind of socialism whatsoever, given the possibility of retrogressive or conservative revolution in some of these countries.

CONTINUITY AND DISCONTINUITY IN THE DEVELOPMENT OF ECONOMIC REFORMS

The new wave of economic reforms in socialist countries, including China, which started at the very beginning of 1980s, has been called 'the third wave' as it has two precedents: a tiny wave of reforms in economic administration in the second half of the 1950s, and more substantial reforms in the mid-1960s. The reforms in the mid-1960s failed to produce any meaningful results, with the possible exception of Hungary. Contrary to the expectations of Hungarian reformers, however, the reforms resulted in an indirectly bureaucratically controlled model which came under fire by reform-minded economists both inside and outside the country.

I have argued elsewhere[1] that the third wave could be applied to character-ise the nature of reforms unfolding in Hungary, Poland and, to some extent, the Soviet Union, which, while lagging behind the former two countries, became more market oriented in its reform trials from the second half of 1987. All of the above-mentioned countries, while differing in degrees, intensified their orien-tation toward a market economy and began to talk about 'market socialism' instead of a 'socialist market economy'.[2]

At the same time, the crucial problem for further development of economic reform will be the extent to which they succeed in switching from the indirectly bureaucratically controlled model to the indicative planning model, that is, a market economy regulated by macro-economic policy.[3] In the case of its more or less successful realisation, the difference between socialism and contempo-rary capitalism will be blurred, at least from the point of view of the functioning mechanism of a contemporary economy.[4]

I had initially considered the problems of economic reform in Central and Eastern European countries mainly in terms of continuity rather than disconti-nuity, as an evolutionary development and extension of the third wave of economic reforms. However, having witnessed the dramatic events in Central and Eastern Europe in the second half of 1989, from September to December in particular, I feel that the above premise should be questioned. At the very least, one must now acknowledge that important elements of discontinuity are apparent in the general picture of the third wave of economic reforms. The reforms still retain the general trend of continuity insofar as three basic directions of pluralisation have been adhered to: pluralisation of ownership,[5] markets (which now include not only commodities, but also capital and labour), and political systems (multi-party systems and coalition governments).

The discontinuity apparent in the course of the revolutionary changes of 1989 focuses mainly on the political systems where the most dramatic changes took place. These changes far exceed the categorisation of the reform movement in terms of an extension of the third wave of economic reform.

It has been the common (or, at least, implicitly common) view that socialism as a socio–political and economic system consists of three fundamental fea-tures: (1) concentration of major political and economic decision-making in the hands of the top leadership of the ruling party, encapsulated in the phrase 'the leading role of the party'; (2) the predominant role of public (state) ownership in the means of production; and (3) planning at the central level associated with the concentration of political and economic power in the hands of the ruling party.

Needless to say, the above three pillars have been modified or weakened over a long period of time from the Kruschev reforms of the mid-1950s to the course of events of the 1980s in Eastern European countries. Although nothing remained in its original Stalinist form, the core of the system remained intact. Not even the most advanced reform trial of the mid-1960s, or the Prague Spring of 1968, questioned the leading role of the party. These reforms aimed to retain the predominant role of the party with the voluntary consent of the people, while giving the people freedom of the press and freedom of association. The most advanced economic reform in the 1960s, the Hungarian reform of 1968, did not touch the political system itself nor put under serious question the predominant role of central planning *vis-a-vis* the market mechanism.

Today the whole system is placed under serious question and scrutiny. What we are now witnessing in countries of socialist Central and Eastern Europe, and to a lesser degree in the Soviet Union, is not a reform but a collapse of one system and its replacement by another. Hence it seems quite appropriate to use the term revolutionary to characterise the changes now occurring there. It is quite stimulating for students of comparative economics in general, and students of Soviet and Eastern European economies in particular, to ponder the implications of these changes for our understanding of economic systems and concept of socialism.

IMPLICATION OF POLITICAL CHANGE

At first glance the provisional programs put forward by the respective temporary political leaderships established after the revolution seem almost the same: renunciation of one-party rule (abandonment of the leading role of the party) and acceptance of a multi-party political system and coalition government, accompanied in some countries by a change of name of the former ruling party and of the state itself; implementation of free elections, as was the case in Poland in June 1989; introduction of market-oriented economic reforms; recognition of the rights of citizens to travel abroad and the introduction of freedom of speech and the press; and reorientation towards integration into the world economy (but initially, into the European economy). Notwithstanding these similarities, there are important differences in the implementation of these revolutionary changes in the countries in question.

Take, for example, Poland, the forerunner of change. In Poland, the prestige and influence of the Polish United Worker's Party was completely lost in the course of events in the summer of 1980. Although the Solidarity movement was banned and outlawed by the declaration of a state of emergency in December 1981, a kind of 'falling together' scenario has been going on since that time, because neither the party–government nor Solidarity was able to exercise leadership individually. Hence a compromise solution emerged between the ruling elite and counter-elite in order to resolve the deadlock in a non-violent form.

Hungary is another special case. Hungary has followed a course of gradual, but more or less persistent, reform trials since the mid-1960s. In this sense, the last 20 years are not completely lost time though the inconsistency and ineffi-ciency of Hungary's reforms is now the target of severe attack by radical reformers and a considerable section of the public. A considerable part of its ruling elite has abandoned the notion of socialism in the traditional communist, Marxist–Leninist mould and embraced the social–democratic brand of social-ism of Western Europe. In the case of Hungary, the political vision of socialism was adapted to market-oriented economic reforms, under which macro-eco-nomic regulation of the market economy will be linked with multiplicity of ownership relations (a mixed economic system) and a clearly-expressed orien-tation towards substantial privatisation.

What occurred peacefully in the GDR and Czechoslovakia could be termed a civil revolution explicable in terms of the maturity of the civil society of these countries. Vaclav Havel, the new President of the Czech and Slovak Federal Republic, called it a 'velvet revolution'.

Bulgaria and Romania belong to quite different categories. In Bulgaria changes occurred as a result of an intra-party *coup d'etat* carried out under strong pressure from mass movements. In Romania it was essentially a military *coup d'etat*, though undoubtedly there were considerable elements of populist revolt. In the latter cases, although the most aggressive and conservative elements were removed from the party leadership, a rather strong framework of the former power structure seems to have been preserved.

The differences mentioned above may not appear considerable but when the time comes for the practical elaboration and implementation of reform schemes, together with the difficult task of economic recovery, the differences will have a major influence in the direction of further economic and political reform.

A crucial problem, however, as a result of free elections from March to June 1990, is that no single former ruling party gained a majority mandate, and few even a relative majority. This is the most eloquent expression of the degree of crisis into which the whole system of real socialism has fallen, and of the extent to which the system of one-party rule has been considered as alien to the politico–cultural traditions of Central Europe.

As suggested earlier, planning at the central level has been associated closely with the concentration of political power in the hands of the top leadership of the ruling party, so with the disappearance of one-party rule (the *first* pillar of real socialism) the *third* pillar (planning at the central level) will be undermined too. What we are now witnessing among the people is a clear tendency towards rejection not only of the whole system of real socialism but also of the whole concept of socialism. There is a very strong aspiration to restore the politico–cultural traditions of Central Europe and return to a West European type of market economy with built-in macro-economic regulation, that is to say, to a social–democratic (or Tinbergen) model for running a contemporary economy. This is the most eloquent expression of discontinuity in the third wave reform trials.

At the same time, political democratisation by means of multi-party and coalition governments presents a dilemma. The implementation of radical economic reforms presupposes the establishment of strong political leadership capable of implementing reform programs which may contain unpopular measures. It is not quite certain whether strong leaderships will emerge from coalition governments based on the multi-party system. In Hungary, for example, there are more than 50 political parties and groups, including very tiny ones, with quite different orientations.

It was both interesting and paradoxical to note the divergence of opinion on the question of coalition government expressed at an informal round-table conference organised by the Advisory Board on World Economy attached to the Hungarian Government in Budapest at the end of September, 1989. While the Hungarian partners emphasised the significance of political democratisation through the multi-party system, the foreign participants stressed the need for a democratic but effective and strong political leadership, and warned against excessive expectations based on multi-party coalition governments.

The countries of Central and Eastern Europe, after an interval of over 40 years, now have freely elected coalition governments. We can only wait to see how the multi-party coalition governments cope with the problems they face.

IMPLICATION OF ECONOMIC CHANGE

As far as the *second* pillar of real socialism is concerned, the tendency from the beginning of the 1980s has been towards further diversification of ownership relations and sectors: co-existence of purely private, collective and mixed (different types of leasehold and subcontract systems) sectors alongside a public sector which will have to undergo substantial change (privatisation of public enterprises). Here we see a continuous development which started in the first half of the 1980s, rather than a discontinuity.

There is, however, a qualitatively new element. The term privatisation, so fashionable in Hungary, Poland and Czechoslovakia today, seems to have two aspects: one is the outright extension of the purely private sector (private enterprises), the other the privatisation of hitherto publicly-owned (state) enterprises which cannot be transferred immediately into the hands of individuals.

In the former case, the share of the private sector in the formulation of GNP is expected to increase in Hungary from about 10 per cent today to roughly 30 per cent by the mid-1990s. Even the Soviet reformers envisage that the share of their state sector will decrease to below 50 per cent in the course of 1990s. In the 'competitive sector', a special Hungarian term to denote the commerce and service sectors as well as the industrial sector producing consumer goods, Hungarian reformers are trying to ensure that it will be dominated by enterprises other than public ones (that is, private, collective and mixed enterprises).

In the latter case, the problem is far more complicated. Though, of course, there are many different ways to privatise publicly-owned enterprises, the general consensus among the reformers, not only in Eastern Europe but also in the Soviet Union, seems to be to turn state enterprises into joint stock companies. Under this system, the state will retain roughly a 20 per cent (in the Soviet Union reformers say a 40 per cent) share of stocks under the guise of state shareholding companies which, in reality, will operate as profit-seeking business organisations. The remaining shares will be held by commercial banks, employees, the public and, to a considerable extent, foreign investors. Under the supervising role of the shareholders' general meeting, a strong and independent top management, capable of taking both risks and responsibility, is expected to be established.

Usually economic reforms in socialist countries are examined in terms of marketisation of the economic system, namely the extension of the coordinating role of the market mechanism. Though undoubtedly it is and remains an essential aspect of any serious economic reform, what lies at the root of attempts to privatise publicly-owned enterprises is the recognition that the socialist economic system has so far failed to form a 'subject of rational economic management and behaviour' capable of taking both risks and responsibility and geared not only to short-term profits but also to the long-term renovation and development of the enterprise's capital assets. This recognition is clear irrespective of the concrete form of economic administration, whether in its Soviet form in which the state (in practice, supervising ministries and agencies) nominates the top management of enterprises, or in its Yugoslav self-management variant under which self-managing councils elect management.

The striking deterioration in the economic performance of the Soviet Union and Eastern European countries can probably be explained not only in terms of insufficient marketisation of their economies but also by the failure to form rational economic management at the enterprise level. This is particularly the case in the new era of high-tech revolution where innovation proceeds rapidly and the needs of consumers and producers change swiftly. In such an environment, an enterprise requires an efficient and skilful management.

The formation of this strong enterprise management, however, involves another serious problem: the formation of an equally strong countervailing power in the form of trade unions. Taken together, this could be called a 'simulation of capital–labour relations' with potentially no small element of antagonism. In this sense, too, the traditional view of socialism will be altered and undermined.

The pluralisation of the market which will be extended to cover all factors of production, from capital to labour, is set to change the traditional concept of socialism. Marketisation of these factors of production, long considered a taboo from the Marxist perspective, means that the allocation of both investment and labour resources will be determined not by centrally-planned procedures but by market forces, while the wage levels and wage relativities will be settled through bargaining procedures, as noted above by the term capital–labour relations.

Claims on 'unearned income' derived from property rights will have to be legalised, which in turn will lead to an undermining of the traditional, though controversial, principle of 'distribution according to work done'.

Overall, the question could be raised of what will remain of the traditionally held view of socialism. It seems quite appropriate and natural, therefore, that Eastern European reformers — and Soviet reformers, even Gorbachev himself — are now talking about a social–democratic vision of socialism, although the meaning of the term itself is far from clear.

WHAT WILL REMAIN OF THE CONCEPT OF SOCIALISM?

If we take, for example, a ten-year perspective, I am inclined to think that some distinction between socialism and contemporary capitalism will remain, in the sense that the share of the public sector of GNP, including public enterprises with state participation, will not be below the level of, say, 40 per cent. This will far exceed the level in West European countries. Macro-economic control of the market economy in Eastern Europe will be tightly exercised as it is placed under the strong pressure of socialist value systems, such as the orientation towards stability and egalitarianism, deeply rooted in the minds of the people.

To justify the existence of the distinction between capitalism and socialism in this way would, however, constitute a rather passive response which does not lead to a productive solution since it clings to the remnants of socialism, which, if consistent reform programs were to be implemented, would disappear or retreat to the background.

The only way to get out of this *Sackgasse* in a productive, positive way is to focus on the quality of macro-economic regulation exercised over the fully-fledged market economy with due attention to long-cherished socialist ideals such as security, stability, equality and solidarity.

Then, and only then, could the difference or competition between capitalist and socialist systems be interpreted not so much in terms of ownership relations and the relative weight allotted to plan and market but in terms of the quality of macro-economic control.

To attain such a qualitatively high level of macro-economic control of the market economy is in itself a very difficult task which leaves little room for a pre-supposed harmonious solution. In this sense, too, the traditionally held distinction between socialism and capitalism will inevitably become more blurred.

PROSPECTS OF A RETURN TO CAPITALISM

I have spent considerable space considering the nature, scope and problems of the reform trials now going on in the former socialist countries of Central and Eastern Europe. To conclude, I will raise a provocative though hypothetical problem, that is, the prospect of some, if not all, of these countries returning to a capitalist system.

Let us recall the transitional state of affairs which prevailed in countries of Central and Eastern Europe during the first years after the end of the Second World War, roughly from 1945 until the end of 1947. At that time, one-party rule was yet to be established. There existed, to a reasonable degree, democratic governments based on multi-party coalitions. The economic systems retained much of the character of a market economy based on multiplicity of ownership though some part of the economy had been nationalised. Censorship of the mass media and police surveillance were not as rigidly exercised as was the case after 1948. The economies were outward-looking and not inward-looking as they were after the foundation of CMEA (COMECON) in January 1949. Overall, these were open economic systems of the NEP type of the early 1920s in the Soviet Union — open in the sense that they were open to change of direction.

After 1948, however, they were absorbed into the Soviet-style Stalinist system under the irresistible military and political influence of the Soviet Union.

If the reforms proclaimed in these countries by the provisional leaderships are brought to their logical consequence, we shall have again a system which is open to a change of orientation. Socially-controlled market economies, usually linked with the social–democratic notion of socialism, would be the best alternative, though in the case of Central and East European countries the economic basis for such an economy has to be created from the very beginning.

If we take a long-term perspective, however, the possibility cannot be ruled out that some countries will return to a capitalist system. East Germany, of course, is a special case of reintegration into the capitalist system. Lithuania is another likely case.

In the Hungarian case there are two possibilities: either a soft or crash landing on the socially-controlled market economy with the retention of some socialist ideas, or the implementation of an advanced reform scheme leading to the formulation of some variant of a capitalist economy. I am mindful, however, of the risk of privatisation resulting in a desire of the people to return to the past. Much will depend on the new correlation of political forces that were formed after free elections.

THE ROLE OF THE WEST

At the outset of this paper, I underlined the significance of the present time as an historic opportunity not only for the success of overdue reforms in Central and Eastern Europe, but also for dismantling the legacies of the Cold War. On the one hand, the radical transformation now taking place has contributed greatly to lowering both political and economic barriers dividing East and West. On the other hand, for the first time in post-war history, both the Soviet Union and the West have a common interest in supporting the aspirations of the peoples of Central and Eastern Europe to establish stable democratic governments and market-oriented economies. We are now witnessing, again for the first time in the post-war period, a positive interaction between the democratic transformation in socialist countries and the New Detente which is now beginning to unfold.

However, the situation is very complicated and contradictory because of the deep economic and political crisis existing side by side with the reform efforts. Moreover, each of these countries has to accomplish a dual transition, the difficulties of which cannot be underestimated, from an authoritarian regime to a parliamentary democracy and from a state-run planned economy to a market economy.

We have learned from the experience of economic recovery and reforms, not only in the East but also in the West, that when radical reforms are introduced, things usually get worse before they get better. The next two or three years (1991–93) will be a most difficult time. Having passed the hurdle of free elections and established by and large democratic coalition governments, the difficult tasks of economic recovery and genuine economic reform will have to be tackled.

Here, we in the West have to step in. We have to concentrate our assistance during this period. But how should we respond, and with what means and from what philosophy? In determining concrete schemes to assist Central and Eastern European countries, we should consider that Gorbachev's *perestroika* — and perhaps even Gorbachev himself — and the subsequent reforms in Central and Eastern Europe have become a factor, firmly built into international relations in which the legacies of the Cold War are gradually melting away. If a big backlash were to occur in the reform process, it would inevitably threaten to destabilise international relations and the world economy. In this sense, to help or not to help is not a choice for Western countries.

Though we should not be over-optimistic about the prospects of successful economic recovery and reforms in these countries and of their integration into the world economy, the possibility of Central and Eastern Europe becoming a source of instability in the world economy (another Latin America) will have to be avoided. In the event of substantial success in overcoming economic difficulties and adopting market economies closely tied with Western economies, these countries, which have long entered the stage of consumer societies, will become positive actors in the world economy, but particularly the European economy, thereby contributing to its vitalisation.

At the same time, however, while helping Central and Eastern European countries break out of the difficult situation in which they find themselves, the West should not behave arrogantly and exploit the opportunity to induce these countries to adopt capitalism. Though there might be some countries that choose this course of development, it is a choice which should not be accelerated from outside.

No foreign economic models should be directly exported to these countries. Nor is it reasonable to impose a textbook solution of the neo-classical school for economic recovery and the creation of a market economy. We should be mindful that we can only help their efforts through a process of self-help. It is unrealistic to expect that countries which have long operated under a state-run planned economic system will be able to adapt easily to a purely market economy, particularly as traditional socialist values are strongly rooted in the minds of the people.

For the reasons above, it will be appropriate to help these countries work out concrete models of a 'socially controlled market economy', adapted to the conditions of each country. Equally important is to help them work out consistent economic policies for the transitional period so as to facilitate a soft landing in the 'safety zone' over the next few years. If this is done, we could expect the reforms now unfolding to take root more or less firmly, thereby lessening the prospect of retreat or reversal.

In conclusion, if the positive interaction between the reforms in socialist countries and the New Detente continue during the coming decade, we can expect that the dividing line between East and West, although it will not disappear completely, will become more like a dotted line, particularly in Europe. With that goal in sight, a great deal of effort and goodwill is required from both sides.

6 Recent Japan-Soviet relations: Gorbachev's dilemma and his choices

Hiroshi Kimura

During a Soviet–Japan ministerial-level meeting held in New York on 27 September 1989, the Soviet Foreign Minister, Eduard Shevardnadze, proposed to his Japanese counterpart, Taro Nakayama, that Soviet President Mikhail S. Gorbachev visit Tokyo in 1991. Gorbachev considered it necessary to visit Japan, 'a key power in the Pacific Region'[1] and a 'power of prime importance'[2] for a variety of political and economic reasons. A question that arises is why did Gorbachev's visit have to delayed until 1991? It is true that Gorbachev had a busy schedule in 1990, including local elections, the United States–Soviet summit and the 28th CPSU Congress. Still, if Gorbachev had wanted to visit Japan in 1990, it would have been possible for him to arrange it. The answer probably lies in the fact that the Soviet leadership had not decided its basic policy towards Japan and particularly towards the Northern Territories issue — the dispute between Japan and the Soviet Union over the four islands (the Habomai group, Shikotan, Kunashiri and Etorofu) off Hokkaido which were occupied by Soviet troops at the end of the Second World War.

THE DILEMMA OF RELYING UPON EXTERNAL ECONOMIC ASSISTANCE

Gorbachev's program of economic *perestroika*, after two years of theoretical formulation, entered the implementation stage around the middle of 1987.[3] Around that time, the economic performance of the Soviet Union began to deteriorate. Ironically, the worsening economic performance occurred at the very time when the necessity and justification of *perestroika* was patently clear. Although economic reform appeared easy to plan, it was, in reality, not easy to integrate selectively capitalist-type market mechanisms into the existing framework of socialism. Based on the results of similar experiments in Yugoslavia, Hungary and China, *perestroika*'s initial difficulties should have been expected.

In any event, since 1987, the depressed Soviet economy has seemed on the verge of returning to the stagnant state experienced under Brezhnev or possibly to an even more critical situation. There are several reasons behind the current shortage of foodstuffs and basic consumer goods in the Soviet Union: poor harvests; the introduction of private and cooperative enterprises; galloping inflation; the huge government deficit; the earthquakes in Armenia and Tadzhikistan; strikes by coal miners and railroad workers; and ethnic–nationalist unrest. For all these reasons, the Soviet economy now faces a critical period.

Of course, it is unfair to ascribe all of these ills to the present government. Many of these problems were due to the failings of previous leaders and are not directly the responsibility of Gorbachev's government. The current economic depression is the accumulated legacy of the era of stagnation, a legacy which cannot be solved easily by any one government. Additionally, the expansionist foreign policy towards Afghanistan, Vietnam, Cambodia and other third world countries, implemented by previous regimes and maintained until quite recently, has cost the Soviets huge amounts of capital in both cash and credit. Nevertheless, these are not sufficient reasons for pardoning the Gorbachev government for being over-optimistic in its expectations for the national economy or for its failed economic policy. The Gorbachev leadership has relied too heavily on relics of 'Andropovistic' spiritual stimuli such as the anti-alcoholic campaign, the tightening of labour discipline, the eradication of official corruption and unearned income, and other injustices. The Soviet government has also been slow to realise the importance of achieving rapid results in agricultural reform and is remiss in not showing the masses the concrete results of *perestroika* in a more tangible fashion.

However, the most serious mistake was the partial and gradual introduction of capitalist-style market mechanisms into the socialist framework of the Soviet economy. The misguided thinking behind Gorbachev's experiments, encompassing both the partial introduction of market mechanisms to an economic system based on central planning and reform through half-measures, has contributed to the worsening of an already bad situation. For example, the introduction of private or cooperative enterprises requires that the Soviets first accumulate a reserve of funds for licence fees, and observe certain stringent regulations regarding the payment of taxes and the procurement of raw materials. Even if profits are realised after negotiating these initial hurdles, Soviet entrepreneurs may be intimidated by amendments to the cooperative laws. The reason behind this fear is their memory of the reversal of New Economic Policy (NEP) in a Stalinist retrenchment and the elimination of 'NEP men'.[4] On the other hand, there will no doubt be people who are willing to act boldly to take advantage of new capitalist opportunities and earn an 'initiator's benefit' in the market. This entrepreneurial wave will lead to price increases, a widening income gap and laxity in work safety regulations. The new entrepreneurs will be held responsible for the harmful effects.

Confronted with domestic economic woes of this type, the Gorbachev leadership responded with four counter-measures. The first measure involved a revision of its original economic policies by, for example, relaxing the fight against alcohol and tightening cooperative laws.

The second involved further relaxation of Soviet socialist economic principles. A good illustration of the second measure was the introduction of a 50-year lease contract system (*arenda*) for farm land and other means of production.

The third measure involved arms control and disarmament. Under Gorbachev, the Soviet Union completed the withdrawal of its troops from Afghanistan in February 1989. The Soviet Union has also begun to withdraw troops from Mongolia and is making serious efforts to improve its ties with China and achieve a resolution in Cambodia. In December 1988, Gorbachev announced to the United Nations plans to implement a unilateral reduction in Soviet ground forces. During a visit to the United States, Soviet Foreign Minister Shevardnadze agreed to proceed with strategic arms reduction talks (START) separately from negotiations on SDI (Strategic Defence Initiative). The main reason behind these decisions is that the Soviet Union has realised, somewhat belatedly, that it is impossible to maintain both the current level of military strength and also achieve growth in the production of goods for private consumption. Considering the national budget, disarmament is a positive method for reducing economic difficulties. On the other hand, a lot of money and time is required to transfer manpower and equipment used in the military sector to the civilian sector. A recent article in *Ogonok* told of plans to convert a factory, which formerly manufactured SS-20 missiles, to produce baby carriages.[5] When I asked a military consultant from the International Department of the CPSU's Central Committee if this was true, I receive an abrupt 'No' with a remark about journalistic exaggeration in the Soviet Union. He suggested such a factory could possibly be converted to manufacture tractors, televisions or lenses.[6] The same official also explained the limitations in transfering technology originally developed for the military sector to the civilian sector. He made the following point: 'The military sector cannot be completely substituted by the civilian sector, but naturally the production of consumer goods should be left to the civilian sector'.[7] This high-ranking Soviet official was admitting frankly that the role of arms control and disarmament has its limitations as a method of relieving the currbnt crisis in the Soviet economy.

The fourth measure to counter economic difficulties involved the acquisition of credit from foreign countries. This measure called for large loans from West Germany and other Western capitalist nations for the purchase of machinery to manufacture consumer goods and agricultural produce. Confronted with considerable economic problems, the Soviet leadership seems to have decided that it is now acceptable to turn to economic exchanges with developed capitalist nations to counter the economic crisis. If this is Gorbachev's policy, it would seem appropriate for the Soviets to assume a more positive attitude in seeking a cooperative economic relationship with Japan. After all, Japan's economy is the second largest in the world. If the Soviets wish to forge such a relationship with Japan, why do they not assume a more flexible attitude regarding the Japan–Soviet territorial dispute?

In seeking *economic* cooperation with Japan, will the Soviets be willing to make some direct *diplomatic* concessions? Looking at the Japan–Soviet relationship in the long term, it is in the Soviet Union's interest to establish a sound relationship with Japan. However, in the short term, it is too early for the Soviet Union to approach Japan. Let me explain.

To begin with, the mutually complementary economic relationship which Japan and the Soviet Union had in the past no longer exists today.[8] After the enlightening experience of two oil shocks, Japan implemented its own *perestroika* and successfully oriented its economic structure from heavy industry to high technology.[9] Japan is therefore less dependent upon Soviet fuel and energy resources. Additionally, due to the increasing oversupply of oil in world markets, Japan is in a position to purchase oil from a number of countries other than the Soviet Union. On the other hand, the Soviet Union wants desperately to purchase high-technology products from Japan but is constrained by the scarce supply of hard foreign currency and the lack of collateral export products.

Even if the Soviets decided to use what little foreign currency they have to purchase the desired technology, it is highly probable that most of the technology they require would violate the COCOM agreement. Japan, being aware of the United States vigilance in this matter, would probably refrain from selling high technology with both military and civil utility for fear of creating another 'Toshiba incident'. Furthermore, the Soviet Union has a low technology absorption factor (estimated to be around 60 per cent)[10] and lacks confidence in its ability to utilise high technology fully.

One identifiable change in the Soviet attitude is that the Soviets no longer claim that development in Siberia and the Soviet Far East can be implemented solely by the Soviet Union. In 1987, the Gorbachev government announced its National Comprehensive Long-Term Development Program to the Year 2000 for the Far East Economic Regions.[11] This program will require approximately 230 billion roubles in capital, with only around 30 per cent supplied by the central Moscow government. How will the rest of the necessary capital be supplied? President Gorbachev said in Vladivostok in 1986 that the Soviet system of economic dependence on central government subsidies should be scrapped.[12] Regional development is to be implemented based on the key principles of economic *perestroika* including independent accounting and self-financing. Although this is intended to encourage self-reliance, one cannot expect these undeveloped regions to be successful single-handedly. The government will, therefore, allow the regions marked for development to engage in international division of labour agreements with neighbouring countries in the Asia–Pacific region. Furthermore, such a division of labour is not limited to socialist countries but is to become a division that 'transcends the capitalist and socialist systems'.

A country that could be considered the ideal partner for the Soviet Union in such an international division of labour is Japan. North Korea or China could supply the manpower but only economically powerful Japan with its surplus liquidity could supply the necessary capital. (Some may consider South Korea as a possible candidate, but the South Korean won is not yet internationally convertible.) Yet, the engagement of Japan in the economic development of the Soviet Union will be difficult to effect. The Japanese economy has developed to such a high level that Japanese companies show little interest in participating in the development of Siberia and the Soviet Far East. Spurred on by the Chinese example, the Soviet Union has permitted joint ventures with foreign enterprises and established special free economic zones as part of its policy to open the Soviet Union to the world. However, even now, the Soviets are ill-prepared to attract companies from capitalist countries to engage in joint ventures. Soviet economists have admitted frankly that they lack a real understanding of terms such as capital, interest, rent, stock and depreciation which represent the key concepts of capitalism. Additionally, a tendency for data secrecy, lack of productivity and bureaucratic inflexibility inhibit the involvement of foreign companies. Obviously, it will take time to effect significant change.

Mr Shigetake Iwata, president of Igilma Continental Trading Company, the first Japan–Soviet joint venture, expressed his dissatisfaction as follows: 'The Soviets are careless in their peripheral corporate preparations. They have yet to meet contract criteria regarding pulpwood quality. Deliveries are late, supply stoppages occur frequently, and statements of receipts and disbursements are always ambiguous'.[13] As a result of such problems, the number of Japan–Soviet joint ventures totals a mere twenty,[14] all of which are small-scale operations. Thus, Japan's large corporations, which view things from the standpoint of profit and loss, feel little attraction to participate in the development of Siberia and the Soviet Far East. The Soviet Union is, of course, quite aware of this situation and has done its best to promote trade with China which will accept barter transactions, and with South Korea and other NIEs as well as countries belonging to ASEAN.[15] The economies of these countries are more complementary with the Soviet Union compared to Japan's highly-developed economy. Ultimately, the Soviets will do what they consider best. The Soviets would naturally wish to develop their economy without the help of Japan's industrial and business circles and thus avoid making any territorial concessions to Japan.

However, even with South Korean participation, I doubt whether Soviet economic exchanges will make much progress. The hesitation by Japanese businessmen may also have had some influence on Korean businessmen's concern over a lack of profitability in trade with the Soviets. Even if Soviet–South Korean trade does develop substantially, the South Korean economy is not strong enough to act as a substitute for the Japanese economy and South Korea will not be able to provide the level of cooperation that Japan could extend. The ultimate Soviet goal is certainly not to tie up with China, South Korea or other NIEs in Asia. According to Viktor Spandarian, an adviser to the Director of the Institute for American and Canadian Studies:

> Among foreign partners involved in establishing joint-venture companies with Soviet enterprises in the special economic cooperative regions located in the Soviet Far East, Japanese business circles could play a very important role. The reason is Japan is the most developed nation in the Asia–Pacific region and would be able to lend the most powerful economic cooperation when participating in these special economic zones. Japan can provide not only the capital for constructing production facilities, but also the machinery and technology required to run such facilities. Additionally, Japan could buy the products produced at such plants.[16]

The successful implementation of economic cooperation between Japan and the Soviet Union would not be merely for the economic development of Siberia and the Soviet Far East, but for *perestroika* in the entire Soviet Union. With the worsening economic crisis in the Soviet Union, the Soviets now seem to have no choice but to approach Japan, a nation of surplus consumer goods as well as surplus liquidity.

THE MILITARY–STRATEGIC VALUE OF THE NORTHERN ISLANDS

From the point of view of improved bilateral relations between Japan and the Soviet Union, the merits of returning the disputed northern islands to Japan far outweigh the drawbacks.[17] However, the Soviets must also consider the effect on the military–strategic situation which the return of the islands might bring about, particularly in regard to relations with the United States.

The Soviet Union under Gorbachev has made a number of diplomatic and military concessions. If I may borrow the words of Professor Jerry Hough from Duke University, Gorbachev has 'surrendered' to China's three conditions. This represents a significant, and heretofore unimaginable, concession from the Soviet Union. Another surprise was President Gorbachev's United Nations speech in which he announced a unilateral cut of 500 000 Soviet ground troops, including 200 000 from Soviet forces in Asia and 120 000 from the Far East. If we are to believe what the Soviets and some Japanese scholars of international politics say, the Soviet Union and the United States are headed for a new detente. President Gorbachev even stated in his address in Vladivostok that the naval port of Vladivostok, the headquarters of the Soviet Pacific Fleet, was to be opened. If Gorbachev is willing to open up Vladivostok then why is it necessary to maintain military bases on the disputed northern islands and continue to aggravate Japanese sentiment? Even if no concessions are made to Japan regarding the northern islands, the removal or reduction of Soviet military installations on these islands would go far in dispelling the deep-rooted image of the Soviet Union as 'an enemy of Japan'.

However, there is no sign that such a move is yet possible. If one queried the Soviets on this issue, they would probably reply with the same official answer: 'The Soviet Union may install whatever it likes on its own territory, and there is no reason whatsoever for foreign countries to interfere. However, if Japan is willing to agree to the demilitarisation of Hokkaido as a condition to the demilitarisation of the neighbouring Soviet islands, then we may perhaps be able to enter into discussions'.[18]

A more realistic reason for the failure of progress is the extremely high military–strategic value of the northern islands. Hitokappu Bay in Etorofu Island was used by the combined fleet of the Imperial Japanese Navy in the Second World War as a rendezvous point for the attack on Pearl Harbour. The islands in the past have thus been of great importance in terms of military strategy. Geopolitically, the Sea of Okhotsk is very important to the Soviet Union and especially to the Soviet Pacific Fleet. These islands have such a pivotal strategic location that there is even debate in the Soviet Union on whether to close the Sea of Okhotsk.

The distinguishing characteristic of the United States' submarine warfare strategy is that submarine tactics are part of a 'forward base strategy'. In contrast, nuclear-powered Soviet submarines patrol relatively closely to heavily-protected bases in Soviet waters from where they can launch their ballistic missiles (a 'bastion strategy'). The Barents Sea and the Sea of Okhotsk would be the main bases for Soviet submarine operations in a nuclear war. Delta-III type missiles with a range of 8000 kilometres, launched from Soviet submarines in the Sea of Okhotsk, can hit almost any target within the United States except the Florida Peninsula. As the four disputed islands rim the Sea of Okhotsk, they fulfil an indispensable role in maintaining strategically important military bases essential to Soviet defence. What makes the situation even worse for Japan is the military–strategic value of the islands has recently increased. Since Gorbachev came to power, fuel economisation programs have been implemented which keep the Soviet Fleet, including nuclear submarines, close to their home ports. Rather than patrol the Indian or Pacific Oceans, the Soviet Fleet now tends to be concentrated in Northeast Asia. The delay in the opening of the port of Vladivostok, despite Gorbachev's promises in his speech at Vladivostok, is probably due to opposition within the Soviet military. If Vladivostok is opened to foreigners, where will the Fleet, or part of it, move? In any event, due to concerns such as these the Soviets will never easily agree to return the four islands to Japan, regardless of possible benefits in the Japan–Soviet relationship.

However, we could possibly refute these weighty theories with the following counter-arguments. To begin with, the Soviet Pacific Fleet is not dependent on the area around the four disputed islands to ply between the Sea of Okhotsk and the Pacific Ocean. Instead, the Soviet Fleet transits to the Pacific Ocean mainly north of Urup Island in the middle of the Kurile chain. A counter to this argument is the importance of the islands to the Soviet Union in a situation where Japan and the United States decided to block the Soya (La Perouse) Strait. In such a situation, it would be a matter of life or death for the Soviets to control the four islands so that they could counteract the blockade. Such discourse will eventually invite the question of how much military–strategic value these islands could have in an age when the Soviet Union has announced that Vladivostok will be opened to foreigners. Furthermore, if the military appraisal of the military–strategic value of these islands is so high, why did the Soviets remove their military installations in the 1960s only to redeploy them after the conclusion of the Sino–Japanese peace treaty?

Another Soviet argument for refusing to return the islands to Japan is that Japan would use them for military purposes. This argument states that due to the close ties between Japan and the United States through the United States–Japan Security Treaty, returning the islands to Japan would give the United States a military–strategic advantage over the Soviet Union. Japan may station P3C long-range maritime patrol aircraft on the islands to maintain surveillance over Soviet nuclear submarines. In doing so, Japan would thus tip the balance of strategic–military strength in the Sea of Okhotsk decidedly against the Soviet Union. Although Japan's sovereignty over the islands would be firmly established if the islands were returned, it would do much to relieve Soviet anxiety about the islands if, upon their return, Japan voluntarily announced plans for their demilitarisation and permitted Soviet inspection of the demilitarisation process.

The most powerful of all counter-arguments (excluding the scenario of nuclear war) is that military power, unless actually used, is nothing more than one method of exerting political and diplomatic influence over other countries. Military power is, in this sense, nothing more than a 'tool of diplomacy'. If a country's military presence brings about negative results diplomatically, that country should reflect upon the military–strategic value of such a presence. Applying this argument to the northern islands issue, we can say that although the islands may have considerable strategic value now, this value is not absolute and unchanging. It is necessary to relegate this problem to a relative position within the overall framework of Japan–Soviet and United States–Soviet diplomacy. The islands may have a very positive military–strategic value in Soviet strategy against the United States,[19] but the Soviets must weigh the negative effects that will surely occur in diplomatic relations with Japan. As such, comparative considerations must be made and the view that the Soviets will never return the islands as long as they have military–strategic value loses some of its persuasiveness.

In calculating the positive and negative aspects of returning the four northern islands to Japan from the Soviet standpoint, there is at least one more important issue to consider: the role of the United States–Japan relationship. Will the United States–Japan relationship move in a direction more favourable to the Soviet Union if the four northern islands are returned to Japan? In the past, when Japan was economically and politically weak, the Soviet attitude towards the return of the islands was clear. The key point in the policy was to separate Japan and the United States which were firmly yoked together under the United States–Japan Security Treaty. In 1960, when the Kishi cabinet signed the revised version of the United States–Japan Security Treaty, Khrushchev's government voiced strong protest and, in retribution, added a new condition to Article 9 of the 1956 Japan–Soviet Joint Declaration. This new condition stated that in return for the Habomais and Shikotan, foreign military forces must be withdrawn from Japan. Not surprisingly, Japan was unwilling to dissolve its security relationship with the United States. The issue, however, provided an indication of the Soviet Union's sensitivity to the United States–Japan Security Treaty. However, as Heraclitus noted, 'all things are in constant flux'. Most Soviet Japanologists agree that it is unrealistic to press Japan to scrap the United States–Japan Security Treaty. They adhere to a view, which is gradually gaining popularity, that the Soviet Union can no longer base its Japan policy on such unrealistic expectations.[20] They advocate that the Soviet Union should recognise fully the reality and permanence of the United States–Japan Security Treaty as a realistic framework from which to improve relations with Japan. Recently, the Soviets have made statements that 'the United States–Japan Security Treaty is no impediment to improved Soviet–Japan relations' and they they 'do not want Japan in any way to sacrifice its relationship with any other country as a result of improved Soviet–Japan relations'.[21] At the Japan–Soviet Foreign Ministers' Conference held in Moscow in May 1989, Soviet Foreign Minister Eduard Shevardnadze made the following comment: 'Even in a situation in which the United States–Japan Security Treaty continues to exist, the Soviet Union will still hold negotiations for a Japan–Soviet Peace Treaty and there is a possibility that such a treaty may be concluded'.[22] This is the first pronouncement in which the Soviet government has actually given official recognition of the United States–Japan Security Treaty.

Such words may reflect a Soviet view that it is preferable to have Japan constrained under the United States–Japan Security Treaty than independent of it. The Soviets may feel that if Japan was released from the bounds of the United States–Japan Security Treaty it may transform itself into an independent militaristic state and thus pose a greater threat to the Soviet Union. Some Soviets therefore view Japan's linkage to the United States through the United States–Japan Security Treaty as the lesser of two evils.

I think it is fine that the Soviets have reached the stage where they can be realistic. It is also natural that the Soviets have begun to entertain doubts regarding the benefit which the return of the northern islands to Japan would bring to the Soviet Union, asking themselves: what would we gain by giving up the islands to Japan? For the Soviet Union, returning the islands would be a heavy price to pay. In the past, the Soviets may have considered the return of the islands as an issue that could be driven like a wedge between Japan and the United States. However, the use of the issue of the northern islands to divide Japan and the United States has become an increasingly unrealistic and undesirable option for the Soviet Union.

OPENING A PANDORA'S BOX?

Glasnost has opened up a political Pandora's box but given little attention as to how to close it. Among the most troublesome consequences of *glasnost* are the ethnic–nationalist movements. Ethnic unrest has not stopped in Central Asia, but spread to Outer Caucasia, the three Baltic states, Moldavia, and the Ukraine. The demands by these ethnic groups for political, economic and cultural freedom have created a great deal of pressure on the Gorbachev government. Additionally, the backlash against these groups by the ethnic Russian population has resulted in a problem which threatens to rock the very foundations of the Soviet Union.

An area of particular significance for the Japan–Soviet relationship is the demands by the many Union republics and autonomous regions that comprise the Soviet Union for revision of national boundaries which were arbitrarily drawn up in Stalin's time. Among these republics are some that demand not only a realignment of national boundaries but also laws that would enable them to reserve the right to become independent of the Soviet Union. Submitting to such demands, however, would be dangerous for the Soviet Union and may precipitate its downfall. Demands by ethnic groups may be more threatening to the Soviet Union than economic bankruptcy. For Gorbachev, the return of the northern islands to Japan at such a critical time would be an act fraught with immense danger. A Soviet specialist on the Northeast Asia told me that 'while the Soviet Union is concerned with the more serious problem of ethnic unrest, it cannot be concerned about territorial issues with Japan'.[23] In February 1946, by decree of the Presidium of the USSR's Supreme Soviet, the Soviet Union established the national boundaries with Japan as existing between the Japanese island of Hokkaido and the Soviet-held islands of Habomai, Shikotan, Kunashiri and Etorofu. From the outset, this was a unilateral measure on the part of the Soviets and something that was incomprehensible to the Japanese. If the four islands were returned to Japan, a new Japan–Soviet border would be drawn up between the four islands and Urup island. The problem with returning the islands to Japan and revising the existing Japan–Soviet boundaries is that such an act would weaken the central Soviet government's stance towards demands from several Soviet republics. If this occurred, leaders of the ethnic–nationalist movements within the Soviet Union would press for an explanation as to why the Kremlin would redraw territorial boundaries with Japan, a champion of Western capitalism and a nation firmly yoked to the United States through the United States–Japan Security Treaty. No doubt they would accuse the Soviet government of signing away Soviet territory to a foreign power, while refusing to consider disputed territorial boundaries on the home front among various Soviet republics. Ultimately, they would accuse the Soviets of extreme partiality.

Given the eruption of ethnic problems in the Soviet Union, are Japan's efforts for the return of the northern islands an exercise in futility? One cannot deny the recent ethnic problems in the Soviet Union have made the issue of returning the islands to Japan a far more difficult and complex affair than before. Still, such events have not completely ruled out the possibility for a reversion of the islands. The Soviet Union cannot use the issue of domestic ethnic strife as an excuse for delaying the settlement of the territorial issue with Japan forever.

My reasons for thinking this way are as follows. First, Japan's demand for the return of the islands is based upon its belief that the four islands are an integral part of the Japanese homeland. To the Japanese, there is little doubt that these islands legally and historically belong to Japan. In comparison to the demands of any of the ethnic groups within the Soviet Union for revised boundaries, Japan's claim on the northern islands is much more worthy and reasonable.

Second, it will probably take several generations to resolve the Soviet Union's ethnic problems. In retrospect, it is obvious that these problems are the legacy of Russia's Czarist past. Marxism–Leninism underscored class divisions and ignored the interests of all ethnic groups. Additionally, Stalin's mistakes added to the mountain of discontent and pent-up protest that has begun to erupt under *glasnost*. These problems will not be solved overnight, and it is unfortunate that the Soviet Union links the reversion of the northern islands to Japan with resolution of their domestic problems which is a semi-permanent undertaking. Even some advisors to the Kremlin would agree that improving Japan–Soviet ties should not wait for a resolution of the Soviet Union's ethnic problems.

Third, even if the Gorbachev government did decide to return the four islands to Japan, this would not set a precedent for making territorial border concessions. The Soviet Union is currently negotiating its common borders with China. During his Vladivostok speech, Mr Gorbachev stated that he would follow the international practice of accepting the major river shipping channels between the Soviet Union and neighbouring countries as the national border. Through this recognition of international law, the Soviet Union and the People's Republic of China have, with the exception of Heischaz and the western region, almost reached agreement on their borders. This makes the Sino–Soviet negotiations, and not the Japan–Soviet negotiations, the precedent for territorial border concessions.

Fourth, Japan could use the Soviet Union's domestic ethnic–nationalist movements to its own advantage. For example, in the 6 September 1989 edition of *Izvestia*, Vytautus Landsbergis, now president of Lithuania's Supreme Soviet, made the following statement to a reporter for the Japanese newspaper *SekaiNippo*: 'We share a common goal and hope with those social organisations which have been requesting the return of "Northern Territories". If we cooperate, it could be beneficial to both parties. The USSR government should be aware that there is an opinion within the Soviet Union that it should cease occupation of the four islands and return them to Japan'.[24] However, the expression of such support from ethnic groups is not necessarily a good thing for Japan. Japan's negotiating partner in the Japan–Soviet relationship will always be the central Soviet government and not regional ethnic groups. Voices of dissent from organisations calling for a united front against the Soviets serve only to provoke antagonism within the central Soviet government and among the general populace of Soviet Russia. As a result, what may appear at first glance to be a positive trend could have a negative effect on Japan–Soviet relations. On the other hand, support for Japan in regard to the issue of the return of the four islands exposes the fact that Soviet opinion is no longer the intractable monolith that it once was. Until now, the Kremlin has derived maximum benefit from its strategy of making the most of the differing stances of Japanese groups in regard to the territorial issue. This strategy was designed to create a rift, for example, between the Japanese government and each of the opposition parties; between the Ministry of Foreign Affairs and the Ministry of Agriculture, Forestry and Fisheries; and between the residents of Japan's main island of Honshu and those of Hokkaido. Although the playing field is still tilted in the Soviet Union's favour, it is no longer true that Soviet opinion is a single, unwavering opinion with Japan having a mixture of opinions.

CONCLUSION

A famous saying of Lenin's was: 'All things come to those who use time wisely'.[25] One characteristic that is often pointed out as illustrative of a major difference between the Russians and Japanese is the concept of time. The Russians are among the most patient people in the world. In contrast, the Japanese are pressured to achieve results within a limited time frame. In the past, this difference in mentality was often used to the Soviet Union's advantage and Japan's disadvantage. The Soviet Union would sometimes insist on discussing the same negotiating point time and time again or defer the tabling of a proposal. In doing so, the Soviets irritated the Japanese greatly. Ultimately, this forced the Japanese to reduce their demands to the bare minimum and even then the Soviet Union used tactics to wrest further compromise from Japan.

Delay in decision-making and action can also produce negative results. The passive use of time, which involves great patience, is but one method of using time. Another method involves the more active use of time. To use time actively, it is necessary to maintain momentum or act with a good sense of timing. Recently, the Soviet Union has not achieved impressive results from its active use of time. Once an incorrect decision is made and implemented in the Soviet Union it is rarely corrected expeditiously, perhaps due to the myth of Soviet infallibility or the intransigence of the Soviet bureaucracy.

Whatever the reasons may be, recent Soviet diplomacy has resulted in needless delays and has had many negative effects. For example, the Soviet Union's military intervention in Afghanistan lasted almost ten years and involved considerable human, psychological and economic loss. Additionally, the removal of SS-20s, the reconciliation with China, and the decoupling of SDI and START negotiations are all decisions which should have all been made earlier to take the pressure off the Soviet economy.

The same can be said regarding Japan–Soviet relations. The delay in President Gorbachev's visit to Japan gave rise to increasing anticipation in Japan and thus had the effect of focusing world attention on the Northern Territories issue. For the past 45 five years this thorn has been festering in the Japan–Soviet relationship, blocking a myriad of potential avenues towards cooperative relations. Even today, this potential has yet to be plumbed and it is the Soviet Union which has suffered most because of it. Enough valuable time has already been wasted. Decisions should be made as soon as possible.

7 Problems and prospects for Japanese investment in the Soviet Far East

EVGENII KOVRIGIN

The problem of the 'Northern Territories' has been a powerful factor complicating Soviet–Japanese relations. Its final resolution will contribute considerably to the improvement of relations, particularly in the economic sphere. At the same time, as Professor Kimura admits, the return of the disputed Kurile islands to Japan at this time is an act fraught with immense danger. The immediate transfer of the islands to Japan will increase friction between the different nations of the Soviet Union and is not supported by a large proportion of Soviet people, especially the Russian people. However, the territorial problem is not the main obstacle to an improvement in bilateral economic relations although its solution will a very important catalyst in that regard.

If I understand Professor Kimura correctly, he intimates that a solution of the problem on Japanese terms will result in an expansion of Japanese economic interest in the Soviet Union, especially in the Soviet Far East. It might be reasonable to connect the present stagnation of Soviet–Japanese economic relations to the political impasse if Japan was a totalitarian state whose government could simply forbid its business interests to deal with the Soviet Union. Of course, the country's authorities are able to influence the business behaviour of their domestic corporations but, after all, Japan is a democratic state and if, let us say, the *Keidanren* was deeply interested in Soviet Siberian and Far Eastern resources, the position of the government would not be particularly decisive.

The resolution of the territorial dispute will, of course, result immediately in an improvement in the psychological dimension of the bilateral relationship. The Japanese government thereafter can, at its own expense through the hands of Japanese corporations, construct infrastructure and industrial facilities in the Soviet Far East. But this will have little to do with real commerce because market forces or economic stimuli will not be involved. Rather, it will resemble economic assistance to a developing country. Neither Japanese corporations nor the Japanese government will use these facilities themselves if there is no real economic gain on their part. Consequently, there will be no increase in commercial interaction until real economic interest arises on both sides. And it is clear that Japanese economic interest has been greatly weakened since the 1980s, though among the Pacific countries Japan is still the Soviet Union's number one trading partner, especially for the Far East.

Japan's prominent position as a trading partner was quite natural while Japan was deeply interested in the raw materials of the region. Since the mid-1960s, in addition to traditional commercial trade, some new forms of economic links have been introduced, including so-called coastal (barter) trade and large-scale compensation agreements involving billions of dollars. For a considerable time, the compensation agreements played an important role for both countries, especially for the Soviet Union and its eastern regions. Even now, up to 70 per cent of Far Eastern exports are directed to the Japanese market. Alongside its positive aspects, this trade pattern has had some negative features. First, it has consolidated the raw materials orientation of Far Eastern exports. The lion's share of the region's exports is accounted for by unprocessed products of the forestry and fishery industries with little or no value added. Moreover, the one-sided orientation to Japan, which had become virtually a monopolistic partner in the region, made vital industries of the Soviet Far East overdependent on the state of relations between Tokyo and Moscow.

The situation deteriorated when Japan, due to the restructuring of its own economy, began to lose interest in traditional Far Eastern products. The increasing discrepancy in economic cooperation has contributed to the impasse in bilateral relations. Trade turnover has not grown, the volume of Far Eastern (and national Soviet) exports to Japan has dropped, and new forms of cooperation are failing to make appreciable headway.

EVOLUTION OF THE OFFICIAL SOVIET ATTITUDE TOWARDS THE IMPORT OF FOREIGN CAPITAL

The situation could be much better if there was sufficient understanding in the Soviet Union of the major trends in international economic relations and the importance of transnational migration of long-term capital as the main source of dissemination of advanced technology. Instead of attracting foreign (and primarily Japanese) capital, Soviet authorities, and consequently official economic doctrine, were until recently totally opposed to foreign investment.

This was not always the case in post-revolutionary Russia. In 1920, when the very existence of the Soviet Union was in the balance, Vladimir I. Lenin himself was bold enough to put forward the idea of leasing the Kamchatka Peninsula to the United States for 60 years. Lenin's idea was not implemented but concessions in primary industries (such as fishing concessions to Japan) became widespread in the Far East and left their mark on the history of the region. The concessions of those times may perhaps be considered a prototype of modern joint ventures.

Thereafter, however, owing to Stalin's primitive views on trading methods, capital exports of any kind became *passe*. From the beginning of Stalin's era, foreign investment was considered a tool of imperialist interference in the internal economic affairs of the other countries. And though this view is not altogether unfounded (take, for example, the 1973 *coup d'etat* in Chile), it was a lop-sided view because the positive aspects of private foreign investment were dismissed.

In the mid-1980s, the new leadership began to revise the Soviet Union's obsolete economic views. It had become clear that the Soviet Union's pattern of external economic ties, based almost exclusively on simple export–import commercial trade, no longer met the requirements of the modern world. This conclusion was particularly valid in regard to the Soviet Far East. The Soviet Union clearly was a Pacific state, in a geographical and military sense, but not in the economic sense of the word. It also became evident that an adherence to old patterns would lead only to the further economic isolation of the Soviet Union in the Asia–Pacific region. The government concluded that the only feasible solution was to open up the region to joint ventures and other forms of international economic cooperation which could bring hard currency to the country, improve the technological level of Far Eastern industry, and help it to produce goods and commodities which would be competitive in international markets.

After Mikhail S. Gorbachev's celebrated speech in Vladivostok in the summer of 1986, a law was enacted permitting the creation of joint enterprises with foreign capital on Soviet territory. Despite its evident drawbacks, the promulgation of the law itself can be regarded an historic event. But the drawbacks were transparent: the clauses of the law were inflexible, reflecting the old strategies. Little wonder that the reaction of the Japanese business sector was rather cool.

Radical amendments were made in 1988 after Gorbachev's speech in Krasnoyarsk. The new resolution of the USSR Council of Ministers gave the Far East a special status for developing external economic relations. The region was proclaimed a zone of favourable terms of investment. The resolution provided that joint ventures in the Far East would be exempt from a tax on profits for the first three years of operation. Thereafter, tax on hard currency profits would be reduced from the unreasonably high level of 30 per cent to a more tolerable 10 per cent. The government also promised to ease the procedure for profit repatriation. The existing ceiling of foreign share in fixed capital joint enterprises (it had been 49 per cent) was abrogated, and foreign citizens were allowed to occupy leading managerial positions in the joint ventures.

PUBLIC OPINION AND JAPANESE INVESTMENT IN THE FAR EAST

The investment regime (that is, official legislation, rules and regulations) in the Far East can be considered rather liberal towards foreign investors, though the period of its application has been very short, and new amendments may follow. But foreign investors are influenced in their behaviour not only by the regime, but also by what may be called the investment climate. The investment climate is the psychological atmosphere which exists in the host country and the conditions under which foreign entrepreneurs must operate. The 'regime' and the 'climate' often do not coincide. For example, the importation of long-term private capital into Japan was theoretically liberalised 10 years ago. But the atmosphere, the climate, could not be defined as friendly, and for many years business for American investors in Japan was anything but a pleasure. Now, in the United States, there is increasing anti-Japanese feeling due to the aggressive expansion of Japanese investment. Many American scholars believe that this could result in the movement of Japanese capital elsewhere.

Of course, the Soviet Union (and its Far East) is a very young host for foreign capital, and one cannot speak of a settled or well-shaped investment climate there. But one cannot ignore the polarisation of public opinion on this matter. At the highest level, the national government regards foreign, and especially Japanese, investment with favour and the national media in general supports the official position. But at the level of the man in the street, there are strong reservations regarding the influx of foreign capital. Speeches at the First Congress of USSR People's Deputies provided glaring examples of these sentiments. They reflect the not uncommon view that it is better not to develop the eastern regions of the Soviet Union at all than to allow foreign penetration with its negative impact on social behaviour and labour relations. The probable establishment of large-scale processing complexes in the Far East may also face an unpleasant reception from the increasingly active, domestic environment movement. At this time when joint ventures are not numerous and when their presence in the region is not so noticeable, talk of 'green' opposition is largely speculative, but it could become a problem with an increase in Japanese and other foreign investment.

There is one more consideration concerning the investment climate. For many decades the Soviet people were indoctrinated to believe it was bad to be rich. Soviet citizens are unlikely to change their egalitarian views overnight. The negative attitude of a large proportion of the Soviet population towards members of the recently-formed cooperative enterprises and farm leaseholders is no secret. (These are individuals who lease land from the state or from collective farms for agricultural use. Their income is usually much higher than those who work on collective farms.) This attitude may, in turn, be focused on Soviet workers in receipt of relatively high wages engaged in joint ventures or special economic zones.

In any case, potential Japanese investors should be advised to exercise what can be called high-energy but low-profile efforts in the region so as not to irritate the conservative elements of Soviet society. A primary objective of Soviet scholars and officials will be to diffuse the population's mistrust of foreign investment.

FAR EASTERN RESOURCES AND OPPORTUNITIES FOR CONDUCTING JOINT VENTURES

There is another crucial and fundamental question: will the Far East again become attractive to Japanese business interests, and if so, in what spheres of its economy? Undoubtedly, the area possesses a wide variety of resources and industries which may be attractive to international entrepreneurs, particularly those from the Asia–Pacific region.

Despite Japan's adjustment to the manufacture of high-technology products, the massive deposits of mineral and biological resources in the Far East cannot be ignored. The most important of these resources are non-ferrous ores, rare and precious metals, diamonds, pit and hydrogeneous coal, phosphorite, apatite, boron, sulphur, mica, semi-precious stones, oil and gas on the continental shelf of the adjacent seas, to say nothing of the enormous biological resources of the Taiga and the Soviet ocean economic zone. Geologically speaking, the region can be called a second Australia, but it may be even richer because a detailed study of its resources will take many years to complete.

These raw materials will eventually become the base for the development of international enterprises producing a wide variety of semi-finished and finished goods. One can also foresee considerable opportunities for joint undertakings by Soviet and foreign entrepreneurs in construction and agriculture, and simultaneously in mechanical engineering, including assembly plants of different kinds. Additionally, the combination of research by Soviet scientists using highly advanced Japanese technology could become a form of mutually beneficial cooperation between the region and its richest neighbour.

Last, but not least, is the sphere of recreation. The Far East is beautiful, unique in its natural characteristics. The landscape and climate differ greatly from one zone to another, from the subtropical in the south of the Primorie (Maritime) territory to the arctic conditions of Magadan *oblast*. The peninsular of Kamchatka, with its volcanoes and geysers, offers extraordinary opportunities for international tourism. Despite all the efforts of the central industrial ministries to spoil its surface, the Far East remains one of the greatest reserves of wildlife on earth. It is natural to think about international cooperation in the development of its recreational facilities.

No one in the Far East wishes to limit international economic cooperation to Japan alone. Nevertheless, for several reasons, it seems natural for Japan to be the region's principal partner. First, the people of the Far East have become accustomed to the Japanese way of conducting business because of their long-standing contact with Japan. Second, Japan's banks and the technological supremacy of its industrial corporations offer enormous financial opportunities. Third, the flow of Japanese funds could help to transform the entire economy of the region and balance its deformed industrial structure. Fourth, Japanese trading companies with their huge marketing networks could become intermediaries between the Soviet Union and the rest of the Asia–Pacific region. Given these reasons, the local desire for Japanese capital is obvious. The crucial element is how to make the eastern part of the Soviet Union economically attractive to Japanese businessmen.

PROSPECTS FOR SPECIAL ECONOMIC ZONES IN THE FAR EAST

Tangible measures aimed at the liberalisation of Soviet investment legislation have already been discussed. The government hopes the creation of special or free economic zones will become an important factor in attracting Japanese capital to the Far East. Thirty years have passed since the first special economic zone in the world was established near Shannon, Ireland. The merits of such zones and their contribution to the development of the newly industrialising countries are well known and widely recognised. But for the Soviet people, they seem to be somewhat exotic and involve some social and political embarrassment.

Nevertheless, the central government finally ventured to launch several special economic zones on Soviet territory, considering them to be a method to improve infrastructure, invigorate the socialist economy to compete with the free-market economies of Pacific states, and raise funds to finance industrial development.

Soon after this decision was made, a rather extravagant proposal was received from Japan. The author of this proposal was Mr Seizo Ota, the elderly head of Toho Mutual Life Insurance Company. It was a typically grand project. Mr Ota proposed the investment of around US$8 billion for a 60-year lease on about 100 square kilometres of virgin soil near the Bay of Posiet, where the boundaries of the Soviet Union, China and North Korea meet. His idea was to build modern infrastructural facilities in the area, partition it into many sites, and to lease these sites to Japanese and other industrialists. However, after Mr Ota's idea had been scrutinised thoroughly, it became clear that it was more a philosophical concept than a business proposal and the central authorities had to reject it.

Instead, the government decided to create a special economic zone in the Pacific town of Nakhodka and at least two more zones in the European part of the Soviet Union (Vyborg and Novgorod). The authorities of Nakhodka themselves proposed that their town and its suburbs be the site of the zone, with a view to seeking an influx of (primarily Japanese) capital. The existence of two big cargo seaports and the diversified, though obsolete and insufficient, infrastructure were the main reasons for choosing Nakhodka as a special economic zone. It is assumed that international business activity will begin with ship repairs and large-scale processing of fish and timber, and then move in a more sophisticated direction to mechanical engineering, assembly plants and so forth. President Gorbachev reported after his visit to the United States in the summer of 1990 that American business circles had indicated a readiness to invest in the Nakhodka free economic zone. (Earlier, some American firms advised that they planned to erect giant warehouses there, primarily to meet the needs of Japanese foreign trade.) There are also indications of South Korean interest in the zone. Paradoxically, the prospect of Japanese participation is less certain.

The details of regulations concerning the proposed special economic zones are yet to be finalised. But one peculiarity is now clear: the Soviet zones will differ from those in many other countries by also providing a favourable regime and treatment to Soviet enterprises and organisations. Some academics propose the introduction of a new currency in the zones — the so-called chervonets, a gold-backed convertible money unit which existed in the 1920s.

Some surprising news came from Sakhalin in mid-1990. Sakhalin's newly-elected local Soviet proclaimed the whole island a free entrepreneurial zone and promised to establish stock exchanges in its northern and southern parts. Sakhalin seems to be a perfect site for this socio–economic experiment due to its relative isolation from other parts of the Soviet Union and its geographical proximity to the Asia–Pacific region.

REASONS FOR CURRENT JAPANESE RELUCTANCE TO INVEST IN THE REGION

As noted above, investment legislation is now quite favourable for foreign investment in the Soviet Far East. Nevertheless, Japanese corporations show little interest in joint ventures in the region. (Frankly speaking, other countries are similarly inactive: in early 1990, of 1,274 Soviet–foreign enterprises throughout the USSR, only 40 were located in the Far East.) But Japanese inertness is most noticeable, particularly if Soviet expectations are taken into account. At the end of 1989, Japan had only 21 enterprises in the whole of the Soviet Union compared with hundreds of enterprises run by European partners. Most of these 21 ventures are small in size, capitalised at US$1 million or less, and located in the European part of the country. Several small, raw materials processing enterprises in the Asiatic part of the Soviet Union are an exception to the rule. The largest of them is the Tairiku–Igirma Timber Processing Company, located in Eastern Siberia, which, incidentally, is now encountering serious organisational difficulties. My own numerous talks with Japanese businessmen and scholars in Vladivostok and Khabarovsk indicate that there are a range of factors for Japan's reluctance to invest in the Far East.

The first, and probably most important, factor is the non-convertibility of the Soviet rouble. This makes it extremely difficult to evaluate the capital contribution of both partners and their profits, to distribute profits between them, and to repatriate profits to Japan. In essence, the Japanese simply do not know what to do with their gains in roubles. Until the rouble is convertible, the problem will persist.

Second, due to the structural changes in the Japanese economy and current patterns of supply, few raw materials from the Far East are of interest to Japan with the exception, perhaps, of oil and gas on the Sakhalin shelf and ores of rare metals. Taking into account the high cost of initial capital investment and production and the high costs of surface transportation compared with that in the European part of the Soviet Union, the prospects of obtaining sufficient profits in the Far East at the present time are rather doubtful.

Third, cautious Japanese businessmen are concerned by the very speed and unpredictability of reforms and political transformation in Soviet society. Many of them are not completely sure of the final victory of reformists in the Soviet Union and say they will be more active when the political situation in the country becomes more stable.

Fourth, the penetration of Japanese companies into the Soviet Union's eastern provinces has been impeded by COCOM limitations, particularly as a result of the 'Toshiba affair'. Under pressure from the Reagan administration, the Japanese over-reacted to the extent that practically all deliveries of machinery and equipment were cancelled in 1987.

Fifth, the poor state of the infrastructure and facilities inhibits the readiness of Japanese industrialists to invest in the Far East.

Finally, there is a shortage of labour. The labour force also lacks skill and discipline according to standard Japanese requirements. Moreover, due to the long-term economic isolation from the outside world, local managers became accustomed to aim at only one goal — to fulfil by all means the state plans set in Moscow. In the Far East there are still very few able and efficient administrators who understand how the market economy functions. Some institutions in the region have begun to train their students in international management and marketing but it will obviously take considerable time to improve managerial skills.

PROSPECTS FOR FUTURE COOPERATION BETWEEN THE FAR EAST AND JAPAN

The picture of Soviet–Japanese economic relations in the Far East is far from optimistic. Quite frankly, the interest of potential Japanese investors is very low and the fear of risk is very high. The situation is aggravated by the lack of political support on the part of the Japanese government resulting from the Northern Territories dispute. But this does not mean that there is no light at the end of the tunnel. There are positive indications of change, maybe even of breakthrough from this impasse. To begin with, both sides recently resumed negotiations on the joint development of oil and gas on the Sakhalin shelf which the Soviet Union suspended after the oil shock of 1980. Further, the Japanese have shown an interest in the conversion of Far Eastern military plants to the production of civilian consumer goods because the technological level of these facilities is sufficiently high to meet Japanese technological requirements.

A further dimension to bilateral relations is currently underway. This is direct productive cooperation on an inter-regional basis. Certain Japanese prefectures (Hokkaido, Kanagawa and Niigata for example) are trying to establish independent trade and cooperative relations with the *krais* and *oblasts* of the Far East, which are also beginning to obtain financial and organisational independence from central planning bodies. They have begun to develop joint projects in transportation (for example, a ferry service between Hokkaido and Sakhalin), fisheries and agriculture. Niigata Prefecture, whose capital is Khabarovsk's sister-city, is particularly active in its drive for economic independence and is attempting to form a vast trading zone embracing those regions of neighbouring counties which are adjacent to the Sea of Japan.

Groups of Japanese businessmen and managers, to say nothing of individuals, frequently visit the Far East seeking investment opportunities in the region. They say that Japanese interest in the Soviet Far East will be awakened and gradually increase as some of the above-mentioned economic obstacles begin to disappear. The notable thaw in East–West relations is an additional and important incentive for future Japanese involvement in Soviet economic affairs.

Japanese businessmen also predict that the Soviet Union will be comparatively more attractive to them if neighbouring China becomes less open to the outside world.

It is impossible to believe that the Japanese industrialists will remain reluctant to invest in the immense natural riches of the Soviet Far East bedded, literally speaking, next door to them. Even if they do not need mineral and biological resources for themselves, the products of joint Soviet–Japanese projects could be sold to third countries.

Another important incentive for investment in the manufacturing industries of the region lies in the Japanese need to diversify their export markets, especially in view of growing anti-Japanese sentiment in the United States and of plans to establish 'fortress Europe' in 1992. Of course, the population of the Far East is small (it will hardly reach 10 million people by the year 2000) but commodities and consumer goods produced there can be easily sold throughout the whole territory of the Soviet Union or, at least, in Russia proper. The Soviet market is dormant for Japan now because of the inconvertibility of the rouble, but potentially it is immense. Each of the Soviet Union's 283 million citizens (including new-born babies) has more than half a year's wage in savings banks, to say nothing of what is hidden under the bed! And this has occurred when the shelves in department stores and supermarkets are nearly empty! The collection of this money when the rouble becomes convertible is an attractive prospect, and it will be no surprise if some Japanese trading companies resolve to conduct unprofitable operations for some years so as to be first to exploit the market.

CONCLUSION

One more critical question arises: is it advantageous for Japan (and the West in general) to support the Soviet Union through direct investment in the Far East? I think the answer is undoubtedly yes. The integration of the Soviet Union in the emerging network of Pacific economic cooperation must result in an increase in the total volume of business activity in the Pacific basin. Such involvement will work as a stabilising factor when changes in market conditions occur in the region, and will facilitate in remodelling the economies of many Pacific states. The world community needs a democratic and prosperous Soviet Union but it cannot be prosperous if it continues to be an economic outsider in the Pacific basin.

Of course, the Soviet Union itself must fight against bureaucratic inertness and lack of initiative resulting from long years of economic and political stagnation. In the long term, the country perhaps could develop its Far East through its own efforts but this would take decades. That is why it is very important to attract foreign investment and technology to the eastern part of the Soviet Union, and it is natural to look first to Japan. This does not mean that development of the Far East will be limited to cooperation with Japan alone. This would not be wise for many reasons. Although Japan is geographically close, wealthy and technically advanced, the need for diversification of partners is obvious. Many people in the Soviet Union are glad that after 25 years of stagnation, economic ties with the neighbouring People's Republic of China are now accelerating quickly. There are also examples of successful cooperation with North Korea and Vietnam. There are also opportunities of trade and cooperation with other countries of the Asia–Pacific region, including the NIEs, Australia, Canada, the ASEAN countries, New Zealand, to say nothing of the United States.

Nearly 300 years ago, Peter the Great, an outstanding Russian reformer, proclaimed the goal of 'cutting out a window to Europe'. It seems strange that the Soviet Union is now pursuing a similar goal in the Pacific at the end of the twentieth century. Of course, it is better late than never. But too much time has been lost. The economic dynamism of the Asia–Pacific continues to widen the gap between it and the Pacific regions of the Soviet Union. The most viable solution to rectify the situation in the Far East is a high level of regional economic independence from Moscow and cooperation with more successful neighbours. The main prerequisite for a turn to the better will be the display of maximum flexibility on the part of the Soviet Union.

8 The Soviet reforms and relations with the Koreas

YU-NAM KIM

The improved relationship between the United States and the Soviet Union in recent years has given hope to Koreans who have historically sought peace and stability on the Korean Peninsula. Unlike the detente of the early 1970s, the current period of superpower detente appears less tactical and more structural in nature. By structural, I mean a more fundamental, long-term response to the international and domestic changes occurring today. Furthermore, the current period of detente now encompasses a number of countries around the globe. It includes much of the Eastern bloc, Mongolia and Vietnam. Notable by exception are North Korea and Cuba and, to a lesser extent, China and Cambodia, where the leadership has yet to carry the 'revolution' to the second generation.

The current trend also demonstrates a general axiom of international politics: relaxation of tensions between bipolar, primary competitors increases the independence of their respective alliance blocs and friends. Mikhail S. Gorbachev deserves a great deal of credit for the current period of detente. The West initially reacted to Gorbachev's new thinking (*novoye myshlenie*) with scepticism and called for deeds to match words. However, with the withdrawal of Soviet troops from Afghanistan in February 1988, the signing of the Intermediate Nuclear Forces (INF) treaty in June 1988 and destruction of SS-20 missiles, and the announcement of unilateral Soviet troop cuts in Europe, the West began to see tangible signs of Soviet change. The United States is now faced with the task of matching Soviet initiatives with its own.

Contemporary American–Soviet superpower politics poses a major policy challenge for the United States. In the coming years, the United States must seize all opportunities to work constructively with an economically beleaguered Soviet Union. At the same time, it must not permit the Soviet Union to restore its otherwise flagging national strength for future direct military expenditure. Equally important, the United States must not let its defence readiness or military–industrial base diminish too far. Indeed, in his first major address on foreign soil after becoming president, George Bush stated before the Korean National Assembly on 27 February 1989 that: 'peace through strength is a policy that has served the security interests of our two nations well... We must

90

complement deterrence with an active diplomacy in search of dialogue with our adversaries'.

With the rise of Mikhail Gorbachev, the Soviet Union has shown great flexibility and energy. With the strong presidential leadership established by the Congress of the People's Deputies in March 1990, President Gorbachev is attempting to seize the political initiative within and without the socialist commonwealth. Although it appears that the underlying objectives of Soviet foreign policy have changed little, improving the image of the Soviet Union in foreign eyes has become an important aspect of foreign policy implementation.

In contrast with previous Soviet leaders, Gorbachev emphasises economic linkages in discussions on international security. Under Gorbachev's leadership, the Soviets explicitly articulate a linkage between the Soviet Union's international agenda and its domestic economic situation. Gorbachev specifically proposed an overall examination of the international security environment as follows:

> The Soviet Union is giving considerable attention to a joint examination, at an international forum as well as within the framework of the Helsinki process, of the world economy's problems and prospects, the interdependence between disarmament and development, and the expansion of trade and scientific and technological cooperation. We feel that in the future it would be important to convene a World Congress on Problems of Economic Security at which it would be possible to discuss as a package everything that encumbers world economic relations.[1]

In general, Soviet foreign policy aims and directions, reflected both in the 27th Party Congress of the Communist Party of the Soviet Union (CPSU) of 1986 and the 19th Party Conference of the CPSU in 1988, emphasise peaceful co-existence, cooperation and interdependence based on mutual respect for territorial and political realities, that is, the recognition of the post-war *status quo* in Europe and Asia. Specifically, foreign policy theses reported to the 19th Party Congress were stated as follows:

> The foreign policy for *perestroika* relies on a new mode of thinking, one that is consistent and based on research and free from historically-hackneyed stereotypes. The mode of thinking reflects the (practical) realities of the modern world, versatile and controversial as it is, a world that questions the very survival of humanity and yet contains a formidable potential for co-existence, cooperation, and a quest for political solutions to urgent issues.[2]

Many in the West question whether the shifts in Soviet foreign policy are mere tactical manoeuvres or signs of a more fundamental strategic change. A study done by the United States Combined Arms Center reports that the changes are 'operational and the overall conception of the East–West struggle has not changed the minds of the Soviet leadership'.[3] Those who believe in this assertion consider that there is a greater Soviet appreciation of the necessity for a flexible shift in the axis of the main effort to shape subsequent operations after taking a breather.

If, on the other hand, we give the Soviet Union the benefit of the doubt, Soviet flexibility has not received a substantial response from the United States. The Soviets have complained that the response to a number of Soviet peace proposals has been inadequate. Two such proposals, among others, were Gorbachev's regional collective security proposal for an Asia–Pacific peace conference made in his July 1986 Vladivostok speech[4] and the seven-point peace initiative made in Gorbachev's September 1988 Krasnoyarsk speech.[5] The third item of the seven-point peace proposal seems to have been aimed at strengthening Soviet security measures in the Asia–Pacific region by dint of multilateral arms negotiations. The proposal specifically suggested that the Soviet Union, China, Japan, North Korea, and South Korea should agree to joint security talks to limit naval and air force activities with a view towards lowering military confrontation in the region.[6]

Is the Soviet *perestroika* merely a respite or breathing space (*peredyshka*)? If it is a breathing space in order to shape subsequent operations, the Soviet new thinking is but one manifestation of a deeper crisis within the Soviet Union. But singularly absent in Gorbachev's speeches were the requirements for strict observance of Marxist–Leninist norms and for ties based on 'socialist internationalism'.

Against this confusing and still-changing background, this study will attempt to address Gorbachev's *perestroika* policy in reference to the two Koreas. It first examines the meaning of Soviet 'new political thinking', then addresses Soviet relations with North Korea and South Korea, and the prospects for Soviet–South Korean economic cooperation. An assumption that runs throughout this study is that Gorbachev's Asian initiatives and the Soviet interaction with other major powers in the region hold important implications for a peaceful settlement on the Korean Peninsula.

SOVIET 'NEW THINKING'

Watching the course of events taking place in the Soviet Union today, one cannot ignore the undeniably important role of ideas in bringing about change (*izmenenie*) in its security policy. The change in Soviet military policy is an important factor because the Soviet Union has traditionally maintained powerful military forces commensurate with its superpower status. A useful starting point in considering Soviet change is to note the shift in Soviet security policy in regard to Moscow's reorientation of military–civilian resources allocation.

Soviet statements in the Gorbachev era indicate that policies are being fundamentally reconsidered for two reasons. First, Soviet economic difficulties necessitated change in the allocation of resources as its ailing economy could no longer sustain its huge military forces. Second, the Soviets found the military capabilities maintained at such great cost were diplomatically counter-productive due to the threat they posed to neighbouring countries: fear of the Soviet Union in neighbouring countries resulted in a strong network of alliances with the United States directed against the Soviet Union.[7]

At the same time, while Moscow's defence cuts aim to reduce the economy's defence burden, they also contain a strong political element. The Soviet Union wishes to constrain Western military modernisation and obtain Western support for its economic programs. In the light of these political implications, the West may have to consider closely the Soviet military–economic reforms.[8]

At the 27th Party Congress of the CPSU, Gorbachev announced that henceforth Soviet military posture would be defensively oriented and force structure would be determined by the principle of 'reasonable sufficiency'. While there is no concrete basis with which to determine reasonable sufficiency, the attempt to set a minimum ceiling on force structure is a major change in thinking.

According to Gorbachev, one of the major Soviet foreign security policy aspects of perestroika is 'new political thinking' (novoye politicheskoe myshlenie). He says that the concept of reasonable sufficiency and a defensive orientation represent a reorientation of the Soviet approach to international relations.[9] In other words, new political thinking is the foreign policy counterpart of the domestic concepts of perestroika and glasnost. A Soviet scholar from the Academy of Sciences describes the new thinking as an approach to solve the problems of the survival of mankind:

> It (new political thinking) is usually referred to as a concept. I would like to say that it is premature to call it a concept. Up to now it is rather an approach. Concept is usually rather rigid, it has its own mythology, and is unlikely to change in the short-term. Approach (or method) is flexible, it can be applied creatively — and that's the source of its power... So the main features of new political thinking as an approach are:
> – the priority of mankind's global human interests over the class solidarity concept;
> – a pragmatic approach to all issues;
> – the end of self-isolation from the world community.[10]

The 19th Party Conference of the CPSU in 1988 adopted a resolution that military expenditure should correspond to economic priorities and not to quantitative (numerical) parameters.[11] The resolution was followed in June 1988 by a decision by the newly-elected Supreme Soviet to cut the 1989 defence budget (77.3 billion roubles or about US$120 billion) by 50 per cent by the end of 1995.

According to the Soviet doctrine of reasonable sufficiency, the goal of the military is not to win a nuclear war, but to prevent it. Reasonable sufficiency requires military procurement, construction, research and development, structure and training to be oriented to the defence of the Soviet Union. In other words, reasonable sufficiency is sufficiency for defence and not for offence. Military superiority, or even numerical equality in all components of strategic force, is not necessary to maintain a strategic equilibrium.

There are three schools of thought in the West about the reorientation of Soviet foreign policy. The first takes a positive view of changes in Soviet international attitudes. The second is the negative view. The third presents a mixed view of the other perspectives.

The positive view of new political thinking reflects a vital concern for the very survival of mankind in the nuclear era. The positive view readily accepts Soviet proposals for peace including Gorbachev's plan for a nuclear free world in the coming century. It sees, as noted by Gorbachev in his public speeches, that the strategy of nuclear deterrence has long outlived its usefulness without offering an alternative to the nuclear genocide of mankind. Soviet new thinking, its proponents maintain, calls for a 'sudden access of planetary consciousness' to ensure human survival on earth.[12] Gorbachev said in his book, *Perestroika*:

> Our new thinking goes further. The world is living in an atmosphere not only of nuclear threat, but also of unsolved major social problems... Mankind today faces unprecedented problems and the future will hang in the balance if joint solutions are not found. All countries are now more interdependent than ever before, and the stockpiling of weapons, especially nuclear missiles, makes the outbreak of a world war, even if not sanctioned or accidental, increasingly more probable, due simply to a technical failure or human fallibility. Yet all living things on Earth would suffer... We are all passengers aboard one ship, the Earth, and we must not allow it to be wrecked. There will be no second Noah's Ark.[13]

The negative perspective, on the other hand, views Gorbachev's pronouncements with scepticism and awaits tangible changes. Gorbachev went to the United Nations General Assembly in December 1988 and surprised the world with his announcement that Moscow will unilaterally reduce conventional forces by 500 000 in Europe.[14] The negative view wants to see the proposal put into action.

The term 'reasonable sufficiency' is questioned. Despite an extensive purge of the Soviet Union's top military hierarchy, the negative critics argue there is no hard evidence to suggest that Gorbachev has been able to curb military spending to finance his economic reforms. The Soviets say that military spending in 1987–88 was frozen and military spending in 1989 was 77.3 billion roubles. This figure is about half American estimates of real Soviet military spending in the period. The United States estimates that the Soviet Union continues to spend 15 to 17 per cent of its GNP on defence, as opposed to about 6 per cent in the United States and considerably less in West European countries and Japan. The United States estimates that Soviet military spending, rather than declining, grew by about 3 per cent in both 1986 and 1987, almost double the rate of the 1981–85 period.[15] The negative view says there has been no discernible change in Soviet military posture, tactics, procurement practices, equipment, deployment of weapons systems or training procedures that can be attributed to Gorbachev's peace initiatives.[16] It says rhetoric is not enough. As if to confound his critics, however, Gorbachev promised a further cut of 10 billion roubles, slashing 14.2 per cent from the defence budget for 1990–91.[17]

In contrast with these opposing viewpoints, the mixed view of Soviet new political thinking sees Gorbachev's foreign policy *perestroika* as a task to be pursued jointly with the United States. While it questions the sincerity of Gorbachev's peace initiatives, it tends to be equally critical of the United States for its lack of cooperation with the Soviet Union. In reality, this view argues, if the West is to come up with any sound options for peace on earth, the United States must join in cooperative endeavours with the Soviet Union.

In particular, the mixed view notes that there has been no substantial change in superpower relations in the Pacific. The present detente is the child of the Atlantic just as the first detente had been in the early 1970s. Practically all interaction between Gorbachev and his American counterparts, including the INF treaty and force reductions, is Euro-centric. There has been little dialogue in the Pacific between the two Pacific superpowers, the very initiators of the arms race in the region.

While these viewpoints differ in their interpretation of Moscow's new thinking, Gorbachev himself describes his initiatives as 'disarmament for development'.[18] He states clearly that his domestic economic agenda necessitates an overall decrease in military spending. If countries in the West cooperate in the creation of a global security system, Gorbachev will then be able to apply Soviet economic and human resources more thoroughly to economic restructuring.[19] Furthermore, engaging other nations in efforts to achieve mutual security will undermine criticism from more orthodox Soviet policy-makers concerned with the military defence of the nation.

NORTH KOREA

Gorbachev's *perestroika* raises several important questions in regard to the Korean Peninsula. Does Soviet new thinking indicate that Moscow views the world, not in terms of a balance of power or balance of forces, but in terms of a balance of interests? Have the Soviets replaced the concept of national security with the notion of universal security? If so, what effect does the new thinking have on Soviet foreign policy towards the Korean Peninsula in general, and North Korea in particular?

When Gorbachev was interviewed by a German weekly, *Der Spiegel*, in October 1989 on the occasion of Chancellor Helmut Kohl's visit to Moscow, he was questioned about the effect of *perestroika* on Soviet foreign policy. His answer to the question bears implications for the Korean Peninsula. He said:

> When we began *perestroika* and looked at the world around us with a magnifying glass, we saw a strange situation. The world had changed, other realities had arisen, yet international conditions continued to be moulded by the principles of the Cold War. The same cliches prevailed. So the need for restructuring here, too, became apparent. We now have a new notion of international conditions, which we call new thinking.[20]

Gorbachev acknowledges that conditions existing on the Korean Peninsula today are drastically different from those in the 1950s. His Krasnoyarsk speech is again noteworthy:

> The situation on the Korean Peninsula remains complicated, even though the outlines of progress to dialogue between North and South have begun to show there as well... The USSR suggests that the question of lowering military confrontation in the areas where the coasts of the USSR, the PRC, Japan, the DPRK and South Korea converge be discussed on a multilateral basis, with a view to freezing and commensurately lowering the levels of naval and air forces and limiting their activity... I think that in the context of general improvement in the situation on the Korean Peninsula possibilities can open up for forming economic relations with South Korea as well.[21]

Although the Soviet Union continues to maintain good relations with North Korea, there are indications that the Soviet Union is beginning to see Pyongyang as a liability, a drain on its resources, and is assigning lower priority to it. In essence, the Soviets are attempting to reassure the Pyongyang regime, maintain a moderating influence on it and retain their competitive position *vis-a-vis* Beijing.

The general economic condition in North Korea seems worse than that of the Soviet Far East. North Korea's recent trade balance with the Soviet Union has widened in favour of Moscow. In the mid-1980s, Pyongyang's trade with the Soviet Union accounted for one-third of its total foreign trade. In the past few years, the percentage has risen to more than 60 per cent. Some Soviet scholars have hinted that Moscow has advised Pyongyang to implement economic reforms, but to no avail. Moreover, the Soviet Union acknowledges that Gorbachev's Krasnoyarsk speech attempted to influence North Korea to initiate change.[22]

A singular characteristic of the North Korean economy is self-reliance in the building an independent national economy. In 1984, North Korea made a move towards an active open door policy in order to create a comprehensive economic complex based on the principle of self-reliance. This move was made in the context of the law on joint venture enterprises. Pyongyang, however, has not been successful in this respect because Western countries lack incentives to invest in North Korea. So far joint ventures have been partly successful only with pro-Pyongyang Korean residents in Japan.[23]

In general terms, the weaker North Korea becomes, the more it becomes dependent on the Soviet Union. With a history of ups and downs in the relationship between North Korea and the Soviet Union, Soviet interests increasingly match those of North Korea. Like Moscow, Pyongyang watched with growing concern the expanding Chinese relationships with the United States and Japan in the late 1970s. North Korea frequently indicated an interest in improved relations with Moscow, a policy consistent with Pyongyang's wish to avoid a heavy dependence on Beijing.

By 1985 there were more North Korean officials visiting Moscow than Beijing. Over the following years, joint celebrations and joint naval exercises continued at an impressive pace. After its successful participation in the 1988 Seoul Olympics, the Soviet Union attended Pyongyang's international youth festival in July 1989 for another gain in the international sporting arena.[24]

Thus far, Soviet policy has concentrated on rebuilding its ties and influence in North Korea while watching closely the rapid changes in South Korea. Moscow has dealt with Seoul with an impressive sophistication whenever it finds an opportunity to do so. Like China, the Soviets favour closer ties between both North and South Korea. The Soviets now find that there is no need for a midwife, either the United States or China, in the birth of a new relationship with South Korea. The Soviet Union continues to compete with China for a closer economic relationship with economically useful South Korea.

The Soviet Union is highly sensitive to North Korean reaction to its foreign policy *perestroika*. Although Kim Il-sung of North Korea has made two visits to Moscow since 1984, Gorbachev has not seen fit to reciprocate and that may well reflect the low priority he attaches to North Korea. Pyongyang was greatly disappointed in September 1988 when the scheduled visit of President Andrei Gromyko, the first by a Soviet head of state, did not materialise at the last moment because he was ousted from the post. The chairman of the Committee for State Security (KGB) went to Pyongyang as his replacement, but Kim Il-sung was dissatisfied with the substitution. North Korea had expected Gorbachev to visit Pyongyang in May 1989 on his return from Beijing, but he did not extend the trip to Pyongyang for unknown reasons.

The dramatic changes in Soviet domestic and foreign policy and Moscow's 'odd affairs' with South Korea, coupled with the recent crackdown and assertion of control by the hard-liners in China after the Tiananmen incident in June 1989, have altered the strategic equation. There is now greater ideological affinity between Beijing and Pyongyang than there has been in a decade and certainly more than now exists with the Soviet Union.

The Soviet Union has begun to press North Korea to become more open. With the liberalisation of the Soviet press in recent months, a reformist weekly magazine, *Argumenty i Fakty* (Moscow) points out that the North Korean economy faces a crisis, and calls the North 'a museum of Kim Il-sung' in its article:

> The Democratic People's Republic of Korea (North Korea) may be called a Kim Il-sung museum. Portraits and bronze and gilt sculptures of him are everywhere. There is an imposing monument personifying the ideas of Kim Il-sung. Unquestioning devotion to the leader is the principal criterion of the merits of the country's citizens. His instructions are studied carefully. Everyone, young and old, wears on his chest a badge with Kim Il-sung's portrait...
>
> Western specialists do not take the economic achievements announced by North Korea as fact and evaluate sceptically the prospects for fulfilment of the next plan also. Noting the decline in production in the basic sectors of industry, they believe that the economic growth rate in 1987–1988 was not more than 2 per cent per annum. The reasons for the crisis state of the economy are the chronic shortage of energy and raw materials, the inefficient management system, and the high military spending.[25]

The rapid development of events in the Soviet Union and Eastern Europe, which has affected even Albania, has stirred North Korea. It is difficult piecing together a clear picture of the situation in Pyongyang from the fragmentary press reports because detailed economic statistics are unavailable and political decisions are made in an atmosphere of secrecy. However, it is important to note that the Soviet Union, for the first time in its long history of partnership with North Korea, has begun to criticise the elusiveness of North Korea.

Affected by Soviet *perestroika* and *glasnost*, a number of North Korean students defected to South Korea in April 1990. Two North Korean students, both attending Leningrad State University, sought asylum in South Korea after becoming disillusioned with life in North Korea under Kim Il-sung. One of them said that the Soviet media often compared South Korea with North Korea and some articles criticised Pyongyang's dictatorship, while they praised South Korea for its economic achievements. Since 1989, six North Korean students have found refuge in Seoul while studying in East European countries including Czechoslovakia, Poland, East Germany and the Soviet Union.[26]

SOUTH KOREA

On the eve of the 1988 Seoul Olympics, Gorbachev publicly acknowledged that conditions exiting on the Korean Peninsula were drastically different from those which existed in the 1950s. His Krasnoyarsk speech in September 1988 was the first public statement which encompassed 'new thinking' on the Korean issue. As noted above, the speech proposed a multilateral conference for arms control to be held with all regional parties, including South Korea, and suggested an opening of economic relations between South Korea and the Soviet Union.

Gorbachev's call for the establishment of a South Korean–Soviet economic relationship and multilateral arms control discussions to include the two Koreas falls within the parameters of new thinking. Due to the Soviet Union's successful 'Olympic diplomacy' and South Korea's pursuance of Northern Politics, the two sides quickly agreed to establish trade offices in Seoul and Moscow and then proceed to upgrade the trade offices to consular level. While no discussions have been held on Gorbachev's proposal for multilateral talks in the West Pacific, the trade and economic cooperation issues between Seoul and Moscow progressed fast enough to surprise North Korea. Total trade volume between the two countries rose to almost $US600 million in 1989 compared to only $US36 million in 1980. Yuri Ognev, the head of Korean studies group in the Institute of the Far East of the USSR Academy of Sciences, declared 'these two Koreas exist, whether we recognize it or not'.[27] But the North Korean official daily *Rodong Sinmun* said it was 'unthinkable' that Moscow should recognize Seoul.[28]

South Korea and the Soviet Union agreed to establish trade offices by April 1989. After eight months, the trade offices were upgraded to consular level.[29] The office of the Korean consular department in Moscow began to issue visas in March 1990 whilst the Soviet consular department in Seoul first issued visas in April 1990. At the same time, Korean Air and the Soviet airline Aeroflot inaugurated their Seoul–Moscow air service on 30 March 1990.

Co-leader of South Korea's ruling Democratic Liberal Party, Kim Young-sam, visited Moscow in June 1989 at the invitation of the Institute of World Economy and International Relations (IMEMO). He visited Moscow again in March 1990. Through IMEMO's political brokerage, he met President Gorbachev in the Kremlin. On his return, Kim Young-sam voiced optimism about establishing formal diplomatic relations with the Soviet Union before the end of 1990. At the same time, Prime Minister Kang Young-hoon told the Korean National Assembly that his government would work to set up formal diplomatic ties with Moscow.[30]

The sudden meeting between President Roh Tae-woo of South Korea and President Mikhail Gorbachev of the Soviet Union in San Francisco on 4 June 1990 came as a surprise. During this, their first meeting, the two leaders exchanged views and ideas on problems of the Korean Peninsula in a friendly atmosphere. The two leaders agreed that the 'fruit of the Korea-Soviet relationship must be brought to ripeness' for it cannot be eaten if it has not ripened well. The Korean–Soviet summit talks were an epochal event that laid the groundwork for a fundamental change in inter-Korean development in addition to the establishment of full diplomatic relations between Seoul and Moscow on 30 September 1990.

It appears that Gorbachev's approach to international relations dealing with the Korean Peninsula is not a simple development of previous trends but rather a radical departure from the previous position. He seeks to build two political bridges with the two parts of Korea, while keeping the allied relationship with North Korea intact. This change in perspective means that Moscow has begun to see its national interest intertwined tightly with peace in the Korean Peninsula and related closely with the economic prosperity of South Korea. Moscow wants the two Koreas to solve the problems of the division and maintain peace and stability on the Korean Peninsula, for a stable Korea serves the interests of the Soviet Union. The Soviet Union is interested in economic cooperation with South Korea. The Soviet Union sees in South Korea a country interested in developing good relations with socialist countries to secure its international position. The Soviet Union wants to see South Korean capital and technology invested in the Soviet Far East.

ECONOMIC COOPERATION

The key to Soviet foreign policy new thinking lies in Soviet domestic economic policy. Every Soviet enterprise now has the right to engage in the international market. The Soviet Far East region is now preparing to experiment in a 'mixed economy'. By a mixed economy, I mean an economy with limited central control and planning mixed with the market mechanism of free enterprise. This measure will undoubtedly create favourable market conditions for joint ventures with the capitalist economies of the Asia–Pacific.

There are a number of considerations which argue for economic cooperation between South Korea and the Soviet Union. Due to geographic proximity, cultural similarity, historical familiarity, and economic complimentarities, South Korea's economic cooperation with the Soviet Union can be concentrated on the Soviet Far East and the East Siberian region.

Most importantly, South Korean–Soviet economic cooperation should take into account the present constraints and conditions of international relations. South Korea has deep-rooted, special relations with the United States and other Western countries, whereas the Soviet Union, as a leading socialist country, has long had a special relationship with North Korea. Because of these constraints, Seoul and Moscow need to have great patience in order to enhance mutual relations. True, a Soviet economist reminds us of the fact that the current economic ties with South Korea are 'taking place against the background of expanding friendly Soviet relations with North Korea in the political, trade, economic, scientific, cultural and other fields'.[31]

Economic contacts between South Korea and the Soviet Union began in 1974 through indirect trade by way of third countries. The possibility of direct economic cooperation between the two countries took real shape following the Gorbachev speeches in Vladivostok and Krasnoyarsk. After Soviet participation in the 1988 Seoul Olympics, the two sides began to intensify efforts to build goodwill and a framework for commercial interaction. With the establishment of trade offices and consular departments in both Seoul and Moscow, talks began in the fields of economic and cultural cooperation. The talks and business negotiations are promising, but the results are disappointing. At the end of 1989, a government source said that only one Korean firm operated two joint ventures with Soviet counterparts, whilst two firms were under consideration for organising six joint ventures in the Soviet Union.[32]

At this stage of the relationship, the two sides must have a balanced view of the roles played by private and government sectors. There should be a close connection and linkage between the development of economic and political relations. The balanced development of relations in both areas is an important factor in the improvement of cooperative relations in the long term.

There are definite needs for new markets for Korean products as well as new industrial resources for manufacturing. As inducements to investment, therefore, certain markets might be opened up, or some of the materials vitally needed for future Korean industrial development might be offered at a competitive price. In this respect, South Korea's importation of enriched uranium from the Soviet Union to fuel its nuclear power plants highlights the developing economic relationship. South Korean nuclear plants recently signed a contract with a Soviet counterpart to import up to 40 tonnes of uranium concentrate over the contract period of 1990–99.[33]

If the two sides wish to expand business transactions further, their governments will have to take official steps to secure and protect their business interests. Korean business investors' confidence in the Soviet Union will be strengthened significantly by appropriate bilateral agreements that protect Korean business interests. In particular, the uncertainties involved in joint venture arrangements need to be reduced, adequate incentives to Korean partners need to be provided and mutual trust between the two sides must be established.

It is said that over the past three years, more than 1,000 joint ventures or enterprises and related investment agreements have been signed between Soviet firms and foreign counterparts. But only some 30 foreign enterprises actually operate in the Soviet Union.[34] This is a clear indication of the uncertainties facing prospective market-oriented foreign partners in dealing with Soviet enterprises operating under a planned economy. On the other hand, Soviet firms also show a lack of understanding about the operations and systems of business firms of the capitalist economy.[35]

At the early stage of economic cooperation, because many may want to avoid the risks of large-scale investment, businessmen may tend to make small capital investments and transfer low-level industrial technology. If their business in the Soviet Union was protected by suitable investment agreements, they would be less hesitant to invest in more risky, larger projects. In short, the maturity of bilateral governmental relations will regulate the depth of bilateral economic cooperation.

Notwithstanding prevailing difficulties in negotiating joint ventures with Soviet firms, there are several prominent cases in which Korean firms are confident of success. The Jindo (Fur) Corporation, in its small-scale joint venture in the field of fur trading and retail sales, has been very successful. Jindo invested US$0.48 million in fur trading and fur coat trading in Moscow. Recently, the Hyundai Construction Company invested US$1 million in a joint logging venture with the Forest Administration of the Soviet Primorsky Kray. Several major Korean industrial corporations including Hyundai, Daewoo, Samsung, Kumsung–Gold Star, and other shipping and forwarding companies have obtained permission to open Moscow and Nakhodka branch offices as they prepare to do business in the Soviet Union. Hyundai disclosed its plan to participate in the development of East Siberian natural gas which will eventually require a gas pipeline to be laid through North Korea for South Korean consumers.

CONCLUSION

Soviet bilateral relations with both North and South Korea appear to be a paradox. On the one hand, the Soviet Union wishes to increase its influence on Pyongyang and has dramatically increased its military assistance to North Korea over recent years. The Soviet Union has conducted a number of joint military (navy and air force) exercises with North Korea and obtained port call and over-flight rights in North Korea. Ironically, recent events in the Soviet Union and East European countries, and at Tiananmen Square in Beijing, indicate the potential for an ideological rift in Pyongyang away from Moscow towards Beijing.

At the same time, Moscow is aggressively pursuing economic, cultural, sci-entific and technological exchanges with South Korea.[36] More than 1,200 Soviet citizens visited South Korea in 1989. The Soviet Union is negotiating everything from tourist exchanges to major plant constructions with South Korea and this trend appears to be gaining momentum.

Vladivostok, the homeport of the Soviet Pacific Fleet, is only 120 kilometers from the border on the Korean Peninsula. The once-closed city has opened its doors a little to allow entry to selected foreign visitors, mostly businessmen, and promised to open to all comers by 1991. In 1986, Gorbachev talked of the naval city becoming a Soviet 'window opened widely on the East' and dreamed aloud of the city becoming a major international centre of commerce. Unfortunately, the dream seems as distant now as it did in 1986. Visiting Korean businessmen are attracted by the vast wealth in raw materials but are disappointed by the gross lack of services, facilities and other socio–economic infrastructure.

The development of commodity trade, even on a barter basis, between the two countries should be recognised as a critically important precondition for promot-ing and facilitating Korean participation in joint investment projects, resource development and infrastructure construction in the Soviet Union. Materials required in such cooperative projects could be sourced through the stimulation of active commodity trade between the two countries.

On the political and security sides of the Seoul–Moscow relationship, the meaning and implications of Soviet 'economic security' in the region remains an essential question. Certainly, South Korea remains concerned about Moscow's ally, North Korea. As Soviet economic and foreign policy interests in the region grow, improvements in Soviet–North Korean relations will accelerate both quantitatively and qualitatively.

At least for the foreseeable future, Soviet initiatives with North and South Korea will continue to proceed along this paradoxical, two-front approach. Neither North nor South Korea appears willing to force the Soviet Union into 'choosing' as the Soviets accept the concept of 'two Korean states' co-existing in the international community. The days of Cold War diplomacy, rigid alliance structures and clearly identifiable foreign policy goals are gone.

Perhaps now is the time for South Korea to respond positively to Gorbachev's proposal made at Krasnoyarsk. Seoul could use such an opening to address North–South force reductions to ease tension along the demilitarised zone, to seek Soviet support for meaningful North–South dialogue and to seize the initiative in the face of the Soviet peace offensive.

9 Sino–Soviet economic and political relations

PU SHAN

Reforms in Soviet foreign policy, in the name of 'new political thinking' in international relations, have been among the most significant factors leading to the change in world affairs from confrontation to conciliation, from tension to relaxation.

With regard to Sino–Soviet relations, changes in Soviet foreign policy have also been a significant factor. The Soviet Union's positive response to China's call for the elimination of obstacles in Sino–Soviet relations finally led to a summit meeting in May 1989 and the normalisation of relations between the two countries. Though the obstacles were not entirely resolved, real progress was made regarding Afghanistan, the Sino–Soviet border issue and, to a lesser extent, the Kampuchean problem. The normalisation of relations facilitated the further development of economic exchange and cooperation between the two countries.

ECONOMIC RELATIONS

Sino–Soviet economic exchange and cooperation have great potential. The two countries share a common border of more than 7,300 kilometres. There is a great deal of complementarity between the two economies, especially in the border areas. Many of the Chinese plants and factories built in the 1950s with Soviet assistance need to be renovated and modernised. While the Soviet Union is paying increasing attention to the development of its resource-rich regions in Siberia and the Far East, China also needs to accelerate the development of its northeast and northwest regions given the rapid development of its coastal areas.

Trade has expanded quite rapidly in recent years though its level is still far below the potential of the two countries, occupying only a small percentage of the total foreign trade of each country. In 1989, Sino–Soviet trade reached close to US$4 billion (see Table 9.1) and the Soviet Union ranks fifth among China's trading partners after Hong Kong, Japan, the United States and West Germany.

In 1989, China's imports from the Soviet Union were valued at US$2.1 billion. Major imports (in US$ million) were fertilisers (510), steel (398),

103

Table 9.1   Sino–Soviet trade and its share in China's foreign trade (US$ million)

	1950	1955	1959	1960	1970	1980	1981	1988	1989
Sino–Soviet trade	338	1 790	2 097	1 664	47	492	281	3 258	3 997
China's exports	153	670	1 118	819	23	228	125	1 476	1 849
China's imports	185	1 120	979	845	24	264	156	1 782	2 147
China's foreign trade	1 135	3 145	4 381	3 809	4 586	37 822	44 021	102 784	111 628
Share of Sino–Soviet trade in China's foreign trade (%)	30	57	48	44	1.0	1.3	0.6	3.2	3.6

Sources: *Yearbook of China's Foreign Economic Relations and Trade, 1984; Customs Quarterly Statistics,* first issues of 1988, 1989 and 1990; *China's Statistical Yearbook,* 1983–88.

transport equipment (370), timber (228), non-ferrous metals (216), machinery (182) and petroleum products (65).

China exports a broad range of commodities and manufactures to the Soviet Union consisting mainly of agricultural products, light-industry products or non-durable consumer goods but more recently extending into machinery, electronics and durable consumer goods. In 1989, the value of China's exports to the Soviet Union was US$1.8 billion. China's major exports (in US$ million) were meat (280), clothing (269), textiles (218), oil seed (170), grain (149) and miscellaneous manufactures (436).

Border trade has expanded greatly, reaching US$540 million in 1989, and new forms of economic cooperation are being implemented. For instance, processing trade has been initiated in which raw materials supplied by the Soviet side are processed into manufactured products, such as leather goods, and then exported to the Soviet Union. China has also exported labour services to the Soviet Union for such work as construction and logging. More than 200 000 Chinese workers are now employed in the Soviet Union under contract.

Joint ventures are also under active consideration. They include, for example, a thermos bottle factory in the Soviet Union and a paper pulp factory in China. In technological cooperation, China has provided some simple but practical help, such as vegetable growing and hog raising in border areas, while the Soviet Union is providing assistance in renovating the old plants built in China in the 1950s and in constructing new power plants. Agreement has been reached on scientific and technical cooperation in agriculture, water management, land improvement, meteorology, fisheries, non-ferrous metals, chemical, oil, gas and machinery industries, railway transport and health services. Plans are being made to develop jointly the water resources of the eastern border rivers for navigation and power generation. The extension and linkage of the railways of the two countries through the western part of the border is now in progress. This could open up a new 'continental bridge' or 'silk road' from the east coast of China through the Soviet Union to Europe. There have also been suggestions that the establishment of free economic zones on the Pacific coast of the Soviet Union will provide opportunities for economic cooperation between China, the Soviet Union, Japan and other neighbouring countries.

There are, however, still many difficulties in the further development of Sino–Soviet economic relations. The rapid expansion of border trade has already led to transport and warehouse congestion in border ports. With the currencies of the two countries being basically non-convertible, trade is conducted mainly on the basis of barter or compensatory trade, and repayments in joint ventures are made mainly in material goods rather than in foreign exchange. The major part of trade between the two countries is still carried out through trade agreements under which the two central governments are responsible for the coordination of the transactions and their balance. Border trade, though increasing rapidly, constitutes a minor part of the total trade, yet it has already created some problems between the central and local authorities in both countries. The present similarity of the economic management systems and the arrangements of economic transactions without the use of scarce foreign exchange may provide a temporary stimulus to the development of economic relations, but there are certainly serious limitations, as the experience of the Council for Mutual Economic Assistance has clearly shown. The use of convertible foreign exchange in Sino–Soviet trade is now being considered. A new long-term agreement covering the period up to the year 2000 on Sino–Soviet economic, scientific and technological cooperation was signed in 1990. Among the cooperative projects agreed upon were the building of two nuclear power plants in China with long-term credit provided by the Soviet Union and the provision of 500 million Swiss francs' worth of consumer goods from China to the Soviet Union on short-term credit. But further development of Sino–Soviet economic relations still depends much on their respective reforms.

POLITICAL RELATIONS

Both the Soviet Union and China have embarked on extensive economic and political reforms. Although they face many similar problems, the two countries have adopted different approaches to reform and achieved different results. There is much that each could learn from the experience of the other. The joint communique of the 1989 summit meeting stated that 'the two sides considered it beneficial to share information and experience regarding their socialist development and reforms'.

With the normalisation of state relations, the communist parties of the two countries also normalised relations. The question is sometimes raised as to whether China and the Soviet Union will again form a kind of alliance as in the 1950s. But the world has changed greatly and both countries have learned from lessons of the past. It was agreed in the joint communique that the two parties would develop contacts and exchanges in accordance with the principles of independence, equality, mutual respect and non-interference in each other's internal affairs. These are also the principles that the Chinese Communist Party adheres to in its relations with political parties of other countries. China is determined to pursue an independent foreign policy to strive for peace and prevent hegemony, and not to enter into alliances with any country. In fact, this stance is reiterated by China in the joint communique.

Rapid change in Eastern Europe and the recent turmoil in the Soviet Union indicate that reform in socialist countries may follow rather different courses. China is determined to continue its own program of reform and openness to the outside world, in spite of the unfortunate events of late spring and early summer in 1989. But China will also guard against foreign interference and the deviation of its reforms from the socialist course. There has been some speculation that reforms in the Soviet Union and in China will become increasingly divergent. Some predict that this will lead to a deterioration in Sino–Soviet relations and to confrontation and conflict between the two countries in the 1990s. But whatever the future course of reform in socialist countries, China believes that it is an internal matter of the countries concerned and that there should be no foreign interference. The Soviet Union has also declared that it holds the same belief and this seems to have been confirmed, at least in relations with China. This being the case, there is no reason that the issue should become a serious one in Sino–Soviet relations.

Events in the Soviet Union and Eastern Europe, however, have profound implications for the international political economy. But the situation is very much in a state of flux, and the outcome is still uncertain. What is apparent is that the post-war bipolar system is being replaced by a multipolar system with new centres of power and new political and economic alignments. The 1990s will be a turbulent period. Under such circumstances, it is all the more important to uphold the principles of respect for the sovereignty and territorial integrity of other states, non-aggression, non-interference, equality and mutual benefit, and peaceful coexistence.

In the normalisation of relations between China and the Soviet Union, these Five Principles of Peaceful Coexistence were accepted as the universal principles guiding state-to-state relations. In fact, the same principles had also been agreed upon during China's normalisation of relations with Japan, the United States and many other countries. What is urgently needed now is to put these principles into practice and thereby establish a new international order.

10 Prospects for reform in the Soviet Far East: agenda and options

PAVEL A. MINAKIR

The reform of the Soviet economy is now a popular theme for discussion, since the connection between the future of the Soviet economy and the international economy is as important as the connection between Soviet foreign policy and international military and political stability.

For the Pacific economic community, one of the most important issues is the prospect of real change in the Soviet Far East. This region is a natural part of the Pacific economic community, a Soviet forefront in the Pacific.

The political and economic changes in the Soviet Far East illustrate the realities of Soviet cooperation in the Pacific market. There is little correlation between official declarations about Far Eastern economic development and actual progress. The main reason is that the regions in the Soviet economy now lie between a partly-reformed economic mechanism at the enterprise level and the old mechanism at the central level. In this situation, the Far East is under pressure from central authorities to solve social and economic problems. But enterprises which are pursuing their own interests in accordance with the Law on Governmental Enterprises adopted in 1988 are under workers' pressure not to accede to all demands from Gosplan and the ministries. The local authorities in the regions are also under public pressure to improve the social and ecological situation quickly. This is an understandable situation given that the reform process in the Soviet Union began from the 'vertical structure' (enterprises-ministries-Gosplan) of the so-called system of industries (*otraslevaya sistema*).

REGIONAL KHOZRASCHOT

It was only in 1989 that discussions began about economic reforms in the regional structure, beginning with the publication of the results of studies and proposals in the field of regional *khozraschot* (self-supporting regions). The pioneers in these studies were Estonian intellectuals who argued for the

108

realisation of regional *khozraschot* to create republican economies quite separate from the Soviet economy as a whole.

The main goal for Estonia and other republics which support this idea (although almost all Soviet republics are now preparing to base their economies on the regional *khozraschot* concept) is to use natural and economic resources for their own needs. This is a natural reaction to the long-standing dictates from Moscow on the republics and regions .

The previous mechanism used to allocate resources was part of this pressure. The mechanism was really rather simple. Practically all profits and the bulk of personal incomes were gathered by the centre, including the majority of depreciation funds. Thereafter, Moscow distributed money according to its own priorities in the areas of social needs and national goals. Ministries attempted to maximise production and minimise costs, and made economic decisions based on the volume of production rather than on market supply. As a result, non-effective enterprises were maintained by the profits of the effective ones, budget funds were distributed between ministries and each ministry made investment decisions based on its own evaluation about maximising profits and production. Each ministry had its own investment policy in the republics and regions because of differences in the effectiveness of industries. On the other hand, each region and republic had its own priorities in social and economic investment policy.

The process of regional investment decision-making consists of a series of unconnected investment decisions made by different ministries. The 'system' that encompassed decision-making in investment policy and the distribution of budget funds led to disproportions in the economies of the regions and republics. It is not surprising, therefore, that the regions objected to this system and that regional *khozraschot* ideas included the following:

—natural resources and economic facilities must become the property of the republics/regions;

—decisions about public investment and the distribution of public funds must be made by republics/regions; and

—republics and regions must have their own tax systems and pay the centre a part of their income instead of receiving money from the centre.

The most important issue is the connection between enterprises and local authorities as well as between enterprises and ministries. Republican or regional freedom is not possible without the freedom of enterprises. However, the adoption of the Property Law in May 1990 may assist in the modernisation of regional policy and regional development.

Initial reforms in the field of territorial planning and development were carried out without regard to the investment distribution mechanism, economic institutions, the production planning system nor the rights of producers and consumers. The concept of regional planning reform was raised in 1987 among economic reform documents published by the CPSU Central Committee. It stressed the need for an improvement of planning technology but made no provision for any radical change in the decision-making process. Because of this, the attempt to reform the Far Eastern economy remained locked into the traditional procedure - namely, Moscow creates a general plan for regional economic and social development in terms of industrial growth and social development goals; the region asks for additional investment and insists on an increase in the number of new constructions; and Moscow makes the final decision.

PROBLEMS IN THE DEVELOPMENT OF THE FAR EAST

This is the situation President Gorbachev had in mind when, in 1986 in Vladivostok, he spoke of a new approach to the economic development of the Soviet Far East and a need to adopt special governmental policy for the region. Following his speech, it seemed that a new era for the Soviet Far East most surely would dawn. According to Gorbachev, the Soviet Far East has the potential for dynamic economic development and effective cooperation with countries of the Pacific rim, for which it is necessary to implement a new strategy of economic development and regional cooperation. Unfortunately, the vision is yet to be implemented, as we shall see from the discussion below.

Undoubtedly, the Soviet Far East has great potential for economic development and international economic cooperation. It covers a large area of some 6 million square kilometres, and is rich in natural resources including coal, gold, silver, tin, other ores, timber, fish, hydroenergy and furs. The Far East contains considerable industry and infrastructure, with regional production reaching about 40 billion roubles, 64 per cent of which is industrial and 27 per cent construction and transport.

For many years the bulk of capital investment in the Far Eastern economy was channelled into extractive industries. This investment policy was understandable because of the high efficiency of these industries. As a result of high growth rates in the extractive industries in the period 1960–74, their share in total regional industrial production is now about 45 per cent. Investment in the extractive sectors of the non-ferrous, forestry, fishing and fuel industries was much more profitable than in the processing sectors because of the low cost of extraction and the high cost of processing natural resources. Total expenses for producing finished products in the Far East are 40 per cent higher than in the European part of the Soviet Union. As investments for planned volumes of commodities were controlled by the ministries, the ministries endeavoured to invest money only in the extraction of natural resources in the Far East. Investments in the processing sector were directed primarily to the European part of the Soviet Union because the cost of processing resources there was much cheaper than in the Far East.

This policy was successful in the 1960s and 1970s. The region had considerable precious mineral resources and fish reserves and the technology required for extraction was rather simple and cheap. During this period, investments in these industries led to high annual growth rates: from 8 per cent in forestry to 14 per cent in fisheries and non-ferrous metals. But whilst increasing profits and compensating for increasing costs, ministries exploited Far Eastern resources with little concern for future production and conservation. As a result, by the end of the 1970s, the situation in the Far Eastern economy had altered dramatically.

The production efficiency and growth rates of the extractive industries decreased, and, by the beginning of the 1980s, annual growth rates in the region were only 2.5 to 3 per cent. The reasons for this fall were the lack of processing industries to provide a stimulant for regional economic growth and the unfavourable international climate for the production of raw materials. Nevertheless, production in the major industries remained profitable but as all profits were taken by Moscow with little return in the form of investment it became impossible to achieve previous volumes of production growth. Investment funds were sufficient to maintain the base of production in the extraction industries. But they were insufficient to improve conditions in the social sphere and develop other industries to balance the regional economy.

The situation in the field of foreign economic ties with Pacific countries has also deteriorated. Exports from the Far East amount to around 1 billion roubles, and 93 per cent of the total export value is derived from timber, fish, coal, furs, oil products and ores of non-ferrous metals. But as conditions in raw materials extraction are worsening, it is not possible to take advantage of the opportunities available for economic cooperation with Pacific countries. Besides, a number of Pacific countries are themselves oriented to the export of raw materials.

The effective integration of the Soviet Far East into the international division of labour in the Pacific rim requires a strengthening of its total economic potential and a substantial rise in the commodity basis of cooperation to create the right conditions for an exchange of commodities and capital. To achieve this, it is necessary to create a dynamic regional economy to attract foreign capital investment and provide the basis for international trade.

By 1985, however, the situation in the Soviet Far East provided almost no opportunities for economic growth and international cooperation. If this situation is to be changed, it will be necessary to solve a range of problems including:
— the lack of capital required to increase the extraction of raw materials and develop the processing sector;
— the labour deficiency and the inadequacy of schemes to attract and retain labour in the region even though wages are higher than in other parts of the Soviet Union (150 per cent of the country's average);
— poor infrastructure in terms of transport, communications, housing and other social conditions; and
— a severe deficit of industrial services such as electric power production, construction and geological prospecting.

To solve these problems it will be necessary to begin the real process of *perestroika* in the Far East. This will involve modernising the regional economy to achieve compatibility with the Pacific market. Because of the lack of capital in the region, as in the Soviet Union as a whole, this goal can be reached only by opening the regional economy to outside investment. Second, it will be necessary to concentrate national investment in the field of infrastructure to create a favourable investment climate not only for foreign investors but also for national investors. Third, it will require that additional authority be delegated to the Far East for the formulation and implementation of economic policy. Such an approach will allow the regulation of the economy through regional economic development as opposed to the traditional method of direct planning with its unpredictable and questionable priorities in the allocation of resources.

LONG–TERM DEVELOPMENT PROGRAM

An understanding of the necessity for such regional economic change emerged only in 1986 when the direction of the radical economic reform in the Soviet Union was somewhat uncertain. But, instead of *perestroika,* the Long-Term Program for Economic and Social Development of the Far Eastern Economic Region was adopted.

This program was adopted by the Soviet government in 1987. At the beginning of 1988, a model for the Soviet economy based on self-finance and self-support was declared for all enterprises and ministries. It meant that the Soviet Union decided to begin the process of decentralisation in the allocation of economic resources using market mechanisms rather than central dictates. But the decision to transfer the management of the Far Eastern economy to the national level was contrary to the principles of self-finance and self-support taken in the long-term program. The program attempted to achieve economic restructuring in the Far East without adapting the method of management to the new economic climate in the country. The government decided to manage the Far Eastern economy using 'the good old method' of direct, detailed targets. Nonetheless, the general goals of the program are sound, among them being:
— the provision of industrial and consumer goods and services that cannot be provided from other parts of the country (energy production, construction, transport services, some consumer goods and services for social infrastructure);
— the construction of new facilities for the renovation and growth of the raw materials sectors; and
— the reinforcement of the export base for traditional commodities and the creation of conditions for international cooperation.

The program envisages the achievement of high rates of economic growth. Within the period 1986–2000, for example, industrial growth is planned to increase by almost 250 per cent while the population is expected to increase by 1.7 million. In order to achieve these goals, however, it will be necessary to invest almost 200 billion roubles from the state budget in the Far Eastern economy.

The program represents the government's stated objectives. Unfortunately, the ministries and enterprises are unable to provide the stimuli to achieve high growth rates. The program consists of a long list of new facilities for different industries and targets for new houses, hospitals, schools and so on. The ministries are expected to invest money in these programs. But in 1988, because of the adverse economic situation, the state budget discontinued the financing of regional projects. In a situation of national economic stagnation, the government was unable to give priority to the Soviet Far East in the investment sphere.

Consequently, the region's development has not achieved the program's goals. Investors (central ministries) have not reacted to Gosplan's commands as readily as in previous years. Enterprises in the region have no real opportunities or incentives for development. Moreover, the government's ability to provide incentives has been decreasing since the beginning of 1988. The budget deficit was about 80 billion roubles in 1988 and 110 billion roubles in 1989. The planning deficit of the state budget for 1990 is about 70 billion roubles but the real figure for the budget deficit will be higher because of the necessity to compensate for the decrease in production, which reached an alarming minus 4 per cent in 1989. To compensate for this, it will be necessary to increase investment funds in the state budget.

The dependence of the Far Eastern economy on the national economy as a whole is rather high. Almost 28 per cent of the total production and consumption resources in the Far East are reliant on imports from other regions and republics. Hence, general economic stagnation and falling production in the Soviet Union has affected the Far East. Some progress in the realisation of goals in the long-term program has been made, for example in housing, but the situation as a whole remains unsatisfactory. The pattern of regional economic development has not changed. Basic disproportions in energy, construction and consumer market funds are no less than three years ago.

The disproportion between the demand and supply of construction facilities has had a negative effect on future regional economic development. By 1991, some 120 new construction facilities are required to meet planned economic development in the Far East. It will be possible to complete only half this number of new constructions. Therefore the planned investments will not be utilised fully by the regional construction industry. This means that capital investments have not yet produced a multiplier effect in the regional economy. Rather, the effect has been to destabilise economic proportions. The reason for this situation is that Far Eastern construction facilities can provide only 10 to 50 per cent of total demand for different materials and constructions. In 1990, the ministry which produced more than 50 per cent of the total construction services and materials came under the Russian Federation. (In previous years it was a central government ministry.) Consequently, real opportunities for this ministry in the field of investments and supply decreased and the situation with regard to construction in the region became more complicated.

In energy production, there is a strong disproportion between the demand and supply of electricity and fuel for electric power stations. For the realisation of the program's long-term targets, it will be necessary to increase the production of electricity from 48 billion kilowatts per hour in 1990 to 100 billion kilowatts per hour by the year 2000. Coal production in the Far East, including export obligations, is planned to reach 80–85 million tonnes from 50 million tonnes in 1990. It will also be necessary to build new electric power stations with a total output of 18–20 million kilowatts. Two nuclear-power stations are planned but the regional population is against their construction because of the fear of a nuclear accident. The 'green movement' is also against the construction of many hydroelectric stations because of the potentially adverse effect on the environment.

In 1989, a reduction of around 30 per cent of investment from the central budget led to a proportional decrease in investments in regional energy systems. As a consequence, prospects for a solution to the regional energy problem are not bright over the next decade.

The problem with the consumer market in the Far East is the same as in the Soviet Union as a whole. In the Far East, the average salary is 1.5 times higher than in the Russian Federation. The growth rates of salaries are similarly higher. But the region has less opportunities to produce the necessary volume of consumer goods by itself than the European part of the Russian Federation. Consequently, the generally bad situation in this field is worse in the Far East. Other regions are ready to export scarce consumer goods to the Far East in return for raw materials (timber, fish and furs). However, the Far East itself has no rights to sell these commodities; ministries in Moscow hold this power. In 1988, regional enterprises received rights to export and import without special permission from Moscow. As a result, export–import operations of regional enterprises in 1988 helped to maintain the 1 to 2 per cent level of monetary emission in Khabarovsk, the Maritime territories and Sakhalin. But in 1989 regional enterprises lost these rights and the general situation in the financial and marketing fields became as bad as in other regions.

According to official statistical information, the annual industrial growth rate in the Far East for 1986–89 was about 103.4 per cent. In reality, the industrial growth rate in the Far East is less than the official figures indicate. The estimate for the growth rate of prices is now about 6 to 7 per cent. This is why the real growth rate of industrial production is around minus 4 per cent. Instead of production increasing as planned, it has ended up decreasing.

INVESTMENT

The reconstruction of the Far Eastern economy will be dependent on investment, which will depend in turn on the creation of a favourable investment climate, not only for foreign but also for domestic investors. When the problem of attracting investment to the region is discussed, people usually think in terms of foreign investment. In fact, it will not be possible to obtain the necessary funds for regional economic development from abroad. The bulk of these funds must be found within the Soviet Union. And they can be found! Soviet enterprises now have considerable capital, particularly in the military sector of the economy. If domestic investors are offered the same attractive investment conditions that foreigners are, it will be possible to organise a capital flow in a west-east direction without orders from Moscow. One of the attractions for domestic investors is the opportunity to deal with foreign partners. In this sense, the creation in the Far East of an open economic regime could be a very attractive incentive for Soviet enterprises.

The creation of an inviting climate for domestic investors depends on the realisation of radical economic reform in the Soviet Union. The government has now put forward a new program for radical economic reform. This program envisages, as a central point, an increase in prices. There is no evidence, however, of any measures to internationalise the domestic market or modernise the financial and foreign exchange systems. Without such measures it will be almost impossible to construct a market economy in the Soviet Union, to create the necessary market mechanisms for an open economy or to provide appropriate incentives for investors.

In addition, the initiative concerning the regional *khozraschot* has some unpredictable consequences. According to this scheme, regions will regulate industry and other economic spheres which are now unprofitable. But real economic decision-making and the control of economic resources will remain in the hands of the government. For this reason, the situation in the field of Far Eastern external ties is not a simple one.

The increase of export-oriented production is linked with the reconstruction of the regional economy and relations between Moscow and the region. Efforts to reconstruct the Far Eastern economy through the central planning mechanism have not been successful. Attempts to increase the volume of regional exports more than threefold by the year 2000 will be unsuccessful also. In accordance with the long-term program, the Far East must export by the end of the twentieth century about 1 million cubic metres of timber, increase the export of machinery goods almost four times, raise exports of (mainly coking) coal to 5.5 million tonnes and so on. But to achieve these goals it will be necessary to reconstruct the raw materials sector. Without considerable investment, this will be impossible. To attract investors to the Far East, it will be necessary to create a special economic climate with conditions more favourable than in other territories. But, at this stage, the new government program for the reform of the Soviet economy precludes the possibility of establishing such an investment climate.

Free economic zones are now under consideration in the Soviet Far East to facilitate the implementation of an open regional economy. In 1989, 16 zones were suggested. Among them were Nakhodka, Wanino, Posjet, BAM, Khabarovsk, Magadan, Blagovestchensk, the Jewish autonomous region, Amursk and other cities and territories. The most feasible project amongst these is the zone in Nakhodka.

The decision to open free economic zones is not a simple one. In the first place, there is strong public opposition. The population is educated on ideals of struggle for independence and many are afraid that with an influx of free economic zones, they will become dependent on foreign capital and lose their land and natural resources. Second, experience with joint ventures in the Soviet Union points to many difficulties in the development of economic cooperation with foreign capital. The most fundamental is the incompatibility of detailed centralised planning in the Soviet Union and the market mechanism of foreign countries. Events of the past five years show that changes in political thinking and an understanding of the necessity for a more market-oriented economy are, by themselves, not enough to convert the centrally-managed economy into a regulated market economy. This is the reason the third difficulty, the non-convertibility of the Soviet rouble, is a lesser problem. Without the creation of comparable economic systems it is impossible to create comparable money systems. The situation with joint ventures illustrates this difficulty very well. In the Soviet Far East there are now around 30 joint ventures. By and large, these have not achieved impressive financial returns. Foreign capital is being invested in the Far East mainly to obtain rights to extract natural resources. The most attractive industries for joint venture activities are the fishery, forestry and mining industries.

Free economic zones can become mini-models of comparable economic systems, and some foreign countries (for example, Japan, Korea, China and the United States) have shown considerable interest in these projects. The first such zone in Nakhodka may well be declared soon. But it will be necessary to invest almost 2 billion roubles on infrastructure in the zone, which covers an area of 30 square kilometres. It is doubtful whether the central government can provide this money and the city itself has none for the project. Thus it is likely that the zone will be a zone in name only. In this case, the result of this experiment will only be apparent after many years.

Free economic zones in the Far East are not the only means to increase the volume of regional exports or solve Soviet currency problems. Their main goal is to construct an operating model for a market economy. But this model can give an impetus to the modernisation of the regional economic system only if ties between the zone and other territories of the Far East can be created. Such connections are necessary to take technological and economic impulses from the zone to the internal market. Joint operations in the zone with domestic producers will help the regional economy overcome traditional approaches and implement market-oriented regulations. Without such progress, cooperation with the Pacific will be impossible.

The formation of free economic zones in the Far East is only one method to open the regional economy. Other methods include concessions, financial cooperation, traditional trade and a special investment regime in the region as a whole. The general strategy is to create an open, mixed economy oriented to both domestic and foreign markets. In December 1988, an attempt was made to open the market by obtaining permission for producers and consumers to trade with foreign partners without the control of the Ministry of Foreign Trade and other ministries. This attempt failed. The reason was that in a situation of economic depression followed by inflation and market deficit, foreign trade took the form of speculation. Previously, speculation on the differences between high internal and low external prices on deficit goods was the preserve of the government. After 1988, many producers and trading companies became involved. In reality, only raw materials can now compete on foreign markets. But raw materials are also included in the list of deficits. This is why the Soviet Union began to export one deficit to decrease the other. These operations were frozen by government regulations in March 1989 which require special licences for almost any kind of export or import operation except for foreign trade in machinery products. These rules did not change the foreign trade situation other than give control to the ministries.

THE TASK AHEAD

Today, in a situation of economic crisis in the Soviet Union, it is difficult, if not impossible, to see real progress in economic cooperation with the Pacific. Many of the substantial problems outlined below will take a painfully long time to resolve.

First, there is the problem of organisational disorder. The granting of licences by ministries has not provided the framework for proper order. On the contrary, it has enhanced bureaucratic red-tape and made local producers and local authorities in the Far East literally bargain for licences instead of purchasing the ministerial services for foreign economic activities. Licensing is desperately needed but it is a task for a single ministry. Except for products of a military or economic–strategic character, the granting of licences should be automatic. Non-licensing is a powerful incentive for a producer to keep strictly to the requirements of quality and timeliness. The Ministry of Foreign Economic Relations is likely to cope with this task perfectly well.

The second problem relates to infrastructure. Everyone agrees that it is the task of the Soviet Union to renew the infrastructure. Up to now there has never been an investment initiative in this direction. Without infrastructure, the establishment of new projects will do little good even if they produce export commodities. Projects that merely add a new item to the list of exports without solving the infrastructure problem are of little benefit. Until infrastructure is improved, the involvement of investors in cooperative business arrangements (financial in particular) will remain difficult. However, the opportunity to solve this problem is available by revising the long-term program. Its revision may provide the needed impetus for the renewal of infrastructure. Of 200 billion roubles assigned for regional development by the year 2000, approximately 150 billion roubles are to be invested through the ministries within the framework of traditional five-year plans, including 50 billion roubles for social programs. However, it is necessary to expend 65 billion roubles on social needs rather than the planned 50 billion roubles. The trouble is that the government is now against the long-term program's revision. Some revision is occurring in the form of the amendment of goals but without any change to the program's priorities.

The third problem is the inflexibility in the forms of cooperation. Few believe that a single form of cooperation will provide a breakthrough in internal economic links. From the point of view of distant planners in Moscow, however, it is possible to pin great hopes on a particular joint venture. The reality is different. The lack of an internal market is a serious obstacle for enterprises able to operate freely and efficiently only within the framework of a market. Attempts to orient joint ventures to third country markets have failed, as each enterprise plays the part of a seller as well as that of a buyer, which requires an internal market. Besides, sales oriented only towards the external market deprive the joint venture partners of a most important impetus, namely production for the capacious Soviet market. There has emerged a tendency to pin the Soviet Union's hopes on free economic zones. However, it will be necessary to promote new forms of cooperation to enhance economic interaction. In this regard, why not review concessions? Why do the North Koreans possess a concession to develop forestry and why are other countries not granted similar rights? Tourism has become a topic of considerable interest. However, to place too much faith in the construction of hotels and the development of tourist services to resolve the economic situation is unreasonable. Tourism is a costly, long-term investment and is unlikely to achieve grand results. However, tourist facilities directed at the hunting and fishing market in the Far East will be more attractive and will give an impetus to the tourist industry as a whole.

The fourth matter concerns the conversion of the military sector of the regional economy to non-military production. Conversion of Soviet military industry offers many favourable investment opportunities. Genuine technological achievements in this industry have opened the opportunity for cooperation in a most efficient sector. At present, technological links with defence enterprises are more feasible for foreign partners than domestic partners due to the great technological gap between the military and civil fields in the Soviet Union. But the advantageous technological opportunities offered by conversion of the military sector demands a solution to the fifth problem, namely information.

One of the most substantial barriers to building links with foreign economies is the shortage of information. Potential foreign partners lack information about conditions and opportunities in the Soviet Union; Soviet partners lack information about the situation of potential markets for Soviet enterprises. Soviet proposals which appear promising are not provided with the necessary information. Seldom is there an enthusiastic response to them. Sometimes they are not even promoted due to the lack of understanding of the realities abroad. Information systems will be developed at the state and commercial levels, but these will not be international systems or systems able to provide the required information exchange. A solution to this problem is of vital importance for the economic development of the Far Eastern region and for the development of international economic cooperation between the Soviet Far East and the Pacific rim.

Notwithstanding these problems, it is pertinent to underline the main features of the favourable investment climate in the region, an important matter for investors. In the first place, foreign investors will have rights and guarantees concerning the repatriation of their profits. Other features include tax reductions, tax holidays, the possibility of foreign investors using the domestic supply system and a reduction of prices and tariffs on infrastructural services and a reduction of land rents.

Hope for the solution of many, if not all, of the problems in the region and in the field international economic cooperation has been tied with the idea of forming of a Far Eastern Republic. The republics were founded in the 1920s and, in the prevailing climate, it is difficult to see the advantages of establishing a Far Eastern Republic comprising the Khabarovsk, Maritime Amur, Magadan, Kamchatka and Sakhalin regions and Yakutia. However, if the new law concerning local government and territorial management adopted in May 1990 is effective and gives proper rights to regions and republics, it will be sufficient for the Far Eastern territories to remain as they are now. If the law does not allow for sufficient change, it may be impossible to resolve the problems even with a Far Eastern Republic. Everything depends on genuine rights and the direction of economic change in the country and regions, not on political games.

11 Economic relations between the Soviet Union and the Pacific: an assessment of opportunities

CHRISTOPHER FINDLAY AND ALASTER EDWARDS[1]

The Soviet leadership has announced changes in policy objectives which have opened the Soviet Union's economy to foreign trade and investment at the enterprise level. The reforms in national policy objectives will create new opportunities for foreign involvement in the Soviet Far East.

The aim here is to review some of the factors which are limiting the development of the capital and trade flows between the rest of the world and the Soviet Far East. It is argued that while attainment of the objectives of the reforms will create new opportunities in the Soviet Far East, the procedures of the reform process have become a source of weakness in exploiting investment opportunities.

In the Soviet Far East, there are opportunities in the exploitation and development of the region's rich endowment of resources and the related infrastructure projects. Traditionally, the region has been a producer of timber and fish. Large reserves of old, and therefore high quality, timber remain. The region is well endowed with many minerals, including iron ore, coal, and gold, as well as a wide range of other non-ferrous metals. In terms of both their tonnage and grade, many of these deposits are world class.[2] Significant tonnages of coal, tin and gold ores are currently mined. In addition, there are large oil and gas deposits offshore from Sakhalin island.

These resources are located in an area larger than Australia but with a population of only about 6 million. The complementarities between the Soviet Far East and the rest of Northeast Asia are therefore striking. Already there is a large movement of guest workers from North Korea and China, as well as from Vietnam and Cuba. Proximity adds to the potential of the region as a supplier of raw materials and products processed to some degree. The geography of the region makes it attractive as a tourist destination, especially for adventure and special-interest travel (such as hiking and hunting), not only for people from Northeast Asia but also from Europe and North America.

In principle, therefore, there is scope for the movement of capital and technology from the rest of the world into the Soviet Far East. These opportunities exist not only for other Northeast Asian economies but also for resource-rich countries like Australia, which have technologies or marketing systems which are relevant to the Soviet Far East. Also, depending on the rate of growth of incomes in the region, new demands for a variety of foods and consumer goods will develop and create further opportunities for trade and investment.[3]

As noted above, the leadership of the Soviet Union has announced a number of changes in policy direction which include the promotion of direct links between Soviet enterprises and foreign partners. However, in practice, there are many uncertainties in the procedures for formalising those links. According to many Soviet enterprises and foreign investors, these uncertainties are inhibiting the exploitation of business opportunities for their mutual benefit. Both groups argue that 'more laws and regulations are required'. People at the local government level say 'We don't know what we can and cannot do. Life was much simpler before *perestroika*'.

The lack of rules and regulations, however, is not the main problem. In other countrie there may be guide-lines for the involvement of foreigners in local economic activity, but typically those rules are negotiable, not at all fixed, and typically, many levels of government would be involved in such negotiations. Examples of the issues involved are given here in relation to the financing of infrastructure and the joint venture guide-lines. The first step is to examine issues in the reforms in the Soviet Union.

ECONOMIC REFORM AND MARKETING SYSTEMS

The reform program announced includes a greater degree of autonomy at local government and local enterprise levels, including the right to do business directly with foreigners. Enterprises can even leave their ministries if they wish and the assets of industrial and service enterprises can be contracted out to cooperatives of workers. Over-quota output is in principle under the control of these enterprises and could be sold for export.

At present, there appears to be little scope to take advantage of these institutional changes because the ministries have retained their monopoly powers over the marketing of intermediate products. Alternative marketing channels have not developed. Thus, an enterprise which decided to leave a ministry could have enormous difficulty in procuring raw materials or other intermediate products. The availability of goods from the over-quota output of state-owned enterprises is said to be minimal. Those enterprises may, for example, in one year exceed their state quota, and thus have a surplus for sale, either to the local market or for export. But in the next year, that surplus will be added to the state quota. Effectively, there is a 100 per cent tax on productivity improvement. Significantly, nearly all the cooperative activities are in the service sector.

Not only intermediate goods but also funds for investment are unavailable to local government and local enterprises. By contrast, in the case of Chinese reforms, the reform program began in the agricultural sector. The huge increases in productivity and income that resulted from the institutional and pricing reforms generated savings in the countryside and a process of accumulation and investment. A similar stimulus to growth has not been found in the Soviet Union. There is stronger resistance to reform in the Soviet economy which is more industrialised compared to China. It has also been hypothesised that, as in the Chinese case, there will be resistance to reform from those parts of the bureaucracy which perceive a loss of power or status as a result of the reforms.

In this environment, the local governments and enterprises in the Soviet Far East are looking to trade with the rest of the world and to obtain foreign investment to break the bottle-necks in the supply of investible funds and of intermediate inputs.

Attempts were made in the Soviet Far East to export primarily to Northeast Asia surplus output of raw materials, especially timber and fish, in return for manufactured goods. Some of this trade was organised as barter, since that avoided the restrictions imposed by the system of allocating foreign exchange in the Soviet Union. Barter trade came into disrepute for the same reason that it existed, that is, the rationing of foreign exchange. The traders were said to be 'profiteering' in markets where prices were driven up compared to world prices, and typically these were markets for 'unproductive' consumer goods rather than investment items. As a result, this barter trade is now described as 'banned'. Trading companies that are involved, many of which still have contracts to fulfil, now have to be licensed to engage in barter trade and also have to have a licence for each transaction. This reaction has cut off, at least temporarily, some opportunities to break the bottle-necks by trade.

A critical component of the next stages of the reform is to create conditions in which productivity will improve and some surplus output can be generated and sold, either within the Soviet Union or to other countries. It seems likely that prior steps needed to achieve increases in the productivity of the existing capital stock of the country include the effective devolution of power, the development of alternative marketing systems and the emergence of competition between those marketing systems. This requires guarantees on the rights to allocate over-quota output, and a greater degree of responsibility at the enterprise level. The reform agenda might also include a more detailed specification of the responsibilities of local governments and their roles in initiating new development projects. There is some discussion of this issue under the title of 'regional self-accounting'. The introduction of elections for the senior officials in local government is a complementary step in developing a system of initiative and responsibility at those levels.

There is also a debate on the extent of enterprise reform required to achieve the growth in productivity that will stimulate the next stages of development. One view is that only private ownership of the assets will achieve this and that private ownership is critical for achieving stable trade and investment relations with firms from capitalist economies. The other view is that complete private ownership is not required and incentives for managers and staff are more important than ownership. In this view, leasing out the assets of the enterprise to staff is a satisfactory first step in enterprise reform. Also, it is observed that capitalist firms have been able to build relations with state and collective enterprises in countries like China or Vietnam.

A higher degree of local autonomy may lead to the emergence of some of the issues that are evident in China in the development of industry in the country-side. One is the confusion of political interests and economic decision-making, since there is not always a clear separation of power between the administrative system and businesses operating within that system. This increases the scope for corruption in local government, especially in the presence of dual marketing systems, where one is controlled by the state and the other is relatively free. It also increases the degree of political influence over the investment decisions of local enterprises. This problem is acknowledged in the Soviet Far East where it is argued by some commentators that a real separation of local enterprise and local government is required, otherwise the issues now present in the region's relations with Moscow will be repeated at the local level between enterprise managers and local officials.

In summary, the next stages of the reform will be characterised by the development of much more complex relations between the centre and local governments, in terms of revenue raising, expenditure and responsibility for the profits and losses of local enterprises. The complication for foreign investors is that they will be dealing with enterprises and their local authorities whose powers and responsibilities will change over the life of a project. Of course, this is highly likely in long-lived resource projects. The main issue in developing these projects is not the absence of rules, regulations and guide-lines but rather arriving at some expectation of the path of the reforms, especially, as argued below, in relation to inter-governmental relations.

INVESTMENT IN INFRASTRUCTURE AND THE TAX RATE

The lack of infrastructure is often held to be a major barrier to foreign investment in the Soviet Far East. The relevant infrastructure includes a wide range of services such as airports, accommodation for foreigners and communications. The development of this infrastructure is important for the tourist sector, and for air freight movements including fresh fish exports and meat and fruit and vegetable imports. Resource projects add to the demand for road, rail and sea transport, energy, and local services for the workers in (possibly) extraordinarily remote locations. The question is how can these developments be financed?

In many cases, the returns on the investment in infrastructure will be higher than otherwise because of the project being considered. The Soviet side could then provide the infrastructure. However, under the joint venture guide-lines, the Soviet side may include a large part of that investment as part of the total Soviet contribution to the equity of the project. There are some problems with this approach from the foreign investor's point of view.

First, the foreign investor's equity may be so diluted that the Soviet side controls the project, that is, has more than 50 per cent of the equity. Despite any advantages in sharing the risks associated with a project, this outcome may be unacceptable to many foreign investors who want to control the use of the technology or set of skills or capital which they bring to the project. Without this control, foreign investors may withdraw from the project altogether, since they fear the abuse of the technological information by their partners or because they wish to control absolutely any project in which some of their funds are at risk.

Second, if the investment in the infrastructure is included in the Soviet equity in the project, then it could be expected that the Soviet government would offer a tax concession to the project. The financial return to the investment in the infrastructure is covered by the return to Soviet equity, so there is less of a case for taxation to finance this particular piece of infrastructure.[4]

At this stage it is not clear which mechanism would be used to account for the infrastructure component of Soviet equity in a project, especially since the Soviet partner is likely to be an enterprise, rather than some level of government. However, whether an equity share or a tax regime is used by the Soviet side to generate a return on its infrastructure investment, not all levels of government, for example, regional and republican, may have access to the profits earned or revenue raised by the project. They may have incentives to impose extra local taxes. Thus the underlying issue is the relationship between levels of government, the allocation of tax and spending powers between them, and the likelihood of changes in the rules governing Soviet federalism during the life of the project.

The alternative is for the foreign partner to finance the infrastructure. Provision of the infrastructure may be attractive to the foreign investor because by using imported materials and construction services, and by managing the construction, the foreign partner may avoid the delays induced by lack of raw materials for such projects in the Soviet Union. Investment in the infrastructure also adds to the scale of the project and so adds to the bargaining power of the foreign investor in relations with governments at all levels, for example, in acquiring goods and services which are obtained more economically from local sources as well as in obtaining the various approvals and licences required.

However, since once again the infrastructure is being provided by one of the joint venture partners, the foreign investor could argue for a tax concession. A tax concession is available to the foreign side in the Soviet Far East where the withholding tax on profits remitted offshore can be negotiated back to zero. Compared to a withholding tax rate of 25 per cent in the rest of the country, the tax rate imposed on the joint venture income by the Soviet government is 10 per cent. The joint venture guide-lines also allow for a two-year tax holiday.

There is an offset to the benefits of tax holidays. Payments must be made from pre-tax earnings into a 'reserve fund' equal to 25 per cent of the value of the total equity in the project over a number of years, as specified in the joint venture agreement. The time at which payments into this fund must commence is unclear but most likely payments will commence only when the original investment has been recouped. This fund of profits on which tax has not been paid is retained in the Soviet banking system, again under conditions which can be specified in the joint venture agreement. However, it is not clear how this fund is treated when the project is wound-up and whether tax must be paid at that time. If not, then the burden of the fund is its opportunity cost which may or may not be less than the tax that would have been paid.

JOINT VENTURE RULES

There is a strong perception in the Soviet Far East, which is apparently shared by people in other countries, that the Soviet Far East can become a stimulus for the development of the economy of Northeast Asia, involving Japan, South and North Korea and the northeastern provinces of China. The complementarities between the Soviet Far East and these countries were noted above. Some of the infrastructure for this development either exists or is under development, such as the free economic zones in the Soviet Far East; a link into North Korea; a new port and a rail link into China at the junction of the Soviet Union, North Korea and China; connections between the Soviet and Chinese power grids; direct flights between the cities of the Soviet Far East and the rest of Northeast Asia (for example, Harbin); and the possible development of Niigata, currently the Japanese (and Korean) gateway to the Soviet Far East, as a freight hub.

Investors from Japan and South Korea have made a number of proposals for resource and infrastructure projects. However, negotiations with investors from these countries will continue to be complicated by the strategic issues that exist between them and the Soviet Union. It is argued by some in the Soviet Far East that, in the short term, it will be easier to negotiate capital flows into the Soviet Far East from Western Europe, North America or Australia.

At present, from the point of view of the foreign investor, the profit from selling to the domestic market in the Soviet Union is restricted by the lack of convertibility of the rouble. Thus, any business venture involving foreign investment in the Soviet Union will require a substantial export component in order to be able to earn foreign exchange.

Furthermore, business opportunities in these sectors will involve some sort of joint venture with the Soviet side. In principle, outright ownership of a project is possible but is discouraged under the guide-lines for foreign investment. Joint ventures are made more likely by the nature of these resource projects where the host country, in this case the Soviet Union, brings the raw material to the project. Thus the regime for regulating joint ventures becomes the critical determinant of the scope for business opportunity in the Soviet Far East.

One feature of the joint venture rules which is especially important for resource projects is that the value of the resource may be included in the equity of the Soviet side in the project, although it is uncertain how this will be applied. For example, an estimate of the value of a mineral deposit in the ground or the value of an uncut timber forest may be added to the Soviet equity. Again, this creates problems of equity shares. It dilutes the foreign partner's share which may not be acceptable for the reasons outlined above.

Any proposal to include the value of the resource also raises some issues of taxation. In projects of this type, the ultimate owners of the resource usually seek some payment for its exploitation. The common approach is to tax the developer of the project by means of a royalty, that is, an amount per unit of output of the project. An alternative would be to auction off the right to explore for resources and to exploit any deposits discovered.

There are a number of differences between these two methods which relate to the size, the level of risk and the timing of the cash flows to the parties. One problem with the royalty method is that the gross revenue flow to the government is uncertain, compared to a bid in advance which is independent of the exploration outcome. A royalty is a tax on output not profits and so it can affect adversely the distribution of returns from the project for the developer. Essentially the government through the royalty obtains a share of the returns regardless of profitability. On the other hand, while a bid in advance is more certain from the point of view of both parties, the revenue (in present value terms) may be less as the size and quality of the deposit is not known.

The Soviet approach is different to either of these methods. The guide-lines suggest that the value of the resource may be brought to the project as equity by the Soviet side. In good years, this arrangement is like a royalty, since the Soviet side receives payment for the resource. But in bad years, the arrangement is more neutral than a royalty since the Soviet side also carries some of the losses.

Accepting that some payment must be made to the owner of the resource, some elements of this arrangement may in fact be attractive to the foreign investor. There are, however, some problems of implementation which may lead the foreign investor to prefer to pay tax instead, or even a royalty.

First, the Soviet joint venture guide-lines do not spell out how the resource is to be valued. In commentary on this proposal, one suggestion was that the value of the Soviet equity would be the present value of the positive net cash flows of the project. However, this extracts all the profit in the project and leaves the foreign investor with no margin for risk, including exploration risk. Other rules have been applied. Apparently in the forestry sector, the timber resource has been valued at the sum of earnings of the first two or three years. On the Russian principle of 'what is not prohibited is permitted', the procedure for valuing the resource appears to be open to negotiation.

The second problem of the procedure is that all terms of the contract are negotiable. The question is whether the terms will be revoked by a policy change, a likely event over the life of a large-scale minerals or energy project.

For example, it seems likely that for minerals which are currently classified as 'strategic' (such as gold, copper, lead or iron ore[5]), the joint venture partner will be a ministry-controlled enterprise, rather that a local government or local enterprise. It may be possible to reach agreement on the value of the resource with this ministry. But later, following the devolution of powers, the local government may become more interested in raising tax revenue from local sources. In the absence of a royalty, government at that level may have the incentive to try to impose one. In anticipation, the foreign investor might therefore prefer a royalty arrangement instead of having a larger Soviet equity in the project.[6]

The problem is that the ownership of the resource may shift between levels of government as a result of the next steps in the reform process. At present, the answer to the question 'who owns the deposit?' is not clear. Local entrepreneurs state vehemently that they can control the resource and its use, certainly if it is not a 'strategic' deposit. Local officials tend to stress the point that even though local enterprises have the right to make direct contact with foreigners, most proposals must eventually be sanctioned by Moscow. The local administrators also stress that issues such as taxation of the resource should be included in the joint venture contract. Thus while the foreign investor may decide that a situation in which there are no precedents and where everything can be incorporated into negotiation of the joint venture contract offers a major opportunity, the risk is that the contract will become obsolete as a result of other policy reforms. This absence of precedents may result in longer and more costly negotiations, at least in terms of management time.[7]

In some cases, foreign partners have asked for guarantees from the Soviet side. The requests have occurred when the foreign partner has organised the bulk of the capital in the project, or at least its share, to be financed by debt and have requested that the debt be guaranteed by a Soviet bank. This is one reaction to the uncertainties created by the process of reform. Obviously this burden is not without cost to the Soviet side, and may be an explanation for the creation of a 'reserve fund' in the joint venture guide-lines.

There may be alternatives to the use of guarantees from the Soviet side. Providers of foreign currency denominated debt would certainly seek some assurances from the project. Underwriting from the Soviet government or at least evidence of long-term contracts for purchases of the output of the project would be required. A foreign investor sufficiently confident about the path of reform might prefer this arrangement, thereby creating some grounds to argue against the creation of the 'reserve fund'.

CONCLUSION

There are opportunities for foreign involvement in resource development projects in the Soviet Far East. The main issue concerns the terms under which that involvement will occur. There are some guide-lines to joint ventures but these do not apply to all types of projects likely to be of interest. Also, the guide-lines are the subject of debate and change. Despite the lack of rules and regulations and the changing nature of the guide-lines, there may be an opportunity for foreign joint venturers to establish suitable contracts. However, there is a real possibility that the contract may be undermined by policy changes, especially changes in the financial relations between levels of government. Such changes are highly likely since they are a critical component of the next stage of reform.

Thus the foreign joint venturer will have to arrive at some expectation of the likely path of development of those relations and design a contract that will resist unfavourable changes. This could involve provision of all the new infrastructure by the foreign partner, a royalty regime instead of Soviet equity being increased by the value of the resource, and long-term contracts with consumers of the project output as a substitute for reliance on Soviet guarantees of the debt.

These suggestions are not consistent with the guide-lines to Soviet joint ventures as currently drafted. However, local officials, who are keen to see new projects, stress that the terms are negotiable. The foreign partner then has the opportunity to set precedents in relation to these sorts of projects. Thus the degree of interest and effort shown by the rest of the world in the process of reform in the Soviet Union is a critical element in the direction of the reforms and their success.

12 Soviet policy in the Asia–Pacific region and economic reforms

VLADIMIR IVANOV[1]

The Soviet Union has entered the 1990s with a greater awareness of itself as a Pacific state. It has discovered anew the Asia–Pacific region, while the countries of the region are giving increasing attention to the Soviet Union. There is an increasing awareness in the Soviet Union of the economic problems of the Soviet Pacific regions and the prospects for development embracing the whole of the Far East. The first cautious step of melting the ice and overcoming the suspicion of neighbouring countries has been accomplished successfully: the Soviet Union has made good progress in the sphere of political and diplomatic contacts.

These changes would have been impossible without the growth of political trust in the Soviet Union's relations with the Asia–Pacific states and without the political process launched in Vladivostok. When Mikhail Gorbachev stated the principles of the new Soviet Pacific policy in Vladivostok in July 1986, it was generally thought that there would no immediate success and that the proposals made would not be realised. Today, it can safely be said that the changes over the intervening years have exceeded all expectations.

As a result of an intensive process of dialogue between states and contacts with scientific and public organisations, favourable conditions were created for business exchanges, meetings and negotiations between economic organisations. Although this process of dialogue started only in 1988, business contacts are gaining strength and creating a new, more favourable psychological atmosphere for the development of trade and economic ties.

A number of Asia–Pacific states are displaying a much greater interest in establishing economic ties with the Soviet Union and its Far Eastern regions. Businessmen and local authorities from Australia, the Canadian Pacific provinces, China, Japan, New Zealand, the Philippines, Singapore, South Korea, Taiwan, Thailand and the West Coast of the United States are looking for new opportunities to interact, exchange information and enter into contracts. As recently as two or three years ago, it would have been difficult to imagine this kind of interest.

During this period, the Soviet Union has developed new attitudes to the problems of regional economic cooperation and expressed its interest in joining the activities of the Pacific Economic Cooperation Conference (PECC).[2]

Notwithstanding these initial results, the most difficult and important task lies ahead: the achievement of real progress in economic cooperation with the states of the Asia–Pacific region and more active Soviet participation in international regional economic organisations.

DOES THE SOVIET UNION REALLY NEED SUPERPOWER STATUS?

The radical changes that occurred in Soviet foreign policy have considerably improved the image of the Soviet Union. Soviet foreign policy now strongly emphasises the 'de-ideologisation' of international relations. In this regard, the long-cherished 'socialist system' has almost ceased to exist. The Soviet Union has made unilateral force reductions in Central Europe clearing the way for similar reductions by the United States in consultation with its European allies.

Soviet–United States relations became part of Moscow's grand strategy to discontinue strategic nuclear confrontation and withdraw from military alliances. By abandoning the traditional power and alliance-oriented international behaviour, the Soviet Union made the first important step away from the deadly cycle of nuclear and military confrontation with the United States, its largest and most powerful adversary in modern history. It may be the first step in a transition to a healthier status for a large country intent to tackle domestic problems rather than retain all the responsibilities of a so-called superpower.

In contrast with the state of euphoria in the West, and Cold War rhetoric from some sections regarding developments in the Soviet Union and Eastern Europe, there is no mention in the new CPSU documents about 'two systems' and 'two social formations', 'the general crisis of capitalism', 'inter-imperialist contradictions' and 'the struggle between the forces of progress and reaction in the modern world'.

During the first five years of Gorbachev's administration, the international climate has altered so dramatically that the Soviet President may find himself uniquely placed to concentrate more on the domestic components of security rather than on the external components. During the current decade, the Soviet Union may declare, as the Chinese did in the 1980s, that the immediate threat of global war has ceased and the country no longer faces a major military threat. With the changed security perceptions and increased strategic confidence of the Soviet Union, there is far less need to emphasise 'superpower' status and old-style international commitments.

The CPSU Platform published in February 1990 and adopted by its Central Committee plenary meeting demonstrates clearly the radical departure from the ideology-based vision of the world and great power rhetoric. In contrast to the documents adopted in 1986 by the 27th Party Congress, the Platform concentrates on the following issues:

— the demilitarisation of the international community;
— a total ban of nuclear weapons and their phased destruction;
— a total ban, destruction and cessation of production of chemical weapons;
— the radical reduction of conventional weapons and military forces in order to exclude the material preconditions for offensive military action;

—the withdrawal of troops from the territories of foreign states and the abandonment of foreign military bases;
—the non-use of outer space for military purposes;
—the reorganisation of military alliances (including their abrogation) into defensively-oriented political groupings designed to enhance common security and international stability;
—significant cuts in military budgets and the conversion of defence industries;
—the gradual development of reciprocal transparency on land, sea, air and outer space; and
—effective control over military activity and compliance with treaties.[3]

Despite the positive changes in the Soviet Union's diplomatic, military and political posture in the Asia–Pacific, including the normalisation of relations with China, there is still much progress to be made in improving relations with Tokyo; expanding Soviet–United States dialogue to the problems of the North Pacific and East Asia; launching multilateral political dialogue between the Asia–Pacific states; and expanding the Soviet Union's economic links with the Pacific sector of the world economy.

Recent developments in Eastern Europe and the official Soviet attitude towards these radical changes proves the sincerity of the newly-born Soviet philosophy of 'freedom of political and social choice'. Perhaps, during the 1990s, the Soviet Union will be trusted more by the West than at any time in the past, though some important areas of misunderstanding and mistrust still remain. Northeast Asia and the Western Pacific have not been affected greatly by the improved climate between the Soviet Union and the United States. Compared to Northeast Asia, Europe is further ahead on the path towards disarmament, dialogue, accommodation and closer economic interaction.

SOURCES OF CONCERN

In Northeast Asia and the Western Pacific, a Cold War mentality still prevails. There is no peace treaty between the Soviet Union and Japan. The Soviet Union and the United States do not conduct bilateral trade across the Pacific despite the geographic proximity and economic opportunities on both sides of the Bering Strait. The United States does not have diplomatic relations with Vietnam or North Korea; nor does Japan have diplomatic relations with North Korea. There are many disagreements between North and South Korea which cannot be isolated from the regional political and strategic scene such as bilateral relations, membership in international organisations, and the reduction of tension on the Korean Peninsular.

Legacies of the Cold War from the 1950s and 1960s are being carried into the last decade of the century. The 1989 Pacex naval exercises conducted in the Northwest Pacific by United States and Japanese forces represent the largest mobilisation of forces in the Pacific since the Second World War. Ironically, these exercises were held during preparations for the Malta Summit. The Asia–Pacific region badly needs its own Reykjavik.

A second problem concerns Japan's foreign policy. Tokyo has had considerable difficulty in acknowledging the Soviet Union as a Pacific country. For example, Japan's *Diplomatic Bluebook*, published by Japan's Ministry of Foreign Affairs, carefully avoided mentioning the Soviet Union as part of the Asia–Pacific region. In the *Defence of Japan White Paper*, on the other hand, the Soviet Union was portrayed as the major threat to the security of Japan.

A third problem is the status of the four islands in the Kurile chain. Disputed by Tokyo since the early 1950s, these territories form part of the long and bitter history of border disputes and broken treaties between Japan and Russia. Although some prominent Japanese individuals and influential organisations recognise that 'these islands are located in an area where the United States and the Soviet navies are in direct competition... and it is necessary for the United States and the Soviet Union to ease tension in this area',[4] the Japanese Ministry of Foreign Affairs is pressing Washington hard to make the territorial issue part of the Soviet–American agenda.

In summary, on the one hand, there are some basic problems that need to be resolved in order to bring about new thinking in the Asia–Pacific. On the other hand, there are deep-seated stereotypes and political restraints to the resolution of these problems. In the case of East–West relations in Europe, however, these inhibitions were dismantled with the active participation of Western countries. In Northeast Asia, a similar mission has been performed since 1988, to some extent at least, only by South Korea.

The progress achieved in relations between Moscow and Seoul since President Gorbachev's Krasnoyarsk speech in September 1988, is one of the rare examples of breaking with post-war tradition in international relations in Northeast Asia. The Soviet approach to the problems of the Asia–Pacific region, explained at Vladivostok in 1986, was based on a readiness to develop relations with all states of the region without exception. Similarly, Seoul's 'Northern Politics' initiative marked a major departure from its previously anti-communist policies.

The spirit of competition and mistrust in Soviet–United States relations in Northeast Asia and the Western Pacific became less acute after the Soviet President's visit to Washington in June 1990 and his meeting with South Korea's President Roh Tae-woo in San Francisco. Although the diplomatic links subsequently established between Moscow and Seoul are important for the future of both bilateral and regional relations, they will not progress fully without basic changes in the the regional climate and better understanding between North and South Korea.

SOVIET MILITARY POSTURE

By the end of the 1980s there remained several major sources of military tension in the region:
— the Soviet–United States naval confrontation;
— the Soviet Union's confrontation with United States forces in Japan and South Korea;
— the tense situation on the Korean Peninsula;

— a considerable level of defence-related activity on the Soviet–Chinese border, which has only recently begun to decline; and

— the gradual, but not yet final, normalisation in Cambodia.

The Soviet Union's superpower status in the Asia–Pacific region is comparatively low. Historically, Soviet forces deployed in the Far East have been divided into two groupings. The first grouping, made up of 326 200 men and the Pacific Fleet, exists to deter the United States and Japanese armed forces in the Pacific area, including American troops deployed in Alaska and the West Coast of the United States. The second grouping (271 400 men) is deployed in the Trans-Baikal military district and the Mongolian and Far Eastern areas adjacent to China.

To counter the American military presence in Northeast Asia and the Western Pacific, the Soviet Union has deployed 870 combat aircraft, including 470 strike aircraft, 4,500 tanks, 4,100 infantry fighting vehicles and APCs, 7,000 artillery pieces, 55 major surface combatants, including two air-capable ships and 48 nuclear-powered submarines other than SSBNs.

Troops deployed along the Chinese border had in their inventory 820 combat aircraft, 8,100 tanks, 10,200 infantry fighting vehicles and 9,400 artillery pieces.[5]

In quantitative terms, the United States and Japanese armed forces are superior to the first grouping of Soviet forces in:

— personnel strength, more than twofold;

— large surface combatants, nearly fourfold;

— surface ships, carrying cruise missiles with a range over 600km, the USSR has no such weapons; and

— strike aircraft, tactical air forces and naval aviation, more than twofold.

The Soviet forces, in turn, are superior to the armed forces of the United States and Japan in:

— tanks, twofold;

— infantry fighting vehicles and APCs, 1.5 fold; and

— artillery systems, 1.5 fold.[6]

It was decided to reduce the Soviet armed forces in the eastern areas of the Soviet Union by 200,000 men by 1 January 1991 including the reduction of army and navy personnel in the Far Eastern zone. The forces deployed in the Far East will be reduced by 120,000 men. Specifically, the Soviet forces are to be reduced by 12 divisions, 11 air regiments and 16 surface ships. There will also be a substantial reduction in Soviet troops stationed in Mongolia followed by their complete withdrawal in 1991.

The primary mission of the Soviet Pacific Fleet is to counterbalance the American attack submarines and aircraft carrier battle groups that can deliver strikes on Soviet territory. Another important mission is to protect the Sea of Okhotsk and its approaches in order to protect Soviet strategic submarines.

A recent edition of the Pentagon's *Soviet Military Power, Prospects for Change* indicates clearly that the United States and its allies hold an edge in the military balance in the East Asia–Pacific region including overall maritime capabilities. It also notes that 'defence is the foremost concern of Soviet military planning in the Pacific region'.[7] In fact, most of the available Western figures and estimates concerning the composition and activities of the Soviet Pacific Fleet make it possible to conclude that the Fleet's primary objective is defensive in nature.

ECONOMIC RELATIONS WITH THE PACIFIC ECONOMIES

The scale of the Soviet Union's involvement in the regional network of economic relations is limited. The Soviet Far East is relatively underpopulated. The lack of infrastructure, both industrial and social, has created many problems including a shortage of housing and a high level of migration. One of the most basic problems is the raw materials orientation of the economy with high exports of unprocessed minerals, timber and fish both to foreign and domestic markets.

Rigidly centralised and ideologically-coloured economic policy prevented the Far East from foreign economic involvement in any form other than trade and compensation deals, primarily with Japanese partners.

In 1988, the volume of Soviet exports to Asia–Pacific countries, excluding the United States and Canada, reached 6,239 million roubles and imports 4,543 million roubles. Priority was given to trade with Vietnam, Mongolia, North Korea, Laos and Cambodia which was in fact subsidised through Soviet exports. From 1980, the Soviet trade imbalance with these states totalled 15,784 million roubles.[8]

In contrast, the total trade deficit with developed economies accumulated since 1980 reached 10,955 million roubles with Japan, 4,337 million roubles with Australia and 1 080 million roubles with New Zealand. The trade deficit with ASEAN countries (excluding Brunei) totalled 4,572 million roubles.[9]

The Soviet Union became the dominant economic partner of Mongolia, North Korea and Vietnam. According to data published by the Finance Ministry of the Soviet Union, their respective debts at the end of 1989 were 9,131 million roubles for Vietnam, 2,234 million roubles for North Korea, 758 million roubles for Laos, 9,542 million roubles for Mongolia and 715 million roubles for Cambodia. The cumulative debt of these states exceeds 23,378 million roubles out of 43,806 million roubles of indebtedness accumulated by all socialist countries.[10]

More than 70 per cent of investment in Mongolia is financed by the Soviet Union. About 55 per cent of industrial output and 20 per cent of agricultural production originates from enterprises built with Soviet assistance. These enterprises provide almost 80 per cent of Mongolian exports. The total number of projects built, modernised or enlarged with the participation of the Soviet Union exceeds 600, including 150 industrial enterprises. With Soviet development assistance, about 70 industrial projects were built in North Korea and more than 300 in Vietnam. Another 200 large projects involving Soviet assistance are underway in Vietnam. The Soviet share in capital investment is as high as 70 per cent. About two-thirds of Vietnam's imports come from the Soviet Union. Throughout the 1980s, the Soviet share in economic assistance received by Laos was about 50 per cent. In Cambodia, 80 different projects were financed and equipped by Soviet partners, 60 of which are already operational.[11]

Although some economic assistance provided by the Soviet Union is ineffective and has evoked criticism from recipients and donor alike, it is quite clear that the net transfer of economic wealth from the Soviet Union to the centrally-planned economies of Northeast and Southeast Asia is substantial and will continue to play an important role in the bilateral relations and socio–economic development of those countries. It is clear for both donor and recipient, however, that the implementation of development assistance should be changed to maximise the use of domestic resources and increase the effectiveness of bilateral economic cooperation. There is also the potential to involve 'third parties' in some important projects financed by the Soviet Union in order to raise their qualitative standards and increase the chances of future economic interaction with regional economies. The gradual transformation of this basically non-commercial channel of Soviet economic involvement in regional affairs may, in the future, be supplemented by certain 'adjustments' in the geography of Soviet trade and its partial reorientation towards the Asia–Pacific at the expense of Europe.

As a large, resource-rich country, the Soviet Union may be associated in the Pacific region not only with the Far Eastern areas but as a country which in 1988 exported to Western Europe 13,107 million roubles of goods including energy resources, which accounted for 7,870 million roubles. In 1988, the amount of imports from Western European countries reached 10,563 million roubles.[12]

The largest trading partners of the Soviet Union are the European CMEA (COMECON) countries, including Yugoslavia, which in 1988 received 34,492 million roubles of goods including 16,736 million roubles of energy resources. In 1988, the total amount of imports from these states was 37,346 million roubles.[13] Some Eastern European countries have expressed dissatisfaction with the way CMEA operates. Others are in the process of utilising Western European countries for market opportunities, sources of investment and technology. It is highly possible that as a result of the domestic and foreign policy changes in Eastern Europe, the Soviet Union may be forced to explore other markets and look for new sources of imports. Indeed, some important changes were recorded in 1989 in trade relations with 'free market economies'.

Finally, let me address the real economic presence of the Soviet Union in the Asia–Pacific region in terms of trade compared to the volume of trade with Western Europe. In 1988, the Soviet Union's total exports to Japan, South Korea, China, Australia, New Zealand and ASEAN reached 2,460 million roubles compared to 5,237 million roubles of goods other than energy resources exported to the Western European economies. In 1988, Soviet imports from ten PECC-member countries (excluding the United States, Canada, Taiwan and Brunei) totalled 3,591 million roubles compared to 10,563 million roubles of imports from twenty Western European economies.

These figures should be seen in the context of the political difficulties the Soviet Union had in relations with China, Japan and ASEAN and the lack of direct economic or official ties with South Korea, Taiwan and Hong Kong. At the same time, Western European political and economic institutions, including the EC, have displayed a positive attitude towards cooperation with the Soviet Union. There is little need to emphasise that individual European states including West Germany, France, Italy, Belgium, the United Kingdom and Finland have cooperated economically with the Soviet Union for the last several decades and since 1985 have developed special policies towards Soviet reforms.

BASIC ECONOMIC PROBLEMS OF THE SOVIET FAR EAST

No scenarios for economic cooperation with Asia–Pacific economies will materialise without basic domestic change on three fundamental levels:

—the management of the national economy from the centre;
—the lack of business, technological and managerial skills at the micro-level in enterprises and factories; and
—the lack of motivation in the work place and cooperative relations between management and labour, and the continuing influence of ideology in organising economic activities.

Without resolving these problems, it will be impossible to change the domestic economic climate to the extent required for foreign companies to invest freely in the Soviet Union. Even more radical changes and liberal regulations are essential for remote and underdeveloped areas such as the Far East and the Soviet Pacific coast.

Unfortunately, by the mid-1980s, an economic crisis became clearly visible in the Far East. There was virtually no increase in the region's share of the country's overall industrial production, while the rates of economic growth were slowing down. Production was growing more slowly than the national average. The high level of migration out of the region persisted. Social problems, related primarily to a lack of modern housing, were responsible for halting the settlement of the Far East. Stagnation in housing construction was aggravated further by the low level of development of the construction industry which suffered from a deficiency of workers and managers. The population of the Soviet Far East found itself dependent on other parts of the country for 50 per cent of its food and 85 per cent of its fuel. The region lacks its own construction materials and engineering facilities and the capacity of its air terminals is less than half the desired level.

The position of the Far East both in the domestic and international division of labour is determined primarily by the raw material resources and extraction industries. These branches account for as much as 30 per cent of all industrial production, and the level of raw materials processing remains low.

The region's industry became alienated from the needs of the region: a large part of its machinery products was taken to the European part of the country, from where technology was imported for local needs. The infrastructure, including its social components, was developed according to the specific requirements of the raw material industries. The establishment of infrastructure was determined by a desire to exploit and export resources rapidly rather than by a consideration for the comprehensive development of the region.

The problem of the loss of marine biological resources is acute. Great disproportions have occurred between the amount of catch and the capacity of facilities for even limited primary processing. The coastal infrastructure of the fishing fleet is clearly inadequate, with a shortage of port and repair facilities. Both the cargo and fishing fleets need to be modernised, renovated and supplied with up-to-date equipment.

In these conditions, the need to turn the Far Eastern economy into a system with elements of 'dual integration' became obvious. This means that the economy of the Far East must become an integral part of the national economy and, at the same time, an element of the international division of labour. This will, in the first place, bring the Far East into line with the country's overall social and economic standards and, secondly, enable the establishment of foreign economic, scientific and technological 'contact zones' with the fast developing Pacific branch of the world economy.

The concept of reorienting the regional economy was put forward by Mikhail Gorbachev at Vladivostok in 1986 during a visit to the Far East. 'The Far East has been traditionally referred to as the country's outpost on the Pacific', Mikhail Gorbachev said. 'This is certainly true. But this view of the region is no longer broad enough. The Maritime Territory and the Far East should be made into a highly-developed economic complex'.[14]

LONG-TERM PLANS AND REALITIES

The long-term state program for the comprehensive development of the productive forces of the Far Eastern economic region up to the year 2000 was issued in mid-1987.[15] It was elaborated by the country's highest planning bodies. The main stipulations of this program, which was approved in August 1987, are:

—the accelerated solution of social problems;
—the setting up of a modern construction industry;
—the expansion of food production;
—the comprehensive use of the mineral and raw material resources;
—the accelerated formation of a fuel and energy complex;
—the further development of ferrous metallurgy;
—the radical technical re-equipment, reconstruction and reorientation of engineering facilities towards the needs of the region's economy;
—the setting up of a complex of industrial branches connected with the exploitation of marine resources; and
—the increase of the Far East's export potential.

According to the long-term program, the economy of the Far East will undergo some important structural changes. Priority will be given to the production infrastructure, processing industries and the services sector. The share of machine-building, chemical and petrochemical industries, the production of building materials and power engineering will all be increased.

It is planned to increase overall industrial production 2.4 to 2.5 times by the year 2000. The amount of capital investment and construction work is to be increased 2.2 times. To achieve these goals, it is planned to allocate a total of 232 billion roubles to these tasks over the period until the year 2000, four-fifths of which is to come from the national budget via various ministries and other agencies.

The social aspect of the program, its most important part, was the first to be addressed. It was stressed that development in the Pacific region of the Soviet Union was dependent on bringing the region up to the country's average standard in terms of the quality of life and on creating attractive living and working conditions.

Although the program's orientation towards bringing the Far East up to the national level in a comprehensive and accelerated fashion cannot be questioned, it is unlikely that this goal can be achieved through the centralised economic mechanism. Indeed, it is precisely with the operation of industrial ministries that the problems in the Far Eastern economy are connected. The program's major weakness is that it leaves this approach intact.

Now that the process of political reform is underway in the country, new opportunities have been opened for the rational reorganisation of the region's economic management. The democratisation of economic life in the Soviet Union is increasingly reliant on the independence of enterprises. These primary economic organisations constitute the foundation of the entire national economy. Yet self-management in enterprises is closely connected with local self-government, which means that the sovereignty of local Soviets must be strengthened, both in the sense of granting them greater legal rights and supporting these rights with material and financial resources. Only then will local Soviets be able to defend their interests in their relations with the ministries and other central agencies.

And what of material backing for local self-government? As in most regions of the country, the Soviets in the Far East have management responsibility primarily over the economic branches responsible for local services, industries and agriculture. The aggregate share of these branches in the total output of the region is just 10 per cent. It is important, therefore, to strengthen the dependence between the revenues of local budgets and the economic results of industrial enterprises and organisations located in the region.

For this reason, the Krasnoyarsk speech outlined a range of special measures to encourage economic development in the Pacific regions. These measures envisage granting state-owned and cooperative enterprises special tax benefits, independent price setting powers and the right to operate directly on the foreign market and utilise hard currency revenues for the social needs of the population.

SPECIAL ECONOMIC REGIME PROPOSAL AND PRINCIPAL AREAS OF COOPERATION

As mentioned above, Mikhail Gorbachev suggested in his Krasnoyarsk speech that state-owned, cooperative and joint enterprises in the Far Eastern region be granted a 'most favoured' status. In the context of creating a special economic regime that will be attractive to foreign partners and profitable to local enterprises, projects are being drafted to set up 'joint-enterprise zones' in the Far East. It is planned to single out territories in the border area of the Soviet Union where the production and processing of agricultural products and the construction of various enterprises will be organised on a joint basis with neighbouring countries.

In December 1988, the USSR Council of Ministers formulated some elements of the special status of the Far East in the development of economic cooperation with foreign countries. Representing a step in freeing the foreign economic activity of the Soviet organisations (the decision, for instance, actually removes the limitations on the share of foreign partners in joint enterprises), the document envisages a three-year tax exemption on the profits of joint enterprises in the Far East with a subsequent 10 per cent reduction of tax and a lower tax rate when profits are taken abroad.[16]

The Pacific region accounts for 40 per cent of all fishing and canned fish production in the Soviet Union. Nonetheless, as noted earlier, the region lacks processing, storage and production facilities, refrigerators and equipment. In recent decades, despite the considerable increase in catches, the quality of fish products has declined steadily. The level of processing is also low. The participation of foreign capital, technology and experience would not only accelerate the filling of the domestic market, primarily the Far Eastern one, with fish products and prepared fish foods, but could also help expand exports and improve its structure. Joint ventures could be established for the technical re-equipping of the Far Eastern fishing fleet, the renovation of existing fish processing plants and the construction of new plants, the modernising of coastal facilities, the re-equipment of small tonnage fleets for shoreline fishing, and the supply of marine facilities with necessary equipment.

Preliminary analysis shows the expediency of orienting the Far East's industry towards developing the production of specialised machinery, construction equipment, equipment for forestry development and fish processing, and for the extraction industry and opencast mining.

It is possible that countertrade agreements will be revived in new forms. Switching the orientation to smaller projects could yield positive results and be instrumental in increasing exports. The traditional large-scale approach to cooperation must be accompanied by a careful search for export opportunities, flexibility, and special efforts to secure a Soviet presence in the market.

It would be expedient to connect the development of imports with the essential needs of the Soviet economy, especially those of the Far East. This would encompass an expansion of imports of industrial machinery, particularly that needed initially, as well as imports to set up production oriented towards meeting the urgent needs of the region, including its traditional export industries.

Most Soviet organisations have little experience with foreign economic ties or knowledge about forms of economic cooperation with foreign partners other than trade. This may explain why Soviet organisations continue to seek contacts almost exclusively with Japanese companies, particularly those with which they are already familiar. In this connection, there is an urgent requirement to set up a service offering enterprises information and advice on participation in the international division of labour. Working with foreign partners also requires the training of a large number of specialists in foreign business practices. This necessitates the setting up of a special system to train personnel, and increasing the number of specialists being trained or retrained abroad.

This raises the difficult question of priority: should the Soviet Union seek foreign capital to manufacture products to replace imports, or to manufacture products for export? The balance between the two kinds of joint ventures will ultimately be determined in the process of cooperation. However, in my opinion, priority should be given to replacing imports, although this approach will initially mean a reduction of hard currency revenues, as well as hard currency expenses. The main goal is to eventually change the structure and quality of domestic production, while the development of export facilities is only a secondary issue. This approach is all the more justified since making domestic industries more competitive will in time improve the prospects of entering international markets.

There are some other matters that need to be considered in the development of economic relations with the Asia–Pacific region. The first is the importance of the particular company *vis-a-vis* the country or the government, since some large multi-national corporations are relatively independent of government control. Second, it is important to choose a specific producer or consumer as a partner, rather than a country. Third, multilateral economic ties should be promoted on the basis of economic complementarity. One version of such cooperation, between the Soviet Union, China and Japan, was suggested by Mikhail Gorbachev in Krasnoyarsk. I believe that major opportunities would also open up if 'third parties' were introduced into Soviet–Vietnamese economic cooperation. Fourth, the trade in services, which could be actively joined by the Far East, is becoming an increasingly important field of economic exchange. Fifth, the experience of many foreign countries that are successfully developing new territories, shows that special regulations tailored specifically for those regions can play a beneficial role.

DOES THE FAR EAST NEED SPECIAL ECONOMIC ZONES?

In the Soviet Union, where many questions regarding the regulation of economic activity and the functioning of enterprises are still being discussed, a key issue is the future relationship between the regions having a 'most-favoured' economic status and the rest of the national economy. In other words, in the case of the Far East for instance, there is the general question of whether the setting up of 'enclaves' with special tax rates, customs and administration should be accelerated.

The advocates of the accelerated approach say that bringing the special regions as close as possible to the conditions of the world market will yield quick and important economic results. Others stress that the gradual transition of the national economy towards a market-oriented one will create a more liberal atmosphere to attract foreign companies whose operations can be targeted to solve economic and social problems in particular regions. In the former case, the principal task is to achieve an accelerated growth of exports and to direct domestic attention towards obtaining profits in convertible currency. In the latter case, the suggested emphasis is on increasing the degree of processing of exported raw materials and developing agriculture, housing construction and the tourist industry.

The Soviet Union is a vast country with a tremendously diversified economic structure. What is suitable for some regions of China and a number of developing countries may not quite fit the conditions of the Soviet Far East. It would be naive to think that the problems of this huge region can be solved by the creation of special economic zones alone. Therefore, it seems that parameters of the 'most favoured' status for the Far East must create conditions that will stimulate the channelling of domestic resources and organisations from the western regions of the Soviet Union to the eastern regions. This is especially important since the government's long-term program for the comprehensive development of the Far Eastern economic region for the period until the year 2000 has not yet proved its vitality.

In regard to the use of special zones to accelerate the development of the Far East and solve its urgent economic problems, it would be expedient to consider the whole Soviet territory to the east of Lake Baikal (with the exception of regions closed for defence reasons) as one integrated 'super-zone of joint enterprise'. This would attract foreign investment, step up industrial potential, change the structure of exports and help solve social problems.

If special economic zones are regarded as a means of economic deregulation, it is reasonable to suppose that favourable economic terms will be introduced selectively so that priority economic or industrial sectors needing an influx of foreign capital and technology will benefit immediately. The industry and functional specialisation of the zones can help the Soviet Far East to reduce exports of unprocessed raw materials.

DEVELOPMENT OF A STRATEGY FOR THE SOVIET FAR EAST

The traditional attitude to the Far East as a resource-rich area and a source of raw materials for the other regions of the country or for export is a consequence of the former 'continental' development concept. It was believed that, for geographical reasons, development would spread from the west to the east.

The regional economic policy shaped both by central bodies and various ministries and agencies was oriented to maximise the exploitation and exportation of raw materials. For example, the desire to obtain access to new sources of minerals and energy, timber and non-ferrous metals, regardless of cost, predetermined the decision to build the Baikal–Amur Mainline (BAM) Railway. It is not difficult to imagine what results the resources poured into this project would have yielded had they instead been invested in developing infrastructure in the Maritime and Khabarovsk territories and the Amur region, where people have been living for many decades, attracted by the better climate, the proximity of waterways and the sea coast. Today, several years after the scheduled deadline for putting BAM into operation, common sense and economic necessity will hopefully ensure the concentration of limited resources on the most promising regions, which will not just absorb such investments, but repay them whilst effecting the desired economic and social changes.

The process of economic development and the encouragement of migration can be stimulated only by improving the quality of life in the already developed regions. This envisages a shift of focus to the larger cities and the developed regions of the Far East. The efficiency of a development pattern 'from coast to inland' is proved by the experience of other countries with vast, undeveloped territories, such as the United States, Canada and Australia.

Stimulating change with the help of a well-considered series of measures can promote the formation of a relatively independent economic centre, whose role in the future may be comparable with such regions as the Urals, Southern Siberia and many other major economic zones in the west of the country. Finally, there is no reason why plans should not be made for the growth of a new Pacific–Eastern Siberian economic centre in addition to the European–Western Siberian one. The size of the country makes this possible, while the area's geographic location and the rapid process of regionalisation of economic life both in the east and in the west point towards such an eventuality.

REGIONAL COOPERATION

In November 1989, a meeting in Canberra, Australia, of government officials of some Asian and Pacific rim countries addressed key issues of trade, investment, and economic policy and prospects for cooperation. This has become known as the Asia–Pacific Economic Cooperation (APEC) process. The Soviet Union, China and Taiwan were not invited. The PECC VII Conference which took place one week later in Auckland, New Zealand, decided not to open the question of membership for the time being and left aside the Soviet application to join this semi-official body. Two points have been raised in connection with the Soviet Union's interest in joining PECC: its sudden change towards regional cooperation in 1986 and its limited economic presence in the Asia–Pacific region.

Since the PECC VI Conference in Osaka in May 1988, a large number of business people, public figures, politicians and scholars from East Asian and Pacific countries have visited Vladivostok, Khabarovsk, Nakhodka and Yuzhno–Sakhalinsk. Major business delegations from South Korea, Taiwan, Japan and other states have made fact-finding trips to the Soviet Far East. The Soviet National Committee for Asia–Pacific Economic Cooperation (SOVNA-PEC), established in 1988 to facilitate interaction with PECC, has been actively involved in efforts to open up the Soviet Union's Pacific areas for trade and economic cooperation.

SOVNAPEC established working groups to deal with various PECC task forces and forums. In 1989, SOVNAPEC delegations participated in the workshops on fishing and trade policies held in Canada, on agricultural policies in South Korea, on transport, telecommunications and tourism in Thailand, and the forum on minerals and energy in the Philippines. In May 1989, a SOVNA-PEC delegation attended the 22nd General Meeting of the Pacific Basin Economic Council (PBEC) in Taipei in an observer capacity. In May 1988 and November 1989, SOVNAPEC delegations attended the PECC conferences in Osaka and Auckland.

SOVNAPEC has additionally sponsored scientific contacts. In July 1988 and December 1989, representatives of the Institute of World Economy and International Relations (IMEMO), took part in the proceedings of the 17th and 18th sessions of the Pacific Conference on Trade and Development (PAFTAD) held in Indonesia and Malaysia respectively.

These Soviet activities support the notion that the key Soviet task is to develop the Pacific and Far Eastern areas of the country as well as to integrate the national economy with the Pacific region through bilateral and multilateral economic cooperation. There is enough evidence that membership of PECC is not a foreign policy matter or propaganda goal but one of the channels to influence the long-term domestic economic strategy and the thinking of those responsible for major economic decisions.

ECONOMIC OPPORTUNITIES AND PRIORITIES

Membership in PECC may help the Soviet Union to understand better existing economic realities and medium-term trends, but it cannot substitute for difficult commercial work in both bilateral economic relations and domestic micro-level activities.

There are some geographic, economic, logistic and political realities which will undoubtedly influence the direction, structure and volume of trade and investment of the Soviet Union and its Far Eastern areas with new Asia–Pacific partners. Amongst these are :

— the geographic proximity of the United States, Canada, Japan, South Korea and China;
— the economic and political importance of the involvement of American corporations in the development Soviet Far Eastern and Pacific areas;
— the experience of Canada in economic development and organising social infrastructure in extreme climatic conditions;
— the prospect of good economic relations with South Korea and other NIEs encompassing trade, investment, joint ventures and technological cooperation;
— the experience of Australia, New Zealand, Canada and the United States in agricultural production, mining and infrastructure development; and
— the prospect of ASEAN countries becoming a bigger market and a source of competitive imports as well as foreign investment in the Soviet economy.

As a major foreign policy and strategic actor, the Soviet Union has accumulated sufficient knowledge and experience to change towards new political thinking and to develop a new approach to security issues. In this age of growing economic interdependence, there is an understanding that a healthy national economy and economic cooperation with the world are no less important for the security of the country than well-equipped armed forces were during the Cold War era.

Both Moscow and Washington face, amongst the emerging realities of the 1990s, a new role for Japan which is now less militarily vulnerable, more politically independent and economically active worldwide. Following the domestic reforms in the Soviet Union and international changes, Soviet perceptions of security and a future world order increasingly view Japan as a key actor. This is why it is critically important for the Soviet Union to normalise and develop relations with Japan. As a neighbouring country, the Soviet Union cannot and must not overlook the economic and political potential of an improved relationship with Tokyo. For the Soviet Pacific areas and the Far Eastern region, Japan is a major element in the immediate military–strategic and politico–economic environment of the Soviet Union. The same might be said of Japan's vision of the Soviet Union in the 1990s. In fact, the proposals made by the Soviet Union to lower military levels in the Far East and the North Pacific potentially are acceptable to those Japanese who would like to see a multipolar, less militarised future world that is not based on nuclear power.

Still, the new political thinking was not for a long time powerful enough to change the course of Soviet–Japanese relations. There was a need for the two countries and their political leaders (not just foreign services) to take another step forward. Such a step was accomplished during Alexander Yakovlev's visit to Tokyo in November 1989 and the successful round of talks with Sintaro Abe in Moscow in January 1990. The Eight-point Program proposed by the leader of the largest ever LDP delegation to visit Moscow is designed to bridge the gap in bilateral relations and increase person-to-person contacts and cooperation for the success of *perestroika*. President Govbachev's visit to Japan in 1991 is a milestone in this process.

If mutually beneficial changes are shaped through multilateral dialogue based on Soviet–United States and Soviet–Japanese understanding and coop-eration, they may alter the whole pattern of regional politics. As noted by Donald Zagoria,

> there are many uncertainties in the rapidly changing strategic situation in East Asia and there will be many barriers on the road towards a more peaceful and stable environment. After 40 years of cold war between the two superpowers, several decades of Sino–Soviet hostility and a century of mistrust between Russia and Japan, suspicions among all the major superpowers are still strong. Nevertheless, the prospects for the breakthrough in easing tension have not been better since the end of World War II.[17]

Notes

Chapter 1

1 Mack and O'Hare (1990, pp.387–8).
2 Stockwin (1991).
3 Drysdale (1988).

Chapter 2

1 Korolev (1990, pp.13–21).

Chapter 3

1 Brus (1972).
2 Grossman (1963).
3 Ellman (1989, p.19).
4 Kornai (1986, p.1690).
5 Sabel and Stark (1982, p.446).
6 Granick (1987).
7 Winiecki (1989, p.62).
8 Winiecki (1989, p.64).
9 Gray (1985, p.22).
10 Littler (1984, p.88).
11 Bensi (1988, pp.60–1).
12 Senghaas (1981, pp.94–115).
13 Kornai (1988: Table 8, p.1719).
14 Winieck (1987, p.16).
15 World Bank (1981, p.99).
16 Winiecki (1987, p.20).
17 Mandel (1989, p.11).
18 *The Times* London, 5 January 1990.
19 There is an interpretation of the Chinese economic reforms which runs as follows: the Cultural Revolution (1966–76) put control of large amounts of resources into local administrative hands. This pattern of existing local and regional control ('localism') shaped the configuration of post-Mao reforms. In particular, the central state authorities have faced continuing difficulties of control over materials allocation. There is a significant degree of truth in this interpretation, but note that control over producer goods (such as steel and cement) does not pass to *enterprises*. Local authorities (provinces, counties

and others) become the economic agents and economic competition is bureaucratic *not* market competition.

20 Kornai (1986, p.1713).
21 Yang (1989, mimeo).
22 Elster (1988).
23 Nuti (1981, pp.35–6).
24 Szelenyi (1989).
25 Yang (1989).
26 In a curious way this point is made by a pre-Gorbachev joke:

> The Soviet locomotive cannot go any further because there are no more rails. The socialist train comes to a stop. Brezhnev instructs the steel industry to make more rails. It is done and the socialist train continues until once more it comes to the end of the track. Andropov is now General Secretary of the Party and discovers there is no more steel to be had. So he orders the track behind the train be put in front of it. The socialist locomotive continues until once more it comes to a standstill. Now there is no track either in front or behind the train. Chernyenko has assumed leadership but there are neither steel nor rails. So he instructs all the communists to get out of the train and rock it backwards and forwards so that the passengers inside should think that the socialist locomotive is once more on its way.

(Quoted by Michael Burawoy in 'Printing By Numbers: Working Class Formation in Hungary and Poland', paper presented at the Aston/UMIST Labour Process Conference, UK, 1990, mimeo.)

27 The rapidly deteriorating economic situation in Poland between 1979–82 generated a momentum towards economic reform. From August 1980 to June 1981, seven different projects for the reform of the Polish economic system were put forward. An official Reform Commission reported in June 1981. However, the effects were very limited given the macro-political context. The system degenerated into a mesh of informal and formal bargaining over resources.
28 *Le Monde* Paris, 7 January 1990.
29 *Reuters* London, 14 January 1990.

Chapter 4

1 Soviet official comments in 'The Vladivostok Initiatives Two Years On' *International Affairs* (Moscow) 8, 1988.
2 Zagoria (1982); Segal (1983); Thayer (1987).
3 See a discussion of these points in Segal (1990).
4 For example, Ivanov (1989).
5 Schiffer (1989). See also the much earlier discussion in Dibb (1972) and Conolly (1975).
6 Rozman (1985).
7 Rozman (1988); Robertson (1988).
8 Robertson (1988).
9 Drysdale (1988).
10 Stephan and Chichkanov (1986).
11 Segal (1989).
12 Segal (1990).
13 Kim (1989).
14 Material in this section is based on the author's *The Soviet Union and the Pacific.*

15 Hasegawa and Pravda (1990).

Chapter 5

1 Sato (1990).
2 The term 'socialist market economy' was used in the report by Deputy Prime
   Minister L. Abalkin at the All-Union Conference of Economists, November
   1989. However, since January 1990, the term 'regulated market economy' has
   been used.
3 Sato (1989).
4 The theme is contained in my IEA paper. I found common ground with Gavriil
   Kh. Popov on this matter. See our joint publication, Sato and Popov (1989).
5 'Diversification' or 'multiplicity', to use the words of L. Abalkin in his report
   at the All-Union Conference of Economists, November 1989.

Chapter 6

1 'Severnye territorii': Chto s nimi delat?' *Novoe vremiia* 49, 1989, p.13.
2 *Pravda* 28 July 1987.
3 Aslund (1989, p.3).
4 Utechin (1964, p.375).
5 Kireev (1989, p.5).
6 Based on author's interview with Andrei Zhykov, consultant on national
   security at the International Department, Central Committee of the CPSU, 8
   September 1989.
7 *ibid.*
8 Bogaturov (1989, p.21).
9 Kuznetsov, Navlitskaia and Sytitsyn (1988, pp.371, 373).
10 Hanson and Hill (1979, p.596).
11 *Pravda* 25 August 1987.
12 *Pravda* 1 August 1986.
13 *Pravda* 10 October 1988.
14 'Vneshnepoliticheskaia i diplomaticheskaia deiatel'nost' SSSR (aprel' 1985vg.
   — oktiabr' 1985 g.) Obzor MID SSSR' *Mezhdunarodnaia zhizn* 12, 1989,
   p.93.
15 'Tretii put' — dialog: interv'iu chlena Politbiuro TsK KPSS, sekretaria TsK
   KPSS Aleksandra Iakovleva' *Novoe vremiia* 48, 1989, p. 11; 'Severnye
   territorii' p.20.
16 Spandarian (1988, p.7). V. Gulii, a people's deputy from Sakhalin *oblast,*
   stated: 'As a resident of Sakhalin, we are seriously interested in Japan's high-
   technology and in Japan's participation in the development of the Far East'.
   'Severnye territorii' p.18.
17 Gulii presented a counter-argument to this matter. See 'Severnye territorii'
   p.18.
18 Based on the author's interview with Georgii Arbatov, Director of the Institute
   for American and Canadian Studies, 16 January 1989.
19 Stating that the northern islands do not have much importance both for Japan
   and the Soviet Union economically and strategically, Gulii argues that the
   Soviet Union would feel much more secure with a peace treaty signed with
   Japan. 'Severnye territorii' p.18.

20 Salkisov (1988, p.147).
21 Bogaturov and Nosov (1989, p.8).
22 *Asahi Shimbun, Yomiuri Shimbun* 4 May 1989.
23 Based on private conversation with Dr Mikhail Nosov, Head of the Asian Section, Institute for American and Canadian Studies, 9 September 1989.
24 'Strannoe zhelanie' *Izvestia* 6 September 1989.
25 Lenin (1964, pp.49–50).

Chapter 8

1 Gorbachev (1986, p.96).
2 *Theses of the CPSU Central Committee for the 19th All-Union Party Conference* (1988, p.27).
3 Kipp et al. (1988, pp.2–6).
4 For a full text, see 'Gorbachev's 28 July Speech in Vladivostok' *Daily Report* FBIS–Soviet Union, 29 July 1986, p.R7.
5 For details, see 'Gorbachev Speech — Foreign Section' *News Release — Communique* Ottawa, Ontario: Press Office of the USSR Embassy in Canada, 19 September 1988.
6 'Vneshnaia politika — Vneshenpoliticheskiy razdel zechi Mikhaila Gorbacheva v Krasnoryarske' *Tass* 17 September 1988, p.8.
7 Nagorniy (1989, pp.7–9).
8 For details, see *Soviet Military Power: Prospects for Change, 1989* (1989, pp.30–3).
9 For a debate on the concept of 'reasonable sufficiency' see Duffy and Lee (1988, pp.19–24).
10 Pleshakov (1989, p.10).
11 *Materiali XIX Vsesoyuznoy Konferentsii Kommunisticheskoy Partii Sovetskogo Soyuza* (1988, p.120).
12 Duffy and Lee (1988, p.19).
13 Gorbachev (1987, pp.11ff).
14 Gorbachev seems to have impressed the United Nations with his 'new thinking'. For a related comment, see 'Moscow on the Hudson' *Newsweek* 12 December 1988, pp.12–15.
15 'Gorbachev, the Army and Perestroika' *Washington Times* 26 October 1988, p.F3.
16 For remarks on the Soviet Reform by Robert M. Gates, Deputy Director of the US Central Intelligence Agency, see 'For the Record' *Washington Post* 2 November 1988, p.20.
17 *Tass Report* 28 (1989, p.18).
18 For a related comment by a senior Soviet commander, see Lushev (1989, pp.14–7).
19 See, among others, Borstein (1981, pp.227–55).
20 'Mikail Gorbachev's Address to the Chinese Intellectuals' *Pravda* 19 May 1989, p.1.
21 *Tass* 'Vneshnaia politika — Vneshenpoliticheskiy...' pp.5, 8, 13.
22 Vorontsov (1990, p.9).
23 Since the establishment of the joint venture law (*Ha-byong-bop*) on 8 September 1984, various joint ventures have been formed with foreign firms. To mention a few, there were French, Swiss, Soviet and other East European

companies in ventures with North Korea in the fields of construction, watch-making, battery manufacturing, mining, gem cutting and shipping. For details, see Kang-suk Rhee (1990, pp.50–2).

24 For the 12th World Festival of Youth and Students, see *Towards the Festival in Pyongyang* (1989, pp.4–8).

25 Mashin (1990, p.5).

26 *Korea Herald* 3 April 1990, p.3.

27 Ognev (1990, p.1).

28 *Rodong Sinmun* 4 April 1990, p.2.

29 For details see, among others, Kim (1989, p.343).

30 *Tong-A Ilbo* 23 February 1990, p.1.

31 Ivanov (1989, p.102).

32 These are the Jindo, Hyundai and Samsung corporations whose joint ventures cover electronics, fur trading, lumber cutting and soap manufacturing.

33 This is the first time that South Korea has imported nuclear fuel from an Eastern bloc country. For details, see *Korea Herald* 6 March 1990, p.1.

34 Bykov (1989, p.8).

35 'Big Deals Hit Big Troubles in the Soviet Union' *Business Week* 14 March 1990, pp.10–15.

36 For details, see Avakov (1989, pp.537–57).

Chapter 11

1 This paper is based on a visit to the Soviet Far East in January 1990. Our hosts were the Institute for Economic Research in Khabarovsk and the Soviet National Committee for Asia–Pacific Economic Cooperation (SOVNAPEC). Conversations with researchers and officials in Khabarovsk and Vladivostok provided background information and assisted in developing an interpretation of events.

2 For further information, see Ivanov and Baikov (1989).

3 Japanese enterprises have shown substantial interest in multilateral joint ventures and in acting as intermediaries in trade. See 'Trade mission targets Manchuria, Soviet Asia' *The Japan Economic Journal* 20 May 1989, p.2. China's initiatives in developing three-way relations with the Soviet Union and Japan are reviewed by Christoffersen (1988, pp.1245–63). A Soviet perspective on relations with the Korean peninsula is presented by Trigubenko and Toloraya (1990, pp.22–3).

4 The alternative would be for the Soviet side to build the infrastructure while the value of the investment is not included in the Soviet equity. This would inflate the share of project net income received before tax by the foreign partner, which could be offset by imposing a higher tax on that income.

5 Other ores are classified as 'local' since they remain under local government control.

6 A royalty is not the only option for taxing resource projects and the options, including profit-based taxes, are reviewed in detail by Garnaut and Clunies Ross (1983).

7 There is scope for mutual gain for both host country governments and foreign investors from the development of more stable rules on joint ventures. Garnaut and Clunies Ross (1983, ch.6) argue that the uncertainties involved for foreign investors in an environment where the rules are not stable will cause them to

discount the returns from any project. As a result, better results in terms of government revenue can be achieved in the presence of a set of general rules which are fixed and announced early in the exploratory process, although this result is subject to qualifications about the manner in which the revenue is collected.

Chapter 12

1 Some of the material in this chapter is based on my article 'The USSR's Pacific Areas: New Approaches to the Development Strategy' in Ivanov (1989, pp.124–60).

2 In his speech at Vladivostok on 28 July 1986, Mikhail Gorbachev pointed out, 'After the plan for a 'Pacific Community' had been rejected, discussions began, on the idea of 'Pacific economic cooperation'. We approached this idea without bias and we are ready to join in the deliberations on the possible foundations of such cooperation; this is, of course, if it is not conceived in a forced, bloc-oriented and anti-socialist pattern, but is rather the result of free discussion without any discrimination'. In reply to a question put by the Indonesian newspaper *Merdeka* on 21 July 1987, M. Gorbachev said: 'The best and the only solid basis for international affairs is equality, mutual respect, non-interference in internal affairs, and mutual benefit. These very objectives will be served by the Soviet Committee for Asian and Pacific Economic Cooperation which is being set up in this country'. In September 1988, in the speech delivered in Krasnoyarsk, M. Gorbachev noted: 'We follow with interest the activity of the Conference on Asia–Pacific Economic Cooperation, have greeted its recent session in Osaka, and are ready to join the work of that international organisation in any form which its members will deem acceptable'.

3 'Towards Humanistic, Democratic Socialism' CPSU Central Committee Platform for 28th Party Congress, draft adopted by February (1990) CPSU Central Committee Plenary Meeting, *Pravda* 13 February 1990.

4 Japan Forum on International Relations (1989, p.31).

5 In May 1989, the Minister of Defense of the USSR, Dmitri Yazov, revealed facts and figures about Soviet armed forces in the Far East. See *Pravda* 28 May 1989.

6 *Disarmament and Security Yearbook 1988–1989* (1989, p.448).

7 *Soviet Military Power, Prospects for Change, 1989* (1989, pp.112, 119).

8 *Foreign Trade of the USSR 1988* (1989).

9 *Foreign Trade of the USSR* various issues.

10 *Izvestia* 1 March 1990.

11 Ivanov (1989, pp.33–60).

12 *Foreign Trade of the USSR 1988* (1989).

13 *ibid.*

14 Speech by M. Gorbachev in Vladivostok, 28 July 1986. See Gorbachev (1986, p.9).

15 'Long-term State Programme of the Far East Economic Region, Buriat Republic and Chita Area' (1987).

16 USSR Council of Ministers (1988).

17 Zagoria (1989, pp.135–6).

Bibliography

Abalkin, L. (1989) Report at the All-Union Conference of Economists, November.

Aslund, Anders (1989) *Gorbachev's Struggle for Economic Reform* Ithaca, New York: Cornell University Press.

Avakov, Rachik M. (1989) 'The New Thinking and Problems of Studying the Developing Countries' Steve Hirsch (ed.) *IMEMO: New Soviet Voices on Foreign Economic Policy* Washington DC: The Bureau of National Affairs Inc.

Bensi, Xing (1988) 'Some Theoretical Problems of the Reform in China' *Far Eastern Affairs* USSR.

Bogaturov, Aleksei (1989) 'Diplomatiia pered vyborom: Sostiazanie v uporstve ili vzaimopriemlemyi pragmatizm' *Novoe vremiia* 32.

Bogaturov, Aleksei and Nosov, Mikhail (1989) 'Treugol'nik bez uglov' *Novoe vremiia* 18.

Bogomolov, O. (ed.) (1990) *Market Forces in Planned Economies* London: Macmillan.

Borstein, Morris (1981) 'Soviet Economic Growth and Foreign Policy' Seweryn Bialer (ed.) *The Domestic Context of Soviet Foreign Policy* Boulder, Colorado: Westview Press.

Brus, Wlodzimierz (1972)*The Market in a Socialist Economy* London, Boston: Routledge and K. Paul.

Bykov, A.N. (1989) 'Recent Changes in the Soviet Economy and Prospects for the Korea–Soviet Economic Relations' paper from an international seminar by the International Private Economic Council of Korea (IPEC), Seoul, October.

Christoffersen, Gaye (1988) 'Economic Reforms in Northeast China: Domestic Determinants' *Asian Survey* 28, 12.

Conolly, Violet (1975) *Siberia, Today and Tomorrow* London: Collins.

Daily Report FBIS–Soviet Union (1976) 'Gorbachev's 28 July Speech in Vladivostok' 29 July.

Dibb, Paul (1972) *Siberia and the Pacific* London: Praeger.

Disarmament and Security Yearbook 1988–1989 (1989) Moscow: IMEMO.

Drysdale, Peter (1988) *International Economic Pluralism* Sydney and New York: Allen and Unwin and Columbia University.

Duffy, Gloria and Lee, Jennifer (1988) 'The Soviet Debate on Reasonable Sufficiency' *Arms Control Today* 18, 8.

Ellman, Michael (1989) *Socialist Planning* 2nd edn, Cambridge: Cambridge University Press.

Elster, J. (1988) 'Jon Elster Goes to China' *London Review of Books* 27 October.

Foreign Trade of the USSR 1988 (1989) Moscow.

Fei, John and Reynolds, Bruce (1987) 'A Tentative Plan for the Rational Sequenc-
ing of Overall Reform in China's Economic System', *Journal of Comparative
Economics* 11.

Garnaut, Ross and Clunies Ross, Anthony (1983) *Taxation of Mineral Rents*
Oxford: Clarendon Press.

Gates, Robert M. (1988) 'For the Record' *Washington Post* 2 November.

Gorbachev, Mikhail (1986a) 'Political Report of the CPSU Central Committee to
the 27th Party Congress' Moscow: Novosti Press Agency Publishing House.

___'Vladivostok Speech, 28 July 1986' (1986b) Moscow: Novosti Press Agency
Publishing House.

___*Perestroika: New Thinking for Our Country and the World* (1987) New York
NY: Harper and Row.

Granick, David (1987) *Job Rights in the Soviet Union: Their Consequences*
Cambridge: Cambridge University Press.

Gray, Jack (1985) 'Is China Creating Its Own Form of Socialism' *China Now* 111.

Grossman, G. (1963) 'Notes for a Theory of the Command Economy' *Soviet
Studies* XV, 2.

Hanson, Philip and Hill, Malcolm R. (1979) 'Soviet Assimilation of Western Technology: A Survey of U.K. Exporters' Experience' *Soviet Economy in a Time of
Change* 2, Washington DC: US Government Printing Office.

Hasegawa, Tsuyoshi and Pravda, Alex (eds) (1990) *Perestroika: Soviet Domestic
and Foreign Policies* London: Sage for the RIIA.

International Affairs (Moscow) (1988) 'The Vladivostok Initiatives Two Years
On' 8.

Ivanov, Vladimir (ed.) (1989) *USSR and the Pacific Region in the 21st Century*
New Delhi: Allied Publishers.

Ivanov, V.I. and Baikov, N.M. (eds) (1989) *The Mineral and Energy Resources of
the Soviet Far East: Material for the Forum on Minerals and Energy of the
Pacific Economic Cooperation Conference* Moscow, Vladivostok and Khabarovsk: The Institute of World Economy and International Relations, USSR
Academy of Sciences.

Japan Forum on International Relations (1989) 'Long-term Political Vision for Sta-
bilization and Cooperation in Northeast Asia' March.

Kim, Roy U.T. (1989) 'Moscow–Seoul Relations in a New Era' *The Pacific Review*
2, 4.

Kipp, Jacob W. et al. (1988) *Gorbachev and the Struggle for the Future* Fort
Leavenworth, Kansas: Soviet Army Studies Office, US Combined Arms Center.

Kireev, Aleksei (1989) 'Skol'ko tratit' na oboronu' *Ogonok* 19, May.

Kornai, J. (1986) 'The Hungarian Reform Process: Visions, Hopes and Reality'
Journal of Economic Literature XXIV, December.

Korolev, Ivan (1990) 'The Problems of the Soviet Union's Involvement in the
World Economy and Economic Relations with Asia–Pacific Countries' *The
Korean Journal of Economic Studies* XXI, 1.

Kuznetsov, Iu.D., Navlitskaia, G.B. and Sytitsyn, I.M. (1988) *Istoriia Iaponii*
Moskva: Vysshaia shkola.

Lenin, V.I. (1964) *Polnoe sobranie sochinenii* Moskva: Gospolitizdat 44.

Littler, C.R. (1984) 'Soviet-type Societies and the Labour Process' Thompson,
Kenneth (ed.) *Work, Employment and Unemployment* Philadelphia: Milton
Keynes Open University Press.

'Long-term State Programme of the Far East Economic Region, Buriat Republic and Chita Area' (1987) Moscow, August.

Lushev, Pyotr (1989) 'Security vs. Dogma' *World Marxist Review* 12.

Mack, Andrew and O'Hare, Martin (1990) 'Moscow–Tokyo and the Northern Territories Dispute' *Asian Survey* XXX, 4.

Mandel, E. (1989) *Beyond Perestroika* London and New York: Verso.

Mashin, A. (1990) 'North Korea: Legend and Reality' *Argumenty i Fakty* (Moscow) 13.

Materiali XIX Vsesoyuznoy Konferentsii Kommunisticheskoy Partii Sovetskogo Soyuza (1988) Moskva: Politizdat.

Mezhdunarodnaia zhizn (1989) 'Vneshnepoliticheskaia i diplomaticheskaia deiatel'nost' SSSR Obzor MID SSSR' 12.

Nagorniy, Alexander (1989) 'Soviet Security Interests in the Pacific and Northeast Asia: New Dimensions and Old Realities' conference paper at *Northeast Asian Security and World Peace in the 1990s* Institute of World Peace Studies, Kyung Hee University, Seoul, September.

Novoe vremiia (1989) 'Severnye territorii': Chto s nimi delat?' 49.

___ (1989) 'Tretii put' — dialog: interv'iu chlena Politbiuro TsK KPSS, sekretaria TsK KPSS Aleksandra Iakovleva' 48.

Nuti, D.M. (1981) 'Poland: Economic Collapse and Socialist Renewal' *New Left Review* 130.

Ognev, Yuri I. (1990) 'Soviet Position on Peaceful Settlement and Reunification in Korea' conference paper at *ROK–USSR Relations: New Developments and Prospects* Institute for Sino–Soviet Studies, Hanyang University, Seoul, April.

Pleshakov, Constantine V. (1989) 'Soviet Foreign Policy and its Implication for the Peace of Northeast Asia' conference paper at *Northeast Asian Security and World Peace in the 1990s* Institute of International Peace Studies, Kyung Hee University, Seoul, September.

Press Office of the USSR Embassy in Canada (1988) 'Gorbachev Speech — Foreign Section' *News Release—Communique* Ottawa, Ontario, 19 September.

Rhee, Kang-suk (1990) 'A Change of Direction in North Korea' *Journal of East Asian Affairs* IV, 1.

Robertson, Miles (1988) *The Soviet Union and Japan* Cambridge: Cambridge University Press.

Rozman, Gilbert (1985) *A Mirror for Socialism* London: IB Tauris.

___ (1988) 'Moscow's Japan Watchers in the First Years of the Gorbachev Era' *The Pacific Review* 1, 3.

Sabel, Charles and Stark, David (1982) 'Planning, Politics and Shop-Floor Power: Hidden Forms of Bargaining in Soviet-Imposed State-Socialist Societies' *Politics and Society* 11, 4.

Salkisov, Konstantin (1988) 'Vladivostokskie initsiativy: dva goda spustia' *Mezhdunarodnaia zhizn* 12.

Sato, Tsuneaki (1990) 'Rethinking Market-Oriented Economic Reforms in Socialist Countries' in O. Bogomolov *Market Forces in Planned Economies* London: Macmillan.

___ 'Comparative Analysis of Economic Reforms in Socialist Countries' (1989) *Contemporary China* volume II, Tokyo: Iwanami Publishers.

Sato, Tsuneaki and Popov, Gavriil (1989) 'Economic Perestroika: Is There a Way Out?' *Sekai* (The World) 535.

Schiffer, Jonathan (1989) *Soviet Regional Economic Policy* London: Macmillan.

Segal, Gerald (ed.) (1983) *The Soviet Union and East Asia* London: Heinemann for the RIIA.

___ (1990) *The Soviet Union and the Pacific* London: Unwin/Hyman.

___ (1989) 'Taking Sino–Soviet Detente Seriously' *The Washington Quarterly* 12, 3.

___ (1990) 'Northeast Asia: All Aboard the Detente Train?' *The World Today* 46, 3.

Senghass, Dieter (1981) 'Socialism in Historical and Development Perspective' *Economics* 23.

Shinju (1989) Tokyo, The Council on National Security Problems, October.

Soviet Military Power: Prospects for Change, 1989 (1989) Washington DC: Department of Defense.

Spandarian, Bikutorii (1988) 'Establish a Special Economic Zone for Enlargement of Cooperation between the USSR and Japan' *APA News* (Japanese), 4 July.

Stephan, John and Chichkanov V.P. (eds) (1986) *Soviet-American Horizons on the Pacific* Honolulu: University of Hawaii Press.

Stockwin, J.A.A. (1991) 'Can Japan and the Soviet Union Sort Out Their Differences?' Australia–Japan Research Centre, *Pacific Economic Paper* 191.

Szelenyi, Ivan (1989) 'Society and Politics in the Transition to Post-Communism in Eastern Europe' paper presented at TASA Conference, La Trobe University.

Tass Report (1988) 'Vneshnaia politika — Vneshenpolitichesiy razdel zechi Mikhaila Gorbacheva v Krasnoryarske' 17 September.

___ (1989) 'On Guidlines for the Home and Foreign Policy of the USSR' report by the Presidium of the USSR Supreme Soviet, 28, 31 May.

Thayer, Carlyle (ed.) (1987) *The Soviet Union as an Asian Pacific Power* London: Westview.

The Japan Economic Journal (1989) 'Trade Mission Targets Manchuria, Soviet Asia' 20 May.

Theses of the CPSU Central Committee for the 19th All-Union Party Conference (1988) Moscow: Novosti Press Agency Publishing House.

Towards the Festival in Pyongyang (1989) Moscow: Novosti Press Agency Publishing House.

Trigubenko, Marina and Toloraya, Georgi (1990) 'The Korean Imperative' *Far Eastern Economic Review* 22 March.

USSR Council of Ministers (1988) 'Concerning the Further Development of Foreign Economic Activity of State, Cooperative and other Public Enterprises, Entities and Organizations' 2 December.

Utechin S.V. (1964) *A Concise Encyclopaedia of Russia* New York: E.P. Dutton and Company.

Vorontsov, Vladilen B. (1990) 'Development in the USSR and the ROK: Impact upon Soviet–Korean Relations' conference paper at *ROK–USSR Relations: New Developments and Prospects* Institute for Sino–Soviet Studies, Hanyang University, Seoul, April.

Winiecki, J. (1987) *Economic Prospects—East and West* London: The Centre For Research into Communist Economics.

___ (1989) 'STE–LDC Comparisons: A Neglected Field of Comparative Systems Analysis' *Communist Economies* 1, 1.

World Bank (1981) *China: Socialist Economic Development* Report No. 3391–CHA.

Yang, Xiaokai (1989) 'Economic Thinking and Reforms in China' Department of Economics, Monash University, mimeo.

Zagoria, Donald (ed.) (1982) *The Soviet Union in East Asia* New Haven: Yale University Press.

___ (1989) 'Soviet Policy in East Asia: A New Beginning?' *Foreign Affairs* 68, 1.

Index

Italicised pages are for tables and figures. References to footnotes are to the page in the text in which they occur.

154